Advance Praise for
Appealing for Justice

"By telling the story of one woman who played a pivotal role in a critical civil rights lawsuit, Susan Casey brilliantly captures the story of an entire generation—indeed, the story of America over the past half century. This book is a must read for anyone who cares passionately about social justice. It explains how epochal change can happen."

–**HELEN THORPE**,
winner of the 2010 Colorado Book Award
for Creative Nonfiction and author of
Soldier Girls and *Just Like Us: The True Story of Four Mexican Girls Coming of Age in America*

"A must-read for fans of the Supreme Court and civil rights, Susan Casey's drama expertly tells the tale of an entire movement through one of its bravest characters."

–**MICHAEL BOOTH**,
member of two
Pulitzer Prize-winning news teams
and winner of the 2015 Colorado Book Award
for Nonfiction

D0048866

Other Books by Susan Berry Casey

Hart and Soul: Gary Hart's New Hampshire Odyssey...And Beyond

Praise for *Hart and Soul*

"There have been millions of words written about New Hampshire primaries but never before a fascinating inside account of one of the campaigns ... a must for political junkies everywhere."

–JACK GERMOND,
nationally syndicated columnist

"A steep snow-covered driveway ... people, slipping and sliding about, finally pushed (a) car up the hill.... One of the men pushing the car in the snow and the muck was U.S. Senator Gary Hart of Colorado.... The car-pushing incident ... serves as a metaphor for a remarkable political story."

–MICHAEL J. BERKNER,
Concord (NH) Monitor

"Her criticism of the press and television is harsh—and probably justified."

–FRANK LYNN,
New York Times Book Review

"Insightful analysis...It is a tribute to the candor and intellectual integrity of Casey's effort that she presents Hart as he really was..."

–CLAUDE R. MARX,
Nashua (NH) Telegraph

APPEALING
FOR JUSTICE

One Colorado Lawyer, Four Decades,
and the Landmark Gay Rights Case: *Romer v. Evans*

SUSAN BERRY CASEY

Appealing For Justice:
One Colorado Lawyer, Four Decades,
and the Landmark Gay Rights Case: *Romer v. Evans*
by Susan Berry Casey

Published by
Gilpin Park Press LLC
792 South Gilpin Street
Denver, CO 80209
www.gilpinparkpress.com

Cover and interior layout by Nick Zelinger, NZ Graphics

The author gratefully acknowledges and thanks the staff of the
Carnegie Branch Library for Local History of the Boulder Public Library
and the staff of the Western History/Genealogy Department of the
Denver Public Library for their assistance and for permission to use
photographs from their various collections.

A very special thanks to photographer John Fielder for permission to use
his stunning image "Maroon Bells-Snowmass Wilderness."

ISBN: 978-0-9976984-0-4 (softcover)
ISBN: 978-0-9976984-1-1 (eBook)
Library of Congress PCN: 2016910762

First Edition
Printed in the USA

To Cyrus, Helen, and Lennon

CONTENTS

APPEALING FOR JUSTICE

One Colorado Lawyer, Four Decades,
and the Landmark Gay Rights Case: *Romer v. Evans*

SUSAN BERRY CASEY

PROLOGUE

For the generation that came of age during the 1960s, those raucous and oftentimes painful years continue to exert a strong hold some fifty years later. For most, the nostalgia surrounding Woodstock continues to define those times, although only a small percentage of that generation actually traveled down those New York country roads to experience rainy days engulfed by pulsating rock bands, free love, and psychedelic fogs.

For many others, it is the searing images of that decade that are etched in memory. Images of local sheriffs unleashing water cannons and attack dogs on young Negroes. Images of gloating, white-hooded Klansmen carrying torches, a burning shack or cross on a lawn in the background.

During the halcyon 1950s in most of America, young people lived a "Happy Days" existence. But for Negroes, as they were called then, the 1950s were not happy days at all. In the Deep South, discrimination, segregation, and poverty was a way of life. States were governed by Jim Crow laws that prevented blacks from sitting at lunch counters, drinking from water fountains, holding good paying jobs, going to school with white children, or exercising their right to vote. Signs everywhere directed "coloreds" to a separate, less-than equal life.

Lynching was common, going virtually unnoticed and unreported, until one hot August day in 1955 when 14-year-old Emmett Till was beaten and hung from a tree in Mississippi for the crime of speaking to a white woman in a store. That same year, Rosa Parks was arrested for refusing to move to the back of the bus. As the decade of the fifties came to a close and a new president came into office, bus boycotts, lunch counter sit-ins, freedom rides, and attempts to integrate public facilities and universities were in full swing in Little Rock and Montgomery and scores of cities throughout the South. But across the rest of the country, nobody really knew what life was like in that part of America.

That all changed with the advent of television. The bulky consoles that arrived in the mid-1950s were initially intended to deliver entertainment of the *I Love Lucy, Davy Crockett,* and *The Guiding Light* sort. But soon television also began to bring images of this other America into living rooms across the country. Still, coverage of the times and events of the day was minimal, barely an afterthought to television executives until the networks' fledgling news divisions made a major breakthrough in the fall of 1959 with the first live presidential debates between Richard M. Nixon and John F. Kennedy. After more than 60 million Americans sat glued to their sets for four nights, one debate per week over a four-week period, network owners suddenly recognized the vast potential for television beyond entertainment.

With the launch of TV satellites in 1963, nightly network news shows expanded from 15 to 30 minutes and the images that began filling the screens were a revelation. America witnessed grainy film footage of farm worker boycotts; of governors standing at school house doors to prevent black students from enrolling; of protestors being pushed and beaten by sheriffs and attacked by police dogs; of federal troops being dispatched to Mississippi and Alabama and Georgia; of the bombing that killed four little girls at the Sixteenth Street Baptist Church in Birmingham.

That year America was also able to watch President Kennedy as he traveled abroad, including his June speech before more than a hundred thousand cheering Germans at the Berlin Wall. It was his assassination, however, that forever changed the public's relationship with television. All networks ceased other programing and for four straight days they provided "live" coverage of all aspects of the assassination tragedy, ending with Kennedy's funeral and burial. For a brief moment in time, all Americans watched as one America.

From that day forward, for thirty minutes every night, and with periodic special reports and documentaries, television provided increasing evidence of what kind of country we were. And the evidence suggested a broad betrayal of values thought to be the essence of our democracy. It was almost inevitable that the long-simmering civil rights movement would now burst out of the shadows of the South and into the national spotlight.

By the end of the decade, the Vietnam War, marked by years of lies by politicians and generals, and the loss of tens of thousand of American lives, fueled a further loss of faith in the country's institutions and leadership. It gave rise to a fierce and raging anti-war movement that paralleled and intermingled with the fight for racial justice. As the sixties rolled into the seventies it was sometimes impossible to tell where one protest movement ended and another began.

Half the population experienced discrimination, inequities, and injustice that was personal. In many states women could not take out a loan or buy a car without the signature of their husband or father. They could not plan their pregnancies or apply for well-paying jobs advertised as "male only," or receive the same pay for doing the same work. Women found little opportunity in the workplace outside of teaching, nursing, or secretarial jobs. Even graduates of the most prestigious law schools were denied entry-level positions in legal firms simply because of their gender.

There were no women CEOs among the Fortune 500 corporations, no female generals or admirals in the United States military, no women on the United States Supreme Court. And the only two women serving in the United States Senate, Senator Margaret Chase Smith of Maine and Senator Maurine Neuberger of Oregon, began their congressional careers succeeding their husbands who had died while in office. All across the country and in all levels of political, professional, and corporate leadership, in the boardrooms and backrooms where decisions were made, women were neither present nor welcome.

For blacks, for the poor, for women, for the hundreds of thousands of young men being sent to war, the injustice, the inequality, and the immorality demanded a response. Social justice movements became that response. Pervasive protests, sit-ins and marches, college take-overs, and growing violence all became part of the mix during the years and times when the country appeared to be coming apart at the seams.

It seemed to happen overnight. Life was good in the post-war fifties, or so it seemed. Then suddenly it wasn't anymore. Not at home, where hope turned to despair as a country tried to make sense of the violence begetting violence, even the assassination of a president. And not in the world that America had supposedly saved from tyranny. An Iron Curtain, symbolic and real, descended upon Europe; the Soviet Union launched Sputnik; and hostilities of monumental proportions seemed possible yet again. In Berlin, in outer space, and on the shores of Cuba, just 90 miles off the coast of Florida, there was suddenly so much at stake and so much in jeopardy. It is a wonder that we found our way back as a country.

Many of us are familiar with the stories of the era's political leaders, of the well-known civil rights champions and anti-war leaders, and of the feminist icons of the women's movement, all who led efforts to right the ship of state. We know far less about the quieter, less visible figures who turned, not to protest or politics or bombs and violence, but to a life of justice. Their stories shine a powerful light into the corners and around the edges of that time in America's history that everybody thinks they know.

This book tells one such story. It is the story of a remarkable woman, Jean Eberhart Dubofsky. Jean Dubofsky's journey through the justice years is one of those stories that nobody knows, although it is much more than her story. It is also the story of that complicated and tumultuous time when one social justice movement blended into another as streams of injustice became a river and ordinary people put their oars in the water to help navigate the country safely to shore.

Jean came of age in the raging heat of these movements at home at the exact same time that the Cold War was at its coldest abroad. The combination of that heat and that cold disrupted the comfortable and traditional life Jean might have been expected to lead. And that disruption led Jean to leave her own indelible mark on our country's journey of justice.

""Liberty and justice for all means ALL. NO EXCEPTIONS!"
–Richard T. Castro

PART ONE

Berlin 1962

Stanford University

From Betty Crocker to Capitol Hill

No Ladies Need Apply

The Tornado

1

Berlin 1962

When the Allies partitioned Berlin after the war, Bernauer Strasse served as one of the dividing lines. The Soviets took control of the eastern half of the city and the United States, British, and French controlled the west. The original agreement guaranteed free movement throughout Berlin, but that changed on August 13, 1961. Overnight, East German soldiers, under orders from the Russians, unfurled rolls of barbed wire down the middle of the streets. When dawn broke, the twisted strands of cutting metal thorns reflected their sinister intent. The soldiers then dug deep trenches at strategic intersections and began constructing a cement block wall, twelve feet high and four feet deep, designed to prevent East Berliners from freely crossing over into West Berlin.

A row of five-story apartment buildings along Bernauer Strasse became part of that dividing wall. The apartments were in the East. The street in front of the building was in the West. Initially, the apartment buildings served as an escape route as East Berliners used knotted sheets and ropes to lower themselves from windows onto the free street of West Berlin. But after one woman died jumping from the fourth floor, the window openings were bricked up.

Just a few months after a physical wall cut Berlin in half, Jean Eberhart, a nineteen-year-old Stanford University junior from Topeka, Kansas, found her way to the corner of Bernauer Strasse and Wolliner Strasse. For an hour she stood beside a parade of Berliners who regularly gathered on that corner to peer over to the East, hoping to see a loved one on the other side. It was one of the few spots left in the city where people could see over the wall. As shouts and waves of recognition echoed back to those around her, it was clear to Jean how valued those tiny threads of connection remained for a people divided by a wall of injustice and, now, despair.

Against the advice of her college instructors, instead of flying, Jean had driven to Berlin. She left from Paris, crossed over the French border and drove through West Germany, into and through East Germany, in order to get to Berlin. She hungered to experience for herself the contrast between the two separate worlds that Germany had become. As she drove through West Germany, she witnessed all the signs of a vibrant post-war country. A modern 4-lane autobahn whisked her past large industrial cities aglow with factories and humming with activity, not a soldier in sight. Until, that is, she reached the East German border crossing at Helmstedt, where she was met with barbed wire and guards wearing long green military coats. Most were carrying rifles; some had police dogs at their side. Once through the checkpoint and into communist East Germany, she drove along crumbling and pitted roads lined not with restaurant stops, filling stations, and modern buildings but by drab brown towns still showing the ravages of the war. Bleak, desolate towns with few signs of life.

Jean had begun her Stanford abroad program with a lark, an earlier trip into West Germany, to Munich during Oktoberfest. But it would be Berlin, where the contrast between East and West Germany was so stark, that Jean would remember most. "One country, one people, and yet two entirely different ways of life existed with only a wall dividing them," was how she described it in a letter home at the time. On one side Germans who were prospering, were free to travel where they wanted, and could govern themselves. And on the other, oppression and deprivation of both freedom and economic survival, with soldiers in the streets, barbed wire and walls, and hopelessness.

Jean traveled with a roommate into East Berlin, and everywhere they went they saw people in uniforms—soldiers, street cleaners, women laborers. Late one night they came across groups of women dressed alike, in overalls or with aprons over long black dresses and headscarves. Some were carrying wicker baskets; others were hand-painting crosswalks on the street. When they stopped to try and talk with one woman, she began to cry. "This happened several times," Jean wrote to her parents. "We'd talk to little old ladies who would begin to cry when they heard we were from America."

Jean would never forget the women weeping for the idea of America. And, when she returned home in the fall of 1962, she began to appreciate that her country fell very short of the "idea" of America held by those women in the streets of Berlin. Jean confronted the cold harsh reality of a country racked by injustice and inequality, with differences just as stark as she had seen abroad: two entirely different ways of life existing with only a wall dividing them. The wall between the two Americas was not made of bricks and mortar or barbed wire. Nor was it simply geographic, though the North/South divide could not be denied. The wall between the two Americas was racism, poverty, privilege, and power.

2

Stanford University

When Jean returned to Stanford after her study abroad, the preppy campus she had left behind had been transformed. "The entire atmosphere was different. It had made a 180 degree turn and justice issues were very much in focus," Jean said. The talk was less of football victories, dating, and fraternity parties, and more of James Meredith, a young black man from Mississippi, who simply wanted to go to his state's university; of sit-ins and marches and freedom rides and other efforts to allow blacks to ride buses and trains, and be served at restaurants and hotels, and sit where they wanted in theatres.

As Jean's generation struggled to make sense of the racism and violence in the South, college campuses across the country became the epicenters of consciousness, dissent, and action. Berkeley and Columbia made more headlines, but the fervor and level of activity at Stanford, Jean's laboratory, came to dominate campus life. "All of a sudden I had a whole new group of friends and there were things going on that took you outside of yourself. The campus became a little incubator for a social movement and I was in the middle of it all."

That change at Stanford seemingly arrived all at once, with the power and effect of a dormant volcano suddenly erupting to dramatically alter the landscape. The name of that volcano was Allard Lowenstein.

Before arriving at Stanford, Lowenstein had been involved in a bewildering array of activities, jobs, and assignments, often simultaneously, in different parts of the country and the world, with connections and relationships that overlapped and intersected in a multitude of different ways. While an undergraduate, he headed the National Student Association. He was later befriended by Eleanor Roosevelt, traveled the world organizing young people on behalf of the United Nations, wrote a book on South Africa, worked for a U.S. senator, held leadership roles on a number of political campaigns, including Adlai Stevenson's presidential campaign, spent time in the army, finished law school, and almost became a candidate for Congress. There is even a debate among Lowenstein's biographers about whether or not he may also have worked for the CIA.

He was a leftist liberal crusader for all manner of causes and a committed anti-war, human rights and civil rights activist who saw peace and justice as the important work of the time. *His* work. He was one of the first to envision student activism as the critical vehicle for change, and he believed that an army of these young activists had to be recruited, engaged, supported, deployed, and directed if the peace and justice agenda was to succeed in America. If there was a common thread through all of his involvements, it was young people. Exciting them, inspiring them, directing them was Lowenstein's passion.

Allard Lowenstein had no academic credentials to speak of, had never taught at a university, and had never trained as an academic administrator, yet he was hired as one of Stanford's first faculty residents in order to assist the university with its efforts to understand, identify, channel, and perhaps contain the growing unrest sweeping campuses across the country. But, instead of channeling or containing or redirecting the awakening energies and passions of students, Lowenstein lit a fuse that led to an explosion of activism. He may not have had the usual academic credentials, but as the head of the National Student Association years earlier, Lowenstein had urged student leaders from campuses across the country to recognize and exercise their acquired power for the purpose of social change. That was his intent at Stanford as well.

His first task was to locate those potential student leaders and bring them together. He had just the place to do that: Stern Hall, a men's residence hall that looked like a military bunker, especially in contrast to the other red-tiled roofs and buff-colored stylish dorms. Stern was where freshmen who failed to receive a bid to their desired fraternity ended up. It was a place nobody wanted to live in.

But Al Lowenstein—no one on campus called him anything but Al—began cultivating a group of freshmen and sophomore men, hoping that they would move into Stern Hall, a place he was determined to remake into a coveted independent dorm. It would be the center for leaders and activists looking for something beyond bourgeois campus institutions like fraternities, a place for young men eager to embrace a life of meaning and action, looking to make an impact on the world. Weeks of recruitment and hours of stimulating and challenging discussions with Lowenstein, usually lasting long into the night, were followed by a weeklong retreat at Big Sur where he hoped to solidify the concept of what he was attempting to organize and implement at Stanford. It worked. Soon he had twenty students committed to live where he lived, to become the nucleus for, and the leaders of, what later became known nationally as the Stern Hall movement.

Al Lowenstein was a constant in the lives of those young men, provoking discussion, challenging assumptions, exposing students to ideas and strategies to fight against injustice, teaching them about their own power and helping them begin to unleash that power. He was a magnet that drew people to him, a pied piper who knew how to turn twenty people into two hundred, and then two thousand, all following behind. The Stern Hall men ran for and were elected to the student legislature and to class office, rising to top positions of power on campus. They then connected with student activist leaders on other campuses, and by year's end, had become national student leaders as well.

Lowenstein left Stanford after little more than a year, but he was never far away from what he had set in motion. The Stern Hall movement leaders continued at full steam. They established something called the Stanford Civil Rights Secretariat, which planned conferences and brought the Rev. Martin Luther King, Jr. and other influential speakers to campus and to the Bay area. When the group moved on to become national student leaders, they remained connected to Lowenstein, who was knee-deep in the planning and execution of many civil rights activities, working closely with Dr. King, Robert Moses, and other civil rights leaders, and with influential civil rights organizations such as the Congress of Racial Equality (CORE) and the Student Non-Violent Coordinating Committee (SNCC).

In the summer of 1963, a large contingent of Stanford students traveled to Mississippi to support a Lowenstein effort to help to register black voters. Organizers were staging a mock election in support of a black Mississippi gubernatorial candidate, Aaron Henry. They set out ballot boxes in communities throughout the state and encouraged blacks to fill out unofficial printed ballots. It was a strategy to disprove the notion promoted by southern government officials that voter registration efforts were a fool's errand because blacks were not interested in participating in elections. This mock election was a precursor to and a model for Freedom Summer in 1964, when thousands of college students staged voter registration drives in a half-dozen southern states. Stanford University contributed more students to those efforts than any other university in the country.

Jean, however, did not join the group of students who went to the South. Not in the summer of 1963 for the Aaron Henry mock election. Not in the summer of 1964, Freedom Summer. It was a noble and romantic idea, going to the South to march or protest or organize voter registration drives. But it was a challenging and dangerous environment. The efforts were often disorganized and the work was difficult. Jean wished she could be like so many of her classmates, but there was a piece of her that understood that she didn't have it in her. She couldn't see herself in rural Mississippi trying to persuade and reassure frightened blacks to come to a meeting or register to vote. "I was just too shy to go up to people or knock on the doors of complete strangers," she said. She couldn't see pushing herself to the head of a picket line, challenging authorities, or speaking before crowds to rally them to the cause.

"By then I knew I wanted to work on civil rights or find a way to help poor people, but going to the South just wasn't something I could do," Jean admitted. Part of it was her innate shyness and part of it was her skepticism about whether or not she would actually be contributing by going. "But I thought if I could have a skill that could be used, that would be a better way to go. Eventually, I began to think that the law might be a way that I could actually do something that would matter."

The college years have always been a time of transition for young people and a key determinant of the direction their lives would take. For students in the sixties, the impact was the same, but more pronounced. More intense. More personal.

Most everyone watched the evening news or saw the headlines and photographs of marches and sit-ins and bombings and blocked schoolroom doors in the daily newspapers. "Those college years were such a dramatic time," Jean recalled. "There was the bombing of the church in Birmingham and violence on the bridge in Tuscaloosa, having to call out the National Guard. And then what happened in Little Rock. And I remember well the Cuban Missile Crisis and what a frightening time it was. Then JFK was assassinated, and all of a sudden life seemed much more serious. I'm sure I became a different person because of all that was going on."

With so much wrong in the world, that different person began to focus on where she might fit in to become a part of making things right. Instead of going to the South as part of Freedom Summer, Jean traveled east to the city where laws were made.

3

From Betty Crocker Homemaker to Capitol Hill

Jean Eberhart grew up in sleepy, unsophisticated Topeka, Kansas. When she first arrived at Stanford in the fall of 1960, she felt totally out of place among students she perceived to be well connected, wealthy, and more worldly. But when her sights turned to finding an internship in Washington, D.C., she did have one valuable connection: a United States senator. How she came to have that connection was an unusual story, and not one Jean ever chose to share with her more sophisticated Stanford classmates. Frankly, it was a little embarrassing and not something she ever wanted to talk about. The truth was that Jean had been introduced to her state's Republican senator, Frank Carlson, by Betty Crocker. And Betty Crocker had come into her life because of Miss Bernice Finley.

It all started senior year at Topeka High School when Bernice Finley, the home economics teacher, asked Jean to fill out an application form in order to take the annual national Betty Crocker Homemaker test. Although some high schools invited every girl in the senior class to fill out the forms and take the test, Miss Finley sought out only the brightest girls in her school and *insisted* they take it. Jean tried to convince Miss Finley that she had the wrong girl, that she was too busy, that she'd never taken a home economics class, that she didn't know how to cook, that it was all a bit silly. But as silly as it sounded to Jean, the Betty Crocker Homemaker program was also a scholarship program, one of the largest in the country for girls. The topic of college scholarships was much on Jean's mind senior year.

There was never any doubt that Jean would go to college. The only questions were: Where? And how would she pay for it? Jean understood her family's finances and knew that a scholarship would be necessary to pay for college, even if she chose the most affordable option, the University of Kansas (KU), twenty miles down the road in Lawrence, Kansas. Jean was fine going to KU. She had already lined up a roommate and picked out the sorority she'd likely join. But Jean was also an adventurer. Because her father was a college professor and had summers off, she and her family were able to spend most summers on long car treks, all across the country, from state to state, and one national park after another. Jean developed a taste of the world beyond Topeka, beyond Kansas, and always held out hope that she would be able to go away for college.

Jean didn't need the help of a guidance counselor, however, to help her decide which colleges to apply to. She knew more from personal site visits than a dozen high school counselors put together because, in addition to exploring national parks during their summer sojourns, the Eberhart family also visited college campuses.

"Any town we went through, it didn't matter how large or how small, if there was a college, we would stop to see the campus. I had probably toured a hundred campuses by the time I was in high school," Jean said. "My first choice was always Stanford. The campus was gorgeous, the weather was warm, and it was California, not Topeka." It was also expensive. If she wanted to attend Stanford, Jean would need significant financial help.

So, despite her misgivings about entering a homemaker contest, on that December day in 1959, Jean, along with the 57 other senior girls that Miss Finley had recruited, took the 50-minute, multiple-choice

Betty Crocker Homemaker of Tomorrow test in the hopes she might do well enough to qualify for a scholarship.

The test contained basic math questions. How many gallons of paint were needed to cover a certain number of walls? Which was less expensive per ounce, a twelve-ounce can of soup costing 35 cents or a 32-ounce can of soup costing 80 cents? Menu and nutrition questions followed. What beverage would best be served with pecan pie? Which food (celery, potatoes, milk, or carrots) provides the most protein?

Jean quickly made her way through section after section, finally reaching the last, apparently designed to test reasoning abilities and relationship skills.

> *Susie finds a rat in the attic. What should she do?*
> A. Scream and run.
> B. Call her husband at work.
> C. Put the rat in a bag.

> *You're having a dinner party and you notice your husband has a spot on his tie. What do you do?*
> A. Point and laugh and make a big noise about it.
> B. Quietly let him know.
> C. Ignore it because you can't do anything about it.

"I'm sure by then I must have been rolling my eyes at the questions," Jean said. She completed the 150 questions[1] and then returned to the rush of other more enjoyable senior year activities. She had all but forgotten about the test when the results were announced and, much to her surprise, she learned that she had earned the highest score of all the 58 girls at Topeka High. The reward was a blue heart-shaped pin; it took winning at the state level to receive scholarship money.

Two weeks later, contest officials notified Topeka High administrators that Jean was one of the ten highest scorers in the state. And, a few weeks after that, the unthinkable happened: Jean had won the Betty Crocker Homemaker of Tomorrow award for the entire state of Kansas. Along with the state title came a $1,500 scholarship. She and her family were ecstatic. It would be enough to cover almost all of the costs at KU.

Jean was knee deep in debate competitions. Her successful high school debate team won the local competitions, then went on to win the district tournament and was ranked third at the state meet, all pretty heady stuff. The first weekend in March she also participated in the extemporaneous speech contest held in Emporia, Kansas. With her Betty Crocker Homemaker of Tomorrow win, her already active senior year became even busier.

She suddenly became a minor celebrity, a role she was not accustomed to. Jean was a writer for the school newspaper and had a regular column in the *Topeka Daily Capitol*. Now, instead of writing about other students' accomplishments, *she* was the one being written about in both papers. In some ways, winning the state Betty Crocker contest threatened to take over her life, adding a whirl of new responsibilities and activities.

Every day when Jean arrived home from school, a pile of mail awaited. "There was a slot next to the door, and the mail would just come through the slot and sit on the floor in the front hall," Jean said. Soon, the floor became overrun with cards and letters of congratulations from people she had never met. It was clear from the newspaper clippings included with the notes of congratulations that stories of her win, along with her official senior portrait, were plastered in papers all across the state. This shy young woman was no longer just a minor celebrity at her school or in her hometown; she was becoming one of the most well known 17-year-olds in the state of Kansas.

There were also official letters from General Mills, the Betty Crocker contest sponsor, outlining rules to be followed, clothes to wear, letters to write, people to meet, schedules of events, contact information, and daily itineraries for a weeklong trip scheduled for April that would culminate in Washington, D. C. with a festive gala featuring all the state winners.

Jean even received a personal letter signed by Betty Crocker herself, which was a little odd considering Betty Crocker was a character created out of whole cloth by General Mills. A fictional homemaker that became the iconic brand for the company, and one of the most famous people to never have existed, Betty Crocker was a comforting role model, kitchen expert, and a fixture in lives of homemakers for decades. Still, she was not a real live person who could actually sign letters to reluctant budding homemakers like Jean Eberhart.

The first assignment for each state's winner was to write letters and make personal phone calls to senators, governors, and congressmen, inviting them to attend the "All-American Table Dinner", the spectacular extravaganza held in Washington later that spring. Apropos of the times, these important people not only said "yes" to attending the dinner, but also invited their state's winner to come by their offices for private meetings. In Jean's first taste of the public arena, her state's elected officials treated Jean as though she was the important person, someone they should know and pay attention to.

When the big Betty Crocker week arrived, Jean and Miss Finley flew to New York City and took what Jean later would describe as a "wild ride" in a cab to the famed Waldorf-Astoria. A wild ride would be an apt description for the entire trip. The four days were a blur of cities, luxury hotels, theatrical shows (including *The Sound of Music* with Mary Martin and even an Ed Sullivan show rehearsal), tours, fancy candlelight dinners, parties, ferry rides, charter flights, and long bus rides. Interspersed throughout their travels were meetings with

General Mills staffers, individual and group interviews, and constant observation and grading by the firm employed to help select one of the 51 girls as the ideal All-American Future Homemaker.

Their final whirlwind day in Washington included stops at the Smithsonian, the Capitol, a special tour of the White House, and a visit with the first lady, Mamie Eisenhower. Before the girls climbed into their petticoats and pastel formals, they gathered in the ballroom of the historic Statler Hilton hotel to "practice" for the evening event. On hand to extend congratulations were Vice President Richard Nixon and Mrs. Nixon. The vice president made brief remarks to the group and then he and the first lady shook a few hands, spending a bit more time chatting with a couple of girls in particular, Jean among them.

The evening went off without a hitch. The girls were introduced with great fanfare, as one by one they paraded across the stage. All of the Kansas senators and congressmen and their wives were in place at Table 19, Jean's table. The Lamplighters sang, ventriloquist Paul Winchell (along with his dummy, Jerry Mahoney) performed, and Olympian Bob Richards delivered inspiring remarks.[2] It was a thrilling night. Finally the drums rolled and a ballroom full of nervous young women held their breaths. Though she herself could hardly believe it, Jean Eberhart from Topeka, Kansas was crowned the 1960 Betty Crocker All-American Homemaker of Tomorrow. The photograph of Jean that ran in papers across the country the next day—eyes wide open, hands to her mouth in shock—suggested that Jean was perhaps the *most* surprised person in the room when her name was called.

Parades and school assemblies and more meetings and picture taking with governors and congressmen and senators followed. Jean took a particular shine to Senator Carlson and he to her. If you ever decide you might like to work in Washington, Carlson told her, you just let me know. My door is always open.

Washington was where decisions were made: to change laws, to send in the National Guard to enforce laws, to create solutions to inequities, to bring the Vietnam War to a halt. It was also a center of protest activity, the place to register opposition, to pressure the Congress and the president to act. Jean was eager to experience all of it. And so she called her friend Senator Carlson and asked if he would be interested in having her come to work in his office.

Even as a lowly intern, her decision to spend time in Washington had a huge impact on her future. Part of it was where she worked, on the Hill, inside of government, learning the ins and outs of lawmaking. And part of it was where she lived once she arrived in the city.

Hidden underneath the Key Bridge on the Georgetown side of the Potomac, a stone's throw from the Potomac Boat Club, was a three-story brick townhouse with balconies on every floor. In 1962, *Life Magazine* made this river-front house on Water Street and the women who lived there minor celebrities when they were included in a photo spread entitled, "How Nice To Be a Pretty Girl And Work in Washington: Glamour, excitement and romance and a chance to serve the country".[3] The photos captured the women playing touch football with their beaus and attending White House state dinners on the arms of congressmen, dressed in gowns and white gloves.

The girls, as they were called back then, were part of the new breed of well-educated young women flocking to Washington in the early 60s. Instead of marrying their high school sweethearts and settling down in their hometowns, they went off to college, and often law school, before beginning their careers. For the first time, possibility was in the air for women who wanted to live a professional life, and the New Frontier of the young dashing president, John F. Kennedy, was the place to be.

The Water Street house where Jean came to live was stunning and luxurious, yet surprisingly affordable if you squeezed eight people into its four bedrooms and split the rent. It wasn't just the fabulous house or the smart, beautiful women who lived there that proved fascinating to *Life Magazine*; it was the glow of excitement around them. They worked as aides to influential powerbrokers by day, and dated rich or famous or powerful men by night, and were caught up in the place and the optimism and the promise of the times.

When Jean landed in Washington for her internship with Senator Carlson, she knew nothing of this house or these women, but she did what every other college intern did when looking for a place to live: she perused the bulletin boards in the Senate office building. There she found an ad describing an opening for a roommate in a house four miles from the Capitol for $65 a month. The address was 3524 Water Street NW, under the Key Bridge.

Jean was the youngest of the roommates, the only one still in college, and while she and Senator Carlson were Republicans, and most of the women in the house were Democrats, a job working on the Hill for a senator made for a comfortable fit.

The Water Street house was part sorority house, part family support system, and part sanctuary for girls living far away from home. They had serious jobs, interesting friends, and attractive boyfriends. Over the course of ten years, women came and stayed a year or two before marrying or moving on. One woman worked as a protocol officer for the State Department, another as a staffer on the Senate Labor committee, and another as a receptionist at the Rhodesian-Nyasaland embassy. Others were lawyers in various federal agencies, staff assistants to senators, teachers, and cabinet secretaries. They had good jobs, but in some ways they were still kids, out on their own for the first time, playing at being grown-ups, and experimenting with the notion that women could be a part of something much larger than themselves.[4]

Jean interned for Senator Carlson in 1964, during the winter term and again that next summer before her senior year. She arrived just a few months after President Kennedy had been assassinated. Much of the glamour, optimism, and sense of possibility that had been a hallmark of the Kennedy years had already dissipated. But the Water Street house still had some of the most active and involved women in D.C. living there. Those women provided each other support and connections. And they provided Jean a roadmap for what was possible.

"I was maybe five or six years younger than most of them. Many had gone to law school and they were all working in very interesting jobs. That really gave me a sense of the kinds of jobs women could get in Washington that they couldn't get anywhere else," Jean said. "And, it gave me a sense of the possibilities if you went to law school."

4

No Ladies Need Apply

When Jean was in high school, her father, a college professor, had warned that the elite colleges and universities in the East, particularly the Ivy Leagues, would not be right for her. If you were from the Mid-West or from the South; if you were from a working class family; if you hadn't gone to a private prep school or a top-notch prestigious high school, you would not fit in, he told her. Jean heeded his advice and instead went west to Stanford.

But when it came to law school, the lure of Harvard was irresistible. Law school would be different, Jean thought. It was a professional school, with students coming from universities all across the country, students who were older, more experienced, young men and women of the world, not impressionable high school students. If they would admit her and provide a scholarship, why not the best law school in the country? Many of her Water Street roommates had gone to school back East, some even to Harvard Law. She felt sure she would fit right in and was no longer put off by her father's admonition that schools "back East" were different. How different could they be?

Jean applied to a handful of law schools but set her sights on Harvard. "I remember that I let out this 'Whoop!' when I opened the envelope from Harvard and it said I had been accepted and that I had gotten a $500 scholarship and a $500 loan."

That same "Whoop!" feeling of excitement about the prospect of Harvard Law School accompanied her as she made the eight-hour drive north along Route 95 from her summer job in Washington. Once she landed on that hallowed Cambridge campus, however, that thrill, that exhilaration that she thought might fortify her for a lifetime, did not last even a day. Not even an hour. In the first ten minutes of her first class on her first day of law school, Jean Eberhart realized that, like Dorothy, she was definitely not in Kansas anymore.

At Harvard Law School she came face-to-face with a world she had never known existed before. A world where women were openly treated as if they were worth less—much, much less—than their male counterparts. A world where the humiliation of women was celebrated by some, condoned by others, accepted by almost everyone. A world where women, all women, not just women from Kansas, were clearly not welcome.

Harvard Law began admitting women in the fall of 1950, but in numbers so miniscule that their presence barely registered. It would take more than fifty years before equal numbers of women and men would be admitted there each fall.

Jean's first year law class, in 1964, was comprised of sixteen women and almost 600 men. Each incoming class was divided into four sections with four women assigned to each. This group would be Jean's cohort for all first year classes for the entire year. When Jean and the three other women marched into their first class on the first day of law school and sat in their assigned seats, they learned in the most blatant way what their proper place would be for the next three years.

Their professor was James Casner, a well-known, very distinguished property law professor, a full professor and associate dean who also served as "acting" dean of the law school for a brief period. Casner wrote the book, literally, used in property law classes across the country. His other claim to fame came later when he was purported to be the model for the irascible Professor Kingsfield, portrayed by John Houseman in the movie *The Paper Chase*.

Casner unapologetically declared that first day that although Harvard Law had admitted women, mistakenly he thought, he felt no obligation to acknowledge their presence or to teach them. They could come to class or not. If they came, they would sit in their assigned seats and they were to remain silent. They would not be called upon in class. Ever.

There was, he later explained, one exception to this never-be-called-on rule, and that would be Ladies' Day. On Ladies' Day only, he would allow the women to participate.

When Ladies' Day finally arrived the following spring, eight months into the academic year, Casner began the class with a question addressed to one of the four female students in the section. "Suppose you were engaged. And I notice you are not," he said, as he ogled one woman's hands in search of a diamond ring, eliciting the desired chuckles from the other students. "But suppose you were. Legally, would you be obliged to give the ring back if you broke off the engagement?" In that full-year property law class, Casner allowed women to participate on only that one day, and the subject he chose would concern an engagement ring, a symbol of the well-accepted presumption that the only reason a woman would possibly want to attend an institution like Harvard Law would be to find a husband.

By the time Jean arrived there, only a handful of faculty members continued Ladies' Day and other practices that directly ostracized or demeaned female students. But such practices were tolerated as a quaint tradition from an earlier era, perhaps an innocent hazing ritual of sorts that women had to endure; or a harmless pedagogical idiosyncrasy, nothing more than an individual professor's choice of teaching method, a scholarly technique, perhaps, like the Socratic method.

To Jean and to many other women law students, Ladies' Day, the refusal to recognize women in class, and other treatment that demeaned women at Harvard Law were neither harmless nor simply a pedagogical idiosyncrasy. "There was this almost overriding sense that you weren't supposed to be there. When Casner announced that women would not be called on, he meant it. It was his way of putting down women. I'd never really encountered this before," Jean said.

Some days Jean made the long walk over to Casner's early morning class, but when she arrived, couldn't always bring herself to enter the classroom. Sometimes she went to the library instead. Sometimes she sat in the hall, just outside the door, listening, but only half-listening. Why go in if I am not going to be able to participate?, she wondered. It was humiliating.

It wasn't simply Casner. Or simply Ladies' Day. The entire Law School experience "was just downright unpleasant," Jean said. "I had such a good experience at Stanford. Maybe that was why I thought the way they treated women at Harvard was just so absurd. And the unpleasantness went beyond being a woman. It was the entire culture, that social element too, why my father thought going back East to college wouldn't be a good idea. There were all these high society, Rhodes Scholar types, the semi-aristocratic old money family folks who wouldn't have anything to do with people like me."

There were other indignities, small and large. Most of the classes were held in Langdell Hall, on the law school campus, three blocks north of Harvard Yard, along Massachusetts Avenue. Langdell had no women's bathrooms. To find the closest bathroom the women had to walk down to the first floor and either go outside and walk across to an adjacent building, Austin Hall, or, during the cold winter months, walk down another flight of stairs "way, way down to the tunnels between the buildings, then down the halls, all the way to the basement of Austin Hall."[5]

Not all professors treated women poorly, but the ethos of the institution permeated the hallways and the classrooms, and the male students took their cues from their surroundings. If you were a woman and you raised your hand in class expecting to be called on, it would not be uncommon to be hissed at by your student colleagues. "One of the women in my section was pretty aggressive, a real talker, and she got hissed at every time she raised her hand," Jean said. If you didn't raise your hand and didn't get called on, you could just fade into the woodwork and nobody would notice you, which was likely the point. "I never raised my hand," Jean said. "So I never had to worry about being hissed at."

Not every woman experienced or handled Harvard Law in the same way. But Jean's story was very much the same story told years later by a former chief justice of the Colorado Supreme Court, Mary Mullarkey, who arrived at the school a year after Jean. Recalling her experiences, Mullarkey used eerily similar, emotionally laden words to describe the experience: Humiliating. Abusive. Devastating. Shocking. Brutal. Her story could be Jean Dubofsky's story.

"I wasn't a sophisticated person," Mullarkey said. "I grew up in Wisconsin in a small town. I went to a small college and it was a very supportive atmosphere. Then I went off to Harvard Law where they had been accepting women for fifteen years. I was 21 years old, so fifteen years was a lifetime to me! I couldn't imagine that after all that time with women at the law school they still did what they did." Hard to imagine, but it all happened, nonetheless.

Faculty members would say directly: We are not going to teach you. We are not going to allow you to speak in class. When women were ready to graduate, advisors in the career planning office would say directly: No law firm will interview you. No law firm will hire you. You are on your own.

"There was a hardcore group of faculty who thought women didn't deserve to be in law school, that they didn't belong there and they had no compunction about making that clear. It was not subtle," Mullarkey said. "My self-esteem was pretty much hammered into the ground by the time I got out of there and it took me years to get over being angry with the way they treated women. It was just an awful, devastating experience. A very difficult thing for me."

It was an odd juxtaposition. These Harvard women were not the slackers of their generation, not even the run-of-the-mill college graduates. These women had stellar academic records. They were at the top of their classes, with expectations for themselves that they would not simply do well, but they would be the best. Suddenly they were plunged into a world where, in addition to not being expected to do well, they were actively discouraged from doing well. Do not even try for Law Review was the message they received. Those positions are meant for the men.

And it was made clear that they should not complain in any way. Not that it would matter if they did complain. "I didn't think there was anything to do, anything that could be done, so you just tolerated things," Jean said. But the impulse to protest, even if symbolically, did tempt her on at least one occasion.

Harvard is famous for its eating and drinking clubs, places that provide students with an alternative to food served in the cafeterias and dormitories. Many of the law students belonged to one particular eating club called Lincoln's Inn. "Of course the women couldn't belong to Lincoln's Inn or any of the eating clubs. So a group of women law students picketed in front of Lincoln's Inn one night. That's as dramatic as we ever got."

Even if protesting would have been effective, there was neither the energy to organize, nor the numbers, nor the relationships with other women law students that might have made taking some action in opposition possible. Women law students simply did not have occasion to know one another. There was no women's law student association, no attempt by the school to introduce the women from various sections or other classes to one another. In many ways it was every woman for herself, isolated and left to maneuver her own way through her experience. The only time, in fact, that all of the women in each first year class were together in the same room was when Dean Erwin Griswold and his wife hosted his annual dinner for the group.

Held at the Griswolds' home, the women came dressed up in semi-formals and high heels. Each year the same beverages and the same meal were served at the same three or four card tables set up in the dining room. Then the women were asked to take their place in a circle of metal gray folding chairs in the living room. It was time for the dean to have "the talk", the same conversation he'd been having with each group of first year women since he became dean of the law school.

Griswold would always start by telling them that although he was the person most responsible for the fact that Harvard Law actually began admitting women, he still wasn't convinced that they would do something useful with this education. He thought of it in this way, he said, that they were in someone else's place—meaning a man—who would go on to do important things. His goal that evening was to impress upon the women how important it was for them to make plans and have ideas about the future in order to justify the fact that they were taking up a slot that should have belonged to another. As was his custom, the dean then went around the circle and, one by one, asked each woman to explain why she deserved to be at the law school when it meant denying some man his rightful place.

Most of the women knew the question was coming because it was the same question asked each year. Some attempted to earnestly outline the impact they thought they might have on the world, while others made light of the question or made up some answer simply to satisfy the dean.

Ruth Bader Ginsburg, now a Supreme Court justice, who had come and gone from Harvard before Jean arrived, often tells of her experience at the Griswold dinner. "It was one of life's most embarrassing moments. I stood up to answer, forgetting that I had a full ashtray in my lap. I watched in horror as butts and ashes cascaded onto the Griswolds' carpet." All she could manage, she said, "was to mumble that my husband was at Harvard too, a 2-L [second-year law student], and it was important for a woman to understand her husband's work." In addition to a husband, Ginsburg also had a fourteen-month-old baby at home, but she kept that fact to herself.[6]

Some women did not take the questioning as lightly and became furious about having to justify their place in law school. They found it simply one more demeaning exercise, especially when Dean Griswold would reply to one student or another that their answer was not a very good one. Occasionally, a student simply did not attend the Griswold dinner, not being willing to go through the charade. Jean was one of those rare students.

"From what I had heard about it, he would talk about how you'd better have a pretty good reason to be here because you are taking up a man's place. I just found all of that so offensive," Jean said. "I just didn't need to go, didn't need to hear that. I don't know if all of the other women went or not. But I just wasn't going to go."

Jean's years in Cambridge were not so totally bleak, however. Law school was just a part of those years in Cambridge, the part to be tolerated. What saved her was all that was going on outside of the confines of the law school. Jean had great roommates and lived in fabulous apartments. Her freshman year she roomed with a third year law student, one of the girls who had lived on Water Street in Washington. Her name was Liddy Hanford. Liddy would eventually marry Kansas Senator Robert Dole and later, when she became known by her new name, Elizabeth Hanford Dole, she too would be elected to the U.S. Senate. Liddy served as a cabinet member in two different Republican administrations, and both she and her husband would become even more well known when they each ran for president in the late 1990s.

Cambridge was also a hub of psychedelic colors, longhaired, bearded hippies, and protestors of all sorts. There was no shortage of sex, drugs, and rock and roll. Even the infamous Harvard Professor Timothy O'Leary, who was experimenting with a new thing called LSD, wandered the streets and kept things interesting.

Most importantly, Jean learned a great deal about the law. She learned how to think and how to organize her thinking. Once she made it through her first year, she sought out other professors with a reputation for treating women as equals. She also had more choices about what courses to take in her second and third years and elected to take as many as allowed outside of the law school, in planning and government and art history.

As the world continued to change, so, too, did Jean. The sexism and prejudice and injustice that she experienced first hand gave her a much deeper appreciation for the injustices that were shaking the country. And her desire to make a difference only grew. Still, she wasn't quite a committed radical or activist yet. Like so many, the impulse to do good was tempered by the enormity of the problems. She felt the same helplessness that many young activists began to feel when it was obvious that participating in freedom marches, voter registration drives, or anti-war protests, or providing legal counsel to the poor, barely made a ripple. And like many, she questioned whether one person could really make a difference. Her internships on Capitol Hill and in the legal aid clinics gave her some hope that through the system, from the inside, there might be a place to make a difference, but she was still testing out who she was and who she would become.

She made it through her first two years of law school, with all their ups and downs, and had lined up a good job in San Francisco for the summer. Her optimistic juices began flowing again. Then two things happened that would be life changing. The first was a tornado.

5

The Tornado

Jean and her younger brother Allan grew up in Topeka, Kansas, a prototypical mid-western town of hardworking, mostly middle-class families, who were dedicated to raising their children in accord with fundamental values of honesty, patriotism, and loyalty to church and country. It was a college town in the typical Kansas small college way, home to Washburn University, a municipally funded affordable school meant to provide higher education to area families.

Washburn was the college that their father, Paul Eberhart, attended and the place he returned to as a young professor. Their mother was a librarian at the Washburn library, and it was there that the two met. Paul Eberhart and Eleanor Taylor soon married, made their home, and raised their family just a few blocks away, so close that a good swing of a bat from their front yard could land a baseball just outside Paul's classroom door.

Eleanor was in many ways the quintessential salt-of the-earth homemaker, wife, and mother. She was responsible for the children, the household, the meals and the good order of the family. And she could never do enough for others. "My mother was just extraordinarily kind and caring," Allan said. "Most people describe her as a saint."

Eleanor also had a great sense of humor; she could poke fun at herself and find great amusement in the peculiarities of others. During baseball season, the St. Louis Cardinals' Dizzy Dean was often the source of her amusement. She had followed the St. Louis team since childhood, mostly because of Dean, and while she loved him as a player, Eleanor loved him even more as an announcer calling the Cardinals' games years later. Dean would say the silliest odd things that would amuse her no end. Often he would mispronounce or misuse simple words, or even make up new words of his own, as in how a player might have "slud" into first base feet first. "Slud is something more than slid," he supposedly once said. "It means sliding with great effort."[7] There was no television in the Eberhart house until the children were much older, so when the Cardinals were playing, the radio would be on with Dizzy Dean doing the play-by-play. And Eleanor couldn't wait for Allan and Jean to come home from school so she could tell them exactly what silly odd thing he might have said that day.

Paul did not always carry with him the lightness and ease in life that his wife did. He could be moody, unusually quiet, and often needed time alone, undisturbed. But while Paul often sought solitude, he also was a very present father. Having a flexible schedule and living so close to the college meant that he could be home a great deal. The family ate all of their meals together almost every day, their father often picking Jean and Allan up at school, bringing them home for lunch, and then taking them back again.

Jean and her father had a particularly close relationship. Their close bond was cemented when Paul became Jean's primary caretaker after Allan was born. Allan battled serious health issues during his early months of life and Eleanor spent almost every waking hour focused on Allan and his health issues, while Paul took almost sole responsibility for caring for Jean. She was only eighteen months old. Paul still had classes to teach each week but when he was not physically in the classroom he was home with Jean or Jean was by his side at school.

After many months, Allan began to recover and by his first birthday he was thriving. Responsibilities at the Eberhart household returned to what would be normal for a family in the 1950s, Jean's mother as the stay-at-home housewife and Jean's father back at work. What didn't return to normal, however, was the bond between Jean and her father. From the time she was very small, he was her greatest champion and closest pal. She could do no wrong in his eyes. He taught her tennis, to love opera, and to never give less than her best. And she never disappointed him.

In many ways it was a 1950s "Happy Days" life, interrupted now and then by a tornado or two. The tornadoes came across the plains with regularity, touching down wherever they pleased. Official record keeping began in the 1890s and, over the next seventy-five years, Topeka suffered a direct hit ten different times, although none struck in heavily populated areas or caused significant damage.

By the 1960s, the local branch of the national weather service had state-of-the-art radar, but the state of the art was primitive; weather radar was not yet capable of detecting tornadoes. Instead, the early warning system consisted of volunteer spotters making phone calls to radio and television stations. On June 8, 1966, when spotters provided the first reports of a tornado touching down southwest of the city and moving in a northeast direction, the people of Topeka did not panic, mostly because Burnett's Mound, the highest point in Topeka, was in the tornado's path. Many believed Burnett's Mound would protect them as it always had.

Burnett's Mound was a sacred burial ground of the Potowatomi Indian tribe and named for a tribal chief. The legend passed down through the generations was that the spirits would protect the city from harm as long as those spirits were left undisturbed. When the winds swept up from the south or west, the myth held, they would dissipate when they ran into Burnett's Mound and Topeka would be spared. Not everyone believed the Indian legend. A water tower and other buildings were eventually constructed on the mound despite strong warnings from Native Americans leaders about disturbing the sacred spirits.

That June 8th was a Wednesday, a warm and muggy early summer evening. Most families were just finishing dinner, putting the dishes away, or sitting down to watch *The Patty Duke Show*. Some were outside chatting with neighbors, their eyes occasionally glancing toward the darkening sky. Just before the sirens went off, the sky turned "a sickening greenish color." Many Topekans recorded their recollections for an oral history project. Most remember the exact moment when an ordinary evening suddenly "felt like something was wrong."[8]

"The sky that evening was unforgettable. I've never seen weather like it before or since," Carol Yoho remembered. She was sixteen years old at the time. "The sky churned green and yellow, and then the air was deathly still. There was no doubt in anyone's mind that a serious storm was developing. The adults were listening to a portable radio when they heard that a tornado had touched down near Burnett's Mound and was headed our way."

Those watching the local evening news on Channel 13 saw TV anchorman Bill Kurtis suddenly step in front of the weather map to urge people to immediately take cover. The tornado was real, it had arrived, and this time Burnett's Mound was not going to stop it. At almost the same exact time, the sirens began to scream and it started to rain as though a "huge black curtain" descended from the sky. "As I looked at it, I could see that the sides seemed to be 'boilin'," according to Jan Griffin, a beauty salon worker, "and I suddenly realized it was a monster tornado on the ground, heading right at us."

The tornado first touched town eight miles south of town, then traveled directly over Burnett's Mound, leaving a path of destruction six or eight blocks wide and 22 miles long. It was on the ground more than a half-hour and, unlike most tornadoes, it didn't hopscotch up and down but just stayed on the ground, tearing up everything in its path. It tore clear through the heart of central Topeka, then angled out over the municipal airport before it sailed off onto the prairie at the far side of town. This F-5 rated tornado, the highest rating given for the most severe, intense tornadoes, had done more damage than any other tornado in United States recorded history.

With an estimated $100 million dollars of damage, Topeka was forever changed that day, and so many lives changed along with it. The city was devastated. A large section of Washburn University lay in ruins.

Paul and Eleanor Eberhart were not in Topeka that day. They were on one of their cross-country jaunts, traveling back from Providence, Rhode Island, after attending Allan's college graduation from Brown University.

On the morning of June 9, with Jean back in Cambridge and Allan in Providence, each picked up their separate copies of the *New York Times* at about the same time, and they saw a picture of Topeka in ruins on the front page. Not just Topeka, but a picture of the Washburn University campus. And not just the Washburn campus, but a picture of the crumbled pile of bricks that previously had been Paul's office and second home.

The Eberhart family home on Lane Street, just two blocks away, was spared that June evening, but Washburn was unrecognizable. The entire family was devastated. "That place had been our life," Allan said. Most devastated of all, of course, was Paul. The building where he taught and had his office for decades was gone. Washburn, his other home, his place with his books and his papers and connections. His anchor. His life. Gone. Within weeks it became clear that more significant than the loss of his books and his papers and his office was that Paul was in the throes of losing his grip on reality.

"It was evident almost from the start that something was terribly wrong," Allan said. He had planned to head for Europe after graduation, but once he arrived in Topeka and saw his father, he understood immediately that his plans would have to change. "We didn't know anything about mental illness then, but what we learned later was that he had all the classic signs of someone falling into a deep depression. My dad just looked haunted."

Neither Allan nor Jean remember having even an inkling that lurking just below the surface of this very high functioning, competent man was this hidden illness. To them he was just Dad, a strong and loving man who cared deeply for his family, even as he clearly had many peculiar ways. He could lie on the living room couch listening to opera, lost in his own little world for hours. He might sit quietly and not participate in conversations when in social settings, or he might speak up loudly to voice his opinion in an almost lecturing tone, ignoring any signals from others that they did not care to listen any longer to his monologue. He bought a brand new car but kept it parked in the garage, only using it on very special occasions. He could seem odd to others, appear uncomfortable or lacking in social skills. But to his children, that was just Dad. It was just the way he was.

"He had some moods. And he would have headaches sometimes and we were told to be quiet. Or he would sit out in the car for hours. Just sit. That's the most I ever knew," Jean said. "I guess mom was so good at disguising any problem that I never knew there was a problem. It touched Mom, of course. But it didn't really touch us, my brother and me."

The clues, however, had been there all along. Comments from colleagues at work that he just wasn't himself lately or he was having one of his bad weeks. The walking-on-eggshells kind of feeling at home, the always-being-careful with what was done and said so as not to upset their father. "There was just so much that you never talked about, never raised, because I guess you kind of knew it would set him off," Allan said. "There were so many undercurrents. He had these moods, and sometimes the anger. I witnessed that quite a bit. It didn't have violence associated with it, but it was scary. Although it was something I don't think Dad ever showed to Jean."

In the years just before Paul became so ill, there were clues, too, in his letters to Jean. He would often mention that he was behind on his work, wasn't sure he'd be able to catch-up, that he had no enthusiasm for getting things done or going to a conference somewhere or traveling. If maybe it should have been obvious that Paul was a troubled man, it wasn't to his children. "He could function, he always kept working. Mom never said a thing to us," Jean said. "I guess she watched over him for many years, but we didn't know until what happened after the tornado."

But even in their not knowing, it became clear as both children looked back, that their mother had been managing, coping, and disguising issues and concerns throughout their lifetime. If friends and family always viewed Eleanor as a saint, part of it was because they could see the burden over the years of dealing with concerns about her husband. Jean and Allan never really knew. And yet, of course, they did know. His depression was totally out of the blue. Yet it all made sense in a way.

After the tornado, Paul's descent into darkness became untenable. He would not dress or bathe. He would get agitated and angry. Eleanor tried to make him eat; had to jar him to get up or go to bed. "My dad wouldn't sleep," Allan said. "He was so despondent." Eleanor felt the need to watch him at all hours of the day and night, fearing the worst, which meant she rarely slept.

During that terrible year, the year of the tornado, the year of Jean's father's illness, there was no more hiding or pretending. He was hospitalized at the famed Menninger Clinic diagnosed with unipolar depression, a recurring cyclical depression characterized by acute episodes usually precipitated by severe loss. As her mother wrote in a letter to Jean, "Yesterday the doctor told us what we already knew." From that point on, there were secrets no more.

Even as Jean returned to Harvard for her final year, her thoughts were never far from Topeka. Those months were punctuated by regular phone calls and many long drives home to check on her father's progress. Jean's mood and sense of optimism varied as the weekly reports on her father's recovery varied. He seemed to make progress and then fall back. The hope that he would recover and be able to return home turned to desperation when he seemed to do the opposite. The prospect of his never coming out of the hospital was devastating. When the experts at the clinic felt stymied, they recommended electric shock therapy, something that seemed a barbaric and desperate measure to Jean. It was to be a year-long roller coaster of heart-wrenching family decisions about treatment options, of Paul getting worse and getting better, before Paul eventually climbed his way back out of his very dark hole and became well enough to return home again, almost a year later, and eventually return to teaching.

Jean often thought of that year not as her last year of law school, but as the year of the tornado and the year of her father. But it also turned out to be the year of two other men: Frank Dubofsky and Walter Mondale.

PART TWO

6

Washington D.C. 1968

Every college campus has students that everybody knows, or knows of. On the Stanford University campus in the early 1960s, Frank Dubofsky was one of those students. He was, first and foremost, a football player. He didn't play one of the flashiest positions, didn't throw long passes or score touchdowns, but he was a star recruit, projected as an All-American, and elected captain his junior year. He was also one of the more recognizable players because of his soft leather helmet, a close replica of the original leather helmets worn by footballers in the 1920s. Frank didn't wear it to gain attention. He wore it because each time he made a tackle, the stiff front edge of the team-issued helmet would cut into the ridge where his forehead and his nose met, and a geyser of blood would erupt. Again and again. The leather helmet fit differently, was softer and more forgiving, and solved the problem. When the leather-helmeted Frank Dubofsky was on the field, you couldn't help but notice him.

Students may have first noticed Frank because he played football, but they came to know him because of the football he *didn't* play. Early in his senior year, when national sports writers predicted he would be a shoo-in for All-American, Frank abruptly quit the team. According to Peter Jan Honigsburg, in "Crossing Border Street: A Civil rights Memoir," it happened this way:

In the fall of 1963, at the start of Frank's senior year, the football coach gave the team a vigorous pep talk before the first game. The coach railed on and on that Saturday's contest would be the most important event of their lives. Yet the more Frank heard, the more he lost heart. Although it was still early in the sixties, it was clear to Frank that the world was changing dramatically. For days during the Cuban Missile Crisis we had anticipated annihilation by nuclear holocaust. Sit-ins at lunch counters had sparked national awareness of the cruelties of segregation; interracial groups of 'Freedom Riders' had risked their lives riding buses into the Southern states; Martin Luther King and his followers had been attacked with police dogs and fire hoses, the brutality spotlighted by national television. And Frank was being told that the football game was the milestone of his life. As the coach droned on, Frank rose, collected his gear, walked out of the locker room, and never returned.[9]

Frank's account differs somewhat. "It was not something I did as flippantly as that story suggests," he said. "It was a very difficult thing, one of the hardest decisions I ever made in my life."

Frank's whole life had been organized around football. It was what he was good at and how he thought of himself: as a football player. Football was at the center of how he and his father, a football coach, related to one another. But once Frank arrived at Stanford, far away from the father/football coach that he loved, and Washington, D.C., where he had grown up, his eyes were opened to much more of life beyond football.

His Western Civilization course freshman year broadened his understanding of the world and may have jump-started a change that would later be fueled by Allard Lowenstein and the Stern Hall boys. Frank always viewed his time at Stanford as divided between the years before and after Al Lowenstein became a part of his life.

"You just cannot overstate how important Al's role was back then. He impacted a lot of people during the short time he was there, including me," Frank said. "He was at the center of protest activities and most responsible for the civil rights movement at Stanford." Frank did not live in Stern Hall but he began spending more and more time with those who did. "They became a big part of my life." And football began to occupy a much smaller part of it. Then, in his senior year, that smaller football part of his life began to turn sour. "I was very disaffected with football by then," he said. "We had a new head coach and I just didn't like him. And I just couldn't respect him, especially after the very tragic accident that never should have happened."

"We had this swinging dummy that weighed maybe 100 pounds, and we had to do drills with it. Three kids had already gotten hurt, had gotten stunned just hitting that dummy. Everyone could see that this was a bad idea and the coach should have stopped it right then, but he didn't. Then one day this young kid, just a beautiful kid, snapped his neck and was totally paralyzed. It was so senseless."

Frank was dealing with a spate of minor injuries that had him playing hurt, and he was being drawn more and more to be involved in civil rights activities. But when his teammate was so severely injured, so needlessly, the questioning about whether he could continue on the team began to gel. "I think all that came together. Football was a big part of who I was my whole life, but I just didn't have the drive, the tenacity anymore," Frank said. "My dad was just not happy about it, and he flew out and said 'you just can't quit'. And I said, 'but I can't do it anymore, Dad. I just can't.' And so I quit the football team and then went down to Mississippi and joined other Stanford students working on the Aaron Henry campaign."

By their junior and senior year, Frank and Jean hung out with some of the same friends and likely had been at the same civil rights or anti-war protests, even to the same parties, but it wasn't until after graduating from Stanford, at a party in Washington, that they actually met. Jean was working at a legal aid job and living on Water Street. Their two circles of Stanford friends working or attending graduate school in D.C. melded into one. When Jean threw a party at the Water Street house, Frank, who had not been on her invitation list, heard that Stanford grads were getting together and he decided to come.

They ran into each other a few more times that summer and from time to time over the next year when Jean was in Washington, or when Stanford friends gathered for a wedding or other social engagements. But she was mostly busy with school and with her friends, dating others and, as it turns out, mostly falling in love with someone else. At the end of her second year at law school, however, when the relationship that she thought was going somewhere ended in disappointment, she picked herself up and began dating others again. And much to Jean's surprise and to the surprise of her friends, the friendship with Frank Dubofsky began to blossom into something more.

Jean's friends did not think this big, burly football player would be her "type". "How could he be a match for her? He went to Stanford to play football; his father was a football coach," said Susan Westerberg Prager, a classmate of Jean at Stanford and a lifelong friend. "Jean was an intellectual, an activist, an independent woman who seemed to know exactly where she was going in life, and she did not seem at all like the football-player type."

But Frank was then, and is today, much more than a football player. "There was always another side to Frank," Jean said. "His decision to quit football and go to Mississippi; his commitment to civil rights work. And he was somebody who could deal with me. He was comfortable with women who might want to accomplish something."

By the summer of 1966, Jean and Frank were a part of each other's life, although living in different cities. Jean interned in San Francisco for the League of California Cities that summer, then returned to Cambridge for her last year of law school. Frank spent the summer in Louisiana, involved in a number of civil rights efforts, including the 20-mile Meredith March. "I thought I would die after the first 10 miles," he wrote in a letter to Jean.

In the fall, Frank returned to Georgetown Law School in Washington. Because he had spent a year traveling before beginning law school, he still had two more years ahead. They saw each other rarely, but their letters during that time provide a glimpse of who they each were becoming.

Jean wrote to Frank of the tornado, of the physical destruction of Washburn and the neighborhood, of the loss of all that was familiar, including the man her father had been. Frank's understanding and sympathy was sometimes poetic, often philosophical, and always deeply sensitive to what he perceived she might be feeling. "After our talks last week I had the feeling this was not quite the same Jean I had talked with last summer," Frank wrote, worried about the toll her father's illness was taking on her. "The change is minor, but noticeable … pushing you farther down on the scale that ranges from optimism to despair. How do you avoid this sliding? God Damn, I wish I knew. But try," he urged.

Jean's letters describing what she was going through, he wrote, made him flash back to a time when he was a little boy struggling with his own worry about his mother, a reference to the tragedy of mental illness in his own life.

Shortly after Frank was born, his father enlisted in the Navy, leaving his mother with a seven-year-old and an infant. Frank's father spent three years in the service, including eighteen months at sea. During the time he was absent, what may have begun as episodes of post-partum depression eventually plunged Frank's mother into such a state of serious mental illness that she became incapable of caring for her children. By the time Frank was four, his mother was living in a locked psychiatric ward. She would spend the rest of her life at St. Elizabeth's Hospital For the Insane in Washington, D.C.

Mental illness was not openly discussed at the time. It was hidden. It was mysterious and frightening and wounding, both to those with the illness and to their families. Jean and Frank did not often discuss or dwell on their families' shared traumas, but their letters showed hints of an uncommon understanding of each other because of those experiences.

Mostly, however, their letters showed them grappling with their places in the world. They wrote about their futures, what they hoped to do to lead a good and meaningful life. They were clearly struggling with just what their relationship could become as Jean crept closer to law school graduation and decisions about what she should do next, what kind of job she might find, and what city would become her next home.

In the end, the biggest factor as Jean weighed job options was Frank. When the time came for Jean to make firm plans about the life ahead of her, "Frank was very much in the picture," Jean said. He had one more year at Georgetown Law School. "And so Washington ended up the place to go."

It had been five years since Jean's first Washington job as an intern with Senator Carlson. Over the course of those years the country had changed. The South was aflame with protests, violence, and growing cries for the federal government to take steps to end the unequal treatment and injustice experienced by blacks. Washington had changed too. Lyndon Baines Johnson was thrown into office after President Kennedy was assassinated, and he immediately put his full weight behind a civil rights bill that had been languishing in the fiercely divided congress. Within two years the Civil Rights Act of 1964, which included provisions granting women equal rights in employment, and the Voting Rights Act of 1965, guaranteeing African Americans the right to vote, had become law.

Despite those efforts and a raft of Great Society programs directed at overcoming poverty and injustice in America, the tumult in the South and on college campuses was at its height by the time Jean was on her way back to Washington.

Campus protests had given way to campus take-overs. Civil rights activists had been joined by militant revolutionaries within the civil rights and anti-war movements, and the actions by the Students for Democratic Society (SDS), the Weathermen, the Black Panthers, and others led to more violence, to bombings of symbols of authority, to murders and assassinations, to soldiers in the streets and on college campuses.

Then body bags began arriving from Vietnam, and arriving on the evening news and into living rooms across the country. Soon enough, almost everyone would know someone impacted by the war in Vietnam. Someone who was going, or arranging their lives around the possibility of getting drafted and having to go. Or someone who went and never came back. Someone's friend, or cousin, or brother.

It was a time that Associated Press reporter Mitchell Landsberg described as "that tragic, traumatic, strangely transcendent year;" [10] a time of movements, revolution, violence, tumultuous race riots, the blossoming of flower children, increasingly confrontational anti-war protests, setbacks in Vietnam, and a pervading sense of rage and anarchy. In the nation's capitol, this boiling cauldron of unrest took on a unique tone and power, as the president and the Congress wrestled with what could be done, should be done, to quell what often appeared to be a growing insurrection in the streets surrounding the White House and Capitol Hill. It was during all of this that Senator Walter Mondale of Minnesota became part of Jean's story.

Without knowing it, the two had first crossed paths years earlier at the Democratic National Convention in Atlantic City in 1964. At the time, Jean was an intern for Senator Carlson, a Republican, yet she was sitting high up in the rafters in the convention hall where Democrats were about to nominate their candidate for president. She came with a friend who worked for a Democratic senator. By then Jean was not so sure she was still a Republican, and when her friend found herself with an extra ticket, attending was an easy choice. New Jersey was close by. Jean had a car. And they knew somebody with a hotel room they could share for a couple of nights. So they drove north, took a right turn at Philadelphia, and landed in Atlantic City just as the convention began on a muggy August evening.

Walter Mondale, then Minnesota's young attorney general, was a key player on the convention credentials committee. In the days leading up to the convention, Mondale had spent long and tense hours alternating between an Atlantic City hotel room and official committee hearings, listening to Martin Luther King, Jr. and Fannie Lou Hamer and dozens of other civil rights pioneers make the case for seating the Mississippi Freedom Democratic Party (MFDP) as official convention delegates. These leaders told stories of the suffering and sacrifices blacks had made to gain equal protections and voting rights in the South; and they made threats to disrupt the convention with demonstrations and protests, even stage a walkout, if the MFDP delegates were not seated.

On the phone and in person, under great pressure, Mondale juggled conversations, proposals, and compromises, trying to resolve an issue likely to blow-up an already volatile party convention. The compromise he was instrumental in forging—seating the regular delegation but offering two additional seats to the MFDP—angered both sides, and Mondale returned to Minnesota with the echoes of bitter criticism still ringing in his ears.

It didn't take long for him to cheer up, however. By fall, Minnesota Senator Hubert Humphrey had been elected vice-president and Minnesota Governor Karl F. Rolvaag appointed Walter Mondale to fill Humphrey's U.S. Senate seat. It was the second time Mondale had been plucked from obscurity. The previous governor, Orville Freeman, named Mondale, his former campaign manager, to replace the state attorney general, who had just resigned. At the age of thirty-two, Mondale was the youngest attorney general in Minnesota history. Four years later he became the youngest and one of the most liberal members of the United States Senate.

By the time Jean graduated from law school, Walter Mondale had settled into his role as a senator, but was impatient with the customs of the Senate that dictated that new senators wait their turn and follow the lead of their elders. "Across the South, African-Americans couldn't eat at a lunch counter, couldn't drink from a public drinking fountain, wouldn't dare to register to vote. Cities were badly divided, black from white, and black children mostly attended segregated schools, often in terrible conditions," Mondale remembered.[11] The country was being torn apart by the continued racial strife and protests over an increasingly unpopular war, and Mondale felt strongly these were concerns that the Senate ought to be focused on. But it wasn't. He was determined to use his time there to push for change even if his elders wouldn't. His focus would be civil rights.

Moderate civil rights leaders pleaded with Congress to pass additional civil rights protections, not simply to undo grave injustice, but because they were deeply concerned that the more radical elements of the civil rights movement would step in to replace those who believed in moderation and non-violence if more progress was not forthcoming. The powder keg of racial division was no longer confined to the South. Mondale and others believed it was about to explode in the North as well, and felt discrimination in housing was the most visible inequity that needed to be addressed. Mondale was at the center of an effort to push a new civil rights act through the Senate to make discrimination in housing illegal.

When Jean heard that Senator Mondale was looking for a legislative assistant, she called over to the Senate office, said she'd like to apply, sent over her resume and was invited to come in for an interview. She didn't know what to expect when she arrived at Mondale's office and had not anticipated that she would be led directly into Mondale's office for a conversation. Nor did she expect that she would soon be debating him over his support for the war.

"Senator Mondale was a protégé of Vice President Hubert Humphrey, who was supportive of the war," Jean said. "So I think Mondale felt he couldn't be against it." Jean, on the other hand, was adamantly opposed to the war and felt obliged to share her views. "I think I spent the whole interview arguing with him about the Vietnam War." She was as surprised as anyone when Mondale's chief-of-staff called her back a few days later and offered her the job.

More than 50 years later, Walter Mondale could not recall that initial interview with Jean, nor that she spent the entire time trying to persuade him that he was wrong about the war. "But it does sound like Jean," he said with a chuckle. According to Mondale, Jean was one of those people you do not forget, mostly because of what he called her extraordinary contribution at a very special time in history. "I was looking for gifted people, smart people, brilliant people and I saw that in her. She could take these tough issues and make sense of them for me. She was not a routine employee doing routine work. She was at the cutting edge of our ideas and what we were going to do and how we would get it done and how we would explain ourselves. Fair Housing was a high hill to climb in those days and she was right in the middle of it, right at the center of the great struggle. She helped me at a crucial time when we changed so much."

When Jean was hired by Mondale, she had no idea what lay ahead. As one of four legislative aides in an office with a dozen staffers, mostly men, Jean began with a general caseload of legislative matters—writing memos, attending committee hearings, and following legislation in a variety of areas. But when two senior staffers left for other jobs, Jean was asked to handle what she called "plum assignments." "There were just so few women working as legislative aides that people noticed you. That's partly why I got to do things so young. If you were a woman and you did your job well, you got noticed. That's just the way it was. Being a woman was a real advantage in some ways." But not all ways.

The Senate was a stodgy place and there were many rules to be followed. When in the Senate chamber, for instance, staff members were required to kneel along the side wall in a certain manner: with one knee up and one down. "But with a short skirt on, you just couldn't kneel with one knee up and one down," Jean said. The sergeant-at-arms had little experience dealing with women staffers kneeling in the Senate chambers and insisted that protocol was protocol, skirts or not. When Jean failed to persuade him that the archaic rules were not going to work anymore, she took the issue to her boss, Senator Mondale. Soon Jean was kneeling on both knees in the Senate chamber without being reprimanded by the sergeant-at-arms.

Jean spent a lot of time in and out the chamber because one of her assignments was assisting Mondale with a new civil rights bill that included addressing discrimination in housing, the next civil rights frontier crying out for attention and the most controversial piece of the proposed new bill. Senate pragmatists judged that inclusion of a ban on housing discrimination in a new civil rights act would doom the chances of any new civil rights bill getting through Congress. The wounds from the bruising fight over the 1964 Civil Rights Act were still fresh, and the party leadership had no appetite for another long and bitter battle that would go nowhere.

Mondale understood their reluctance. A federal ban on discrimination in housing would force every city in America to end the common practice of real estate agents and apartment owners refusing to rent or sell to black families in certain neighborhoods. It was "civil rights getting personal," Mondale recalled. "It wasn't just some abstract cause down South, this was bringing desegregation into neighborhoods in northern cities."[12] Most members of Congress feared a backlash in their home districts if the federal government banned the practice. It was no surprise then, when the Civil Rights Act of 1968 was being drafted, that the controversial housing discrimination language was left on the cutting room floor, the same place it had landed with previous civil rights efforts.

A small group of Senate liberals were dissatisfied with the leadership's desire for a symbolic civil rights bill containing only small, incremental additional protections. They began to meet regularly as an informal civil rights caucus to find ways to push for more. Whenever the caucus gathered, each senator brought along a staff person. Walter Mondale brought Jean Eberhart. "We would meet frequently to help shape the strategy, do nose counts, and connect with outside groups, like the NAACP or the White House," Mondale said. "Jean was in all those meetings and with me on the floor of the Senate." Just months out of law school, Jean Eberhart was spending her days in the backrooms of the Capitol devising strategy to end discrimination in housing with senators Jacob Javits of New York, Philip Hart of Michigan, Ted Kennedy of Massachusetts and other giants of the Senate.

It was not lost on Jean's boss how extraordinary an experience it was for her, the youngest in the room, and the only woman. After one such session, Mondale turned to Jean as they were leaving and said, "You should pay me for this job!" To breathe the same air as these men of consequence at a time of such great possibility, and to be part of the decision-making process, was a heady experience for Jean.

One of the early the decisions made by the group turned out to be key in ensuring that housing discrimination remained part of the discussion as the civil rights bill was making its way through the process. They decided that Mondale, the youngest senator, ranked 87th in Senate seniority, should take the lead. In the arcane world of Senate protocol, they reasoned, his lack of seniority and perceived lack of power would allow his efforts to be dismissed or ignored by the more powerful senior senators. Mondale could take the fair housing bill through his obscure sub-committee of the Banking and Commerce Committee, a committee with more liberal members than the Judiciary Committee, where civil rights bills ordinarily belonged.

While the civil rights caucus had little reason for optimism about their chances of forcing the fair housing provisions back into the civil rights bill making its way through the Senate, they were determined to tell the story of one of the most serious remnants of discrimination still in existence. In the 1960s, congressional hearings were a common and effective venue for gaining attention on important issues. Mondale scheduled hearings in his sub-committee and caucus members intended to use the evidence presented at those hearings to press the case for including a ban on discrimination in housing.

The months' long journey of the fair housing legislation was filled with twists and turns, intrigue and maneuvering, the introduction of various amendments, threats of filibusters, a series of vote counts and floor debates, a few strategic successes, and many failures along the way. The senators and their staffers met daily, sometimes two or three times a day, constantly adjusting tactics and making plans for what else or what next could be done.

When the Civil Rights Act of 1968 finally reached the floor of the Senate, however, senators opposed to including housing discrimination prevailed, as expected. The bill was the same symbolic minimalist version that had passed the House, which did not include a ban on discrimination in housing. In March, against the advice and with the resistance of the Democratic congressional leadership and the White House, Walter Mondale made one final try to attach a housing discrimination amendment to the bill by enlisting Senator Edward Brooke as a co-sponsor. Brooke, a recently elected Republican from Massachusetts, was the Senate's only African American and the first black since Reconstruction. He made an impassioned plea on the Senate floor that ultimately forced his colleagues to formally debate their motion to amend the bill to deal with housing discrimination. In the Senate at the time, debates often went on for days and often influenced the outcome of a given vote. And this debate, when the only black senator stood to make the moral arguments against the vestiges of discrimination still very much alive in the country, moved the institution of the Senate in unexpected ways. "Senator Brooke spoke with special heat and intensity," Mondale said.

It was high drama and the highest of high stakes in the battle for civil rights. After 100 hours of debate, when senators on both sides were exhausted, and with no resolution in sight, they turned to Senator Everett Dirksen, a Republican from Illinois, hoping he could broker a compromise. Dirksen had stepped in at the last minute four years earlier to find a compromise that resulted in the passage of the Civil Rights Bill of 1964. His colleagues hoped he could once again salvage another civil rights bill.

Dirksen refused to act as a negotiator between those supporting or opposing the Mondale/Brooke amendment. Instead, he told both sides that if they wanted his help in breaking the stalemate, he would provide a substitute amendment of his own. And he would expect both sides to accept his version. "Mondale was ready to give up big parts of what we had been fighting for, ready to compromise, to settle for some little thing, anything to at least start down the road towards some protections against discrimination in housing," Jean said.

Within days, after more procedural wrangling and a series of cloture votes that finally forced an up or down vote on the Dirksen amended bill, a comprehensive new civil rights bill passed the Senate. Much to the shock of Senator Mondale and the fair housing advocates, the new bill not only included the federal ban on housing discrimination that they had fought so hard for, but Dirksen had provided a new title for the legislation: The Fair Housing Act of 1968.

It was a stunning, almost miraculous, turn of events. Yet it was too early for a victory celebration. The Senate had done the unthinkable, but in order for the bill to become law, it had to return to the House for a vote there. It was an election year and House members had already made clear that they would not vote for a ban on discrimination in housing. March rolled into April and it appeared likely that House leaders would not even allow the bill to come to the floor for a vote. "No one thought this blockbuster would make it through the Senate," Jean said. "And then, no one in the House even wanted to have to vote on it."

It was a month that Jean would never forget. A month that the country could never forget. Everything was happening at the same time. Labor leader César Chavez, who had led striking farmworkers and boycotts against grapes and lettuce, ended a hunger strike that had captured the national conscience. Former attorney general Robert F. Kennedy was with Chavez the day he ended his hunger strike. Kennedy was in the Senate by then and had been traveling from Appalachia to South Africa to highlight the shame of poverty, inequality, and injustice.

The Senate passed the Fair Housing Act on March 11. The New Hampshire presidential primary was held on March 12 and Senator Eugene McCarthy, the only anti-war Democrat courageous enough to challenge the sitting president, shocked the country when he won 42% of the vote. After the New Hampshire primary results made clear that the Democratic Party would welcome an anti-war candidate, on March 16 Robert Kennedy then announced his own candidacy for the presidency from the Caucus Room of the Old Senate Office Building. Two weeks later, President Johnson addressed the nation, announcing a halt to the bombing campaign and a renewed commitment to find a peaceful way out of Vietnam. Then he stunned the nation by revealing that he would not seek another term as president. But it was four days later when the truly unthinkable happened. Again.

On April 4, 1968, on an overcast and balmy Thursday evening in Memphis, an assassin's bullet killed Martin Luther King, Jr. King's murder and the violence that followed tore an even deeper hole in the heart of the country. Overnight, the pent-up frustration about the war and poverty and the breadth of inequities and injustice that had been lying barely below the surface, exploded into riots and looting and burning in sixty cities across the country. There was rage over King's death, rage from waiting so many decades, rage because Dr. King, the man who had preached non-violence as the vehicle for change, was now dead, a victim of violence.

"When Martin Luther King was killed, I felt like I did when President Kennedy died," Jean said. She was in Washington, in the heart of a city that blew up overnight. It was the fires, more than the rioting and looting, that she remembers most. "The fires started at Fourteenth and U Street, in the heart of black neighborhoods, not far from the night club where jazz musician Charlie Byrd played. I had a friend who had an apartment at the epicenter of those fires. I ran over to the library where he worked, found him in the stacks, and told him he'd have to come stay with me; he couldn't go home." Jean lived out near the National Cathedral, several miles north, away from the fires.

And like everyone else in Washington, for the next few days, home was where they would remain. "We couldn't go anywhere. There was a total curfew and we all had to stay at home. All we could do was watch on television."

With the South and cities all across America in flames, chaos and fear about what might come next gripped the nation. President Johnson and congressional leaders were desperate to do something, anything, to calm the waters, begin the healing, and get through the next weeks and months. It was under that strain, and in the midst of that trauma and tumult, that on April 10 the leaders of the House of Representatives reversed course and brought the Senate's amended version of the civil rights act to the floor of the House. With unprecedented speed and without debate, the Fair Housing Act of 1968 passed the House that same day. The very next day, President Lyndon Baines Johnson signed the supposed "bill-that-would-never-pass" into law.

The country weathered the trauma of the winter and spring of 1968. But any satisfaction that civil rights advocates felt over achieving their goal of making discrimination in housing illegal was tempered by the tragedy that spurred the bill forward. No one doubted that absent the assassination of Martin Luther King, and the intense political heat felt by elected officials, the bill would never have become law.

The experience of those intense months left Jean exhausted and exhilarated, filled with mixed emotions and changed in ways she would only fully appreciate decades later. "Working for Mondale and working on the fair housing bill was one of the more extraordinary experiences. It showed me what somebody who is interested in civil rights issues and poor people's issues could do," she said. And it showed her that even though she was a woman, at a time when few women were allowed to play significant roles in public life, there were times and places and bosses who welcomed women at the table. "If I had worked for another senator, I would not have had nearly the responsibility I had been given by Mondale; it just wouldn't have happened. I was young and I was a woman, but I was treated like someone who was respected, and I realized later that that was quite a remarkable thing at the time."

7

Confronting Slavery

In Washington Jean worked behind the scenes; few people outside of the small circles of Senate colleagues knew her name. But in Topeka, Kansas, eight years after graduating from high school, people not only knew her name but continued to view her as a shining and rising star. She had written a weekly column for the *Topeka Daily Capital* while still in high school, had achieved fame as the Betty Crocker Homemaker award winner, and her reports of her European student abroad travel adventures were regular features in the Sunday paper. Recent notice of her job with Mondale and her work on the civil rights bill also made the local papers.

It was not a surprise, then, that in the spring of 1968, when Topeka High decided to invite a recent graduate who had gone on to some success to give the graduation keynote address, Jean was an obvious choice. Obvious maybe to those responsible for the choosing, but not to Jean. When she received the official invitation letter her immediate reaction, she said later, was "Why in the world they would want me?" But she was planning a visit home and she could fit it into her schedule, so she accepted the invitation.

The principal urged Jean to select a subject she felt graduates would welcome and Jean chose student activism, one of the hottest topics of the year. *Time* and *Life* and many other weekly magazines regularly reported on the unsettled times and the role that young activists had come to play, often in depth and occasionally with cover stories. Young people were at the forefront of protest and of change, through university sit-ins, take-overs, and voting rights marches; anti-war demonstrations on campuses and in the street; and through organizations such as the Poor People's Campaign, the Students for Democratic Society (SDS) and the Women's Liberation and Black Power movements. Jean's message to the high school graduates would be that there was a role for them, that they could make a difference if they decided to get involved and stay involved.

The Topeka High School commencement exercises were held at Moore Bowl on the Washburn University campus. Jean felt at home when she walked out on to the stage. She had notes sketching out various thoughts, but no written speech in front of her as she stood at the podium. She knew what she wanted to say and aimed her message directly at the six hundred graduates in the audience. Seek your place, find a role, and understand your own power to make a difference, she told them.

It was nothing revolutionary, she thought. Nothing incendiary. Just telling it the way it was. She received a fine round of applause and initially it seemed that her remarks had been well received. The story on the front page of the next morning's *Topeka Daily Capital* was positive, more a personal profile than a review of her speech. Jean was invited to speak because of her many achievements, the article noted, but "Jean didn't preach the time-worn topic of striving for higher peaks of achievement.... Instead, she drew from a topic that was uppermost in her interests at the moment and one many of the graduates will confront face-to-face in the very near future: social protests."[13] The article reported that Jean told the graduates that the social movements like the Poor People's Campaign in Washington, student protests against the Vietnam War, and campus uprisings such as at Columbia University "have definitely had some effect" and were methods that allowed people without power a chance to be heard.

The Rev. Charles Erickson of the First Congregational Church shared the stage with Jean that evening; he gave the closing prayer. He penned a note to Jean that same evening to let her know "the joy of hearing your speech." He had spoken with some of the graduates, he wrote, and "they were extremely pleased with your forthright presentation of 'telling it like it is.' More power to you in your marvelous early days of your career. Topeka is blessed by having had your presence in words and feeling conveyed so well in your address. Thank you for being who you are."

Jean received other messages of praise, appreciation, and acclaim, the kind of positive support she was accustomed to receiving in her hometown. But there were other voices, louder voices, voices not of praise but of condemnation. Angry phone calls, shaking of heads, questioning and criticism, letters to the editor. And soon a public ruckus ensued.

"I attended the Topeka High School commencement exercises. I was shocked and very disgusted with the topic that was presented by Miss Jean Eberhart," one letter-to-the-editor writer wrote. "I, for one, was sorry that I made the drive from Kansas City to hear the illustrious speaker," wrote another. "I...hope she stays in Washington."[14] A former classmate later captured the mixed views: "My mother got up and walked out" but the student body was for you.[15]

Under pressure from and at the insistence of school officials, Jean begrudgingly agreed to prepare a written response to the furor. They wanted her to clarify exactly what she said and meant. Jean's response ran three pages.

Her remarks were meant to be descriptive, she wrote, not prescriptive. Meant to detail what was happening in the world and how young people were key participants, using the tool of protest to express their views and attempt to influence policies they disagreed with. The inequities and injustice of the war, and of discrimination and poverty, were real and ripe for protest, she wrote. "I advocated nothing except an attempt to understand" the world as it is, and the role young people are playing. She concluded by taking direct aim at her critics.

> To my knowledge the only critics who have identified themselves have been a right-wing Nazarene minister and several of (his) friends… I listened for over an hour to the objections of the Nazarene minister. He is conservative and I do not agree with him. I hope that the questioning that I have been subjected to was motivated by more than that man's questions. I do not retract anything I said; nor will I add to it…. I felt honored to be asked to speak at Topeka High's commencement. I was invited to speak to the graduating seniors, and I was told that they were interested in the issues I discussed. I spoke to them and not to their parents. I invite your attention to the lead article in this week's issue of *Time Magazine,* a conservative and Republican publication. Placed in the context of that article and of what is happening throughout the country, what I said was not out of place. I have lost respect for the men who question my right to say what I did, and when Topeka schools are subject to such fear and censorship, I fear for America.

The speech and the furor that followed gave her a taste of speaking her own mind, being out in front. By that summer, Jean had been working in D.C. at least part of the time for four consecutive years, long enough to be convinced that it was time to consider moving on. "When you work for another person, they are the one that is out there, not you. You are doing their things, not your own," she said. She was eager to become a part of a real community, a place where she could make a contribution more directly. She began to contemplate how best to carve out a life where her work would directly make a difference.

"I thought then that the job with Mondale was likely to be the best job I ever had, that I would never have an experience quite as heady. But I also thought that if I had stayed, it was very unlikely there would ever be issues again quite as great as the things I'd worked on." It was difficult to think about leaving, to give up being in the center of power and influence. But it was time. And it wasn't just about her going off on her own. It was about Frank, too.

Jean had returned to D.C. after law school to be near Frank while he completed his last year of law school. And what a year it had been. They were both intimately involved with issues of justice, on the front lines of protests and marches, and with landmark legislation. Frank was the more overt political activist. He led campus reform efforts at Georgetown Law, participated in Dr. King's March on Washington, and organized protests for the 1968 Democratic convention in Chicago.

Frank and Jean loved their work and loved Washington; it was exciting and the work was important. But it was not real life to them and they never envisioned a future as permanent members of the government bureaucracy. By that summer of '68, as Frank was about to graduate from law school, he and Jean were both preoccupied with questions about the next job, where they would go, and what they would do. They both yearned to find a community where they could become involved politically and continue to do a piece of the social justice work that had become a passion for each of them. When they began to inquire about jobs in other parts of the country, however, the last place they thought they would find themselves was Palm Beach County, Florida.

———

Palm Beach was a barrier island that sat just off the Florida coast. With its posh town center, wide boulevards lined by palm trees, and block after block of stone mansions facing the equally stunning waters of the Atlantic coast, it was one of the wealthiest towns in America. It was founded at the turn of the twentieth century as a resort and playground for the rich and famous, becoming a second home to the wealthiest people of America who came to enjoy the quiet and the warmth and to live in the lap of luxury. The Rockefellers and the Kennedys were perhaps the most famous of those wealthy people with homes in that celebrated enclave of wealth and privilege.

Just a few miles inland, however, lived thousands and thousands of the poorest of America's poor: the migrant laborers who harvested the crops, picked the citrus, and enabled the agricultural interests in South Florida to thrive. Sometimes entire families banded together as a group in the orchards and sugar cane fields, working hard, long hours. There were others, like the celery harvesters, called stoop workers, who bent to cut celery stalks, six hundred stoops an hour, hour after hour, day after day, turning their twenty and thirty-year-old bodies into frail, bent specimens. If you wondered how old they were, you might have guessed that they were in their sixties or seventies.

These migrant workers lived in one of the hundreds of different camps, in shacks or houses consisting of little more than four walls and a roof, many without plumbing or running water. Most structures were condemned by local authorities as uninhabitable. And many of the children in the camps had never seen a physician, yet were "not only hungry and malnourished, but obviously and seriously ill."[16]

It is likely that the wealthy citizens of Palm Beach were totally unaware of the world beyond their luxury escape. When reporting on the camps at the time, researchers Robert Cole and Harry Huge observed that "one can drive the major roads of Palm Beach County or Collier County and get no idea what is happening down those dusty pathways that lead to fields and camps."[17]

The secret world down those dusty pathways became less of a secret in 1960 when Edward R. Murrow, one of television's most influential pioneers in broadcasting, produced and narrated a biting documentary entitled *Harvest of Shame*.[18] He pulled back the curtain for the first time on one of the great unknown stories of abject poverty in America, shining a spotlight on Belle Glade, Florida, fifty miles inland and a world away from Palm Beach. A decade later broadcaster Chet Huntley went back to the same little town of Belle Glade, to do a follow-up to Murrow's *Harvest of Shame*. In his special report, *Migrant*,[19] Huntley demonstrated that, in the ten years since Murrow's exposé on those conditions, almost nothing had changed.

Belle Glade came into existence in the late 1920s after a federal project drained parts of Lake Okeechobee to make way for much needed agricultural land. The soil left behind provided just the kind of "muck" perfect for cultivation, especially for sugar cane growers. Over the next forty years, as the sugar cane interests flourished, so too did migrant camps with deplorable living conditions.

Robert Coles and Harry Huge brought additional focus and attention to that same stretch of America when they spent two years living among and studying the working, housing, and health conditions of the children and farmworkers of the migrant camps. In 1969, they documented their findings in a lengthy investigative report titled *Peonage In Florida*.[20] Peonage, meaning involuntary servitude or being held against one's will, is not a word used often in everyday conversation. A more familiar word would be slavery.

The vivid portraits of the people and the places and the lives they lived varied from report to report and migrant camp to migrant camp, but only in the particulars. All of the accounts detailed shockingly similar conditions. Sometimes as families, sometimes as groups of teenagers from the same towns, laborers were brought from as close as Texas, or as far away as Jamaica or Puerto Rico. They came by boat and by bus and were deposited at 'loading zones' "where human beings are picked up and left off"[21] for whatever period of time they were needed, before they were put on buses again to be moved to the next place and the next crop. Growers would give crew bosses up to fifty dollars per head for each of the workers delivered to camp.

Because of the pittance they were paid, even the most experienced pickers made less than $2,000 a year. Then, when it came time to be paid, they were often charged so much for meals, housing and transportation that, once all those fees were deducted from their meager earnings, they were left with little, barely able feed their families. Even worse, the ledgers were kept and held by the camp owners, and often the workers would find themselves in debt to the camp owners or to the farmer, owing more than they could ever pay.

"I was born in south Texas and…when I was about fifteen I was sold….They came and got a whole group of us," was how one worker described it. Then "they tell you that you owe them for the food and the transportation and the mattress on the floor you use for sleeping and they tell you if you try to leave, they'll get you thrown into jail and you'll never get out…so you're their property….They own people, that's what, unless they escape, like I did."[22]

Sometimes packed in buses, sometimes herded into trucks like cattle, they were supervised by crew leaders with guns. There were guns on the trucks. Guns in the camps. Guns in the fields.

The story of the migrant camps and the small rural towns that stretched across South Florida from Fort Myers to Palm Beach wasn't just about the poverty or the desperate conditions. It was about being left behind in America during the era when child labor advocates and labor unions had been making progress for workers in urban America. Through legislation and successfully organizing and bargaining with employers, workers achieved safer working conditions, shortened work days, better wages, and unemployment and disability compensation for work related injuries. It was also a time when federal and local programs had begun providing services to the poor, the hungry, the sick, and the forgotten in cities and towns across the country. But in rural America, these migrant farm workers were "denied just about every benefit that 30 years of struggle achieved for other workers."[23]

When a legal services program that grew out of President Johnson's War on Poverty efforts advertised jobs for lawyers to help some of these underserved populations, Jean and Frank applied. When the call came with an assignment for both of them with South Florida Migrant Legal Services, they did not hesitate. They wanted to go. Although they knew nothing of South Florida, nor much more about the plight of migrant farm workers, they felt lucky to be called. Their only hesitation was that if they were going to go to Florida, there needed to be a wedding first.

After a year in Washington with Frank, Jean was sure Frank was the man she wanted to marry. Frank was less sure. Jean, however, was not prepared to move to Florida with him unless there was a commitment to a future together. That commitment was called marriage.

"That's how I felt about it. If we were going to go to Florida, we were going to get married first. Frank was fine with it," Jean said later, although he may have only come around to being "fine with it" after she suggested that she had a standing offer of a job in San Francisco, and perhaps a romantic relationship there that could be rekindled.

"My recollection is that Jean got really adamant about getting married. Either we get married or I'm going to California was the way she put it," Frank said. "The way she looked at it was that she was not going to follow this guy around the country without being married. Basically it was fish or cut bait." So, yes, in the end, Frank was "fine with it."

They planned a small wedding. "I wasn't such a big fan of large ceremonies," Jean said. "I'd been in enough weddings. Big weddings were not for me." Jean found a church in Washington for the ceremony and a quaint country inn in Maryland for the reception lunch. "The only people there were Frank's father and his sister, and my parents and Allan and Uncle Bob, and then we each had a friend stand-up for us," Jean said. "It was a lovely, lovely day."

Frank and Jean went off to Mexico for a two-week honeymoon adventure, then returned to Washington. They packed up their collective lives into Jean's tiny blue Volkswagen Beetle and Frank's roomier cranberry red Volkswagen bus. Then they headed south to begin their married and professional life together.

They soon found a little bungalow nestled in between sand pine trees and scrub, within a couple of football fields of the dunes and Atlantic Ocean. The small wood-framed cottage, located in a hidden neighborhood accessible only by negotiating a narrow unpaved sandy lane, was three miles up the coast from the local office of the South Florida Migrant Legal Services.

The non-descript one-story cinder block building that housed the small but busy legal services office sat just a few blocks off a mostly rundown main street, not far from the railroad tracks that bisected Delray Beach, a sleepy town south of Palm Beach. When Jean and Frank began their work in the fall of 1968, they were part of a new breed of idealistic young lawyers, almost all of whom had come from Washington to places like Delray Beach "because this was now the civil rights thing to do," Jean said. They believed their job was to use the law to bring about social change, even if it meant ruffling feathers. Even if it meant taking on powerful interests.

It didn't take very long for Frank and Jean to discover the depth of the meaning of the word "injustice". The reality of the shameful plight of the migrants and their deplorable living and working conditions was shocking. On top of that, the powerful interests and the politics combined to prevent these activist attorneys from doing the work they thought they were hired to do.

There was so much poverty, so much sadness, so many issues for these young idealists to deal with, they didn't know where to start. "It was just so very depressing," Jean said. "There was this extraordinary wealth right along the coast, all these rich people in their big houses, then maybe ten blocks of apartment buildings where mostly the elderly lived. And then came the huge farms and orchards and fields, miles and miles of them, where people who were the most incredibly poor people you could imagine lived."

Frank and Jean settled into their jobs and before long had a slew of clients needing help. The lawyers worked to ensure that workers receive their wages, and battled to force camp owners to provide basic sanitation and abide by other health and housing codes. It wasn't just poverty and dreadful living conditions that needed to be addressed, nor simply demanding that owners of camps and farms follow various regulations or laws. To Jean it quickly became clear that one of the things they were witnessing and what they needed to address was something more fundamental, more pernicious, and more shocking.

"One of the largest landowners in Palm Beach County was holding kids at gun point to pick oranges—fifteen and sixteen-year-old boys from Puerto Rico. These were black kids and it was a remnant of slavery in many ways. That kind of thing was going on all over that part of Florida," Jean said. Before the legal services staff arrived, these workers had never had advocates willing or able to speak on their behalf. Jean's way of speaking on their behalf was to bring a slavery lawsuit against one of the most powerful, most connected, most successful agribusinesses in South Florida.

The suit[24] filed in federal court made news not only in South Florida but across the state and across the country. The *Chicago*

Tribune, the *Detroit Press,* and other big city and local newspapers carried stories with the following headlines: "Suit Says Workers Enslaved At Camp,"[25] "Farmer Is Accused of Labor Peonage,"[26] "Plantation Terror Charged,"[27] "Terror of Migrants: Death Threats and Machete Beatings."[28] The charges included bringing Puerto Rican workers into the country illegally, forcibly preventing them from leaving the camps, illegally deducting charges for food and transportation from their wages, preventing their lawyers from meeting with their clients, and "bondage, peonage and involuntary servitude." Felipe Pagan Vidal, the named plaintiff and one of the migrant workers who escaped from the camp, testified in court; he described death threats and being hacked with a machete when he attempted to leave the camp.[29]

At the age of twenty-six, in her first job as a lawyer, in her first appearance in a courtroom before a judge, Jean Dubofsky brought the first slavery case in the country since the post Civil War era. "I think the whole notion of bringing this lawsuit was really all about not having any experience at all," Jean said, looking back. "You don't know what you can't do. So I went just charging off and thought, well, I don't know what else to do so I'll just bring this lawsuit."

On the day of the court proceedings, "the judge wanted to know how old I was, and was my husband in the courtroom, and where did I go to law school, that kind of stuff," Jean said, laughing now many years later in the telling of that story. But at the time, it was no laughing matter at all. "I was worried when we brought this case. The crew leaders that worked for this farmer were really tough guys, and I was a little concerned that they would show up at the office and do us some harm," Jean said.

"We went to court asking for a temporary restraining order, and we got our temporary order and all the workers were put on a bus and sent back to wherever they came from. I'm not sure this is what they wanted, but at least they weren't being held at gunpoint to pick oranges and then not be paid; at least they weren't being held against their will."

It was a risky strategy and not one welcomed by the local judicial system or business leaders. The attention shined a harsh light on the business practices of people and companies thought to be pillars of the community. And those pillars of the community responded to being challenged in such a public way, by people they perceived to be outside northern liberal agitators, by unleashing the full force of their political power. In this homogeneous part of the South, dominated by the large agricultural interests, anyone with power and influence knew everybody else. "It turned out that the judge was good friends with the farm owner," Jean recalled.

Richard Nixon was now president, and the head of the Office of Economic Opportunity, which funded the legal services office, was Donald Rumsfeld. The powerful agricultural interests in Florida and across the country had friends in these high places. They used their influence with the governor, with members of Congress, and with the White House to begin the unwinding of the Florida legal services program even before its first lawsuits made their way all the way through the judicial process. Soon Jean and Frank and all the legal service attorneys had to face the harsh reality that their battle was not just with local growers, or with the local officials and judges turning a blind eye to enforcing employment, health, sanitation, and safety laws; the battle was with their own agency, their own bureaucracy, and their own government that sent them there.

Jean remembered well what they were up against. "The first judge, who was friends with the owner, ruled against us. But we appealed and the Fifth Circuit Court of Appeals that covered all of the South ruled for us. We won that case, but in a way we lost, too. The farm owner and his Congressional buddies used their influence and got our legal services program defunded. The program was just barely starting up and then we were told that the decision had been made to cut a large portion of the funding. The funding for lawyers like us."

The funding cuts and the newly revised federal regulations left South Florida Migrant Legal Services with half the staff and a more circumscribed mission. There would be no more organizing, no more law reform work, no more class action suits on behalf of migrant workers, and no more lawsuits challenging government inaction or discriminatory practices. With a mixture of emotions, Jean and Frank packed their bags, re-stuffed their worldly goods into their two VWs, and turned out the lights in their Florida beachside bungalow. "I felt guilty about doing something that caused the program to be defunded," Jean said. "But that was what we were there for. That was what we were supposed to do—shake things up. And we did."

8

Heading West to Colorado

As the sixties were coming to a close, astronauts Neil Armstrong and Buzz Aldrin walked on the moon, but battles closer to home over racial injustice and the Vietnam War showed little signs of abating. If there was any change in the country's concerns over justice, it was the addition of other voices challenging the prevailing social order: those of women no longer willing to accept the norms or rules or expectations that made them "less than" men.

Restrictions on a woman's ability to fully participate in many aspects of economic and social life varied from state to state. In most states, women could not legally keep their own name after marrying, could not obtain credit or buy a car, and were often fired when they became pregnant. Women everywhere were being paid less, not allowed to apply for certain jobs, and not able to participate in many economic transactions without the permission of their husbands.

There were still no laws forbidding Harvard law professors from excluding women from full participation and equal treatment. No expectation that law firms would find themselves in any kind of legal trouble by stating unabashedly that they simply did not hire women lawyers. No regulations prohibiting employers, including the federal government, from routinely listing a large swath of the mostly higher paying and higher responsibility jobs as "For men only".

County clerks and local judicial officers seldom questioned laws that excluded women from serving on juries. Doctors and hospitals were not allowed to provide safe and legal abortions. And women had no recourse when a husband told his wife where she could or could not work. It was just the way it was, all across the country. Until it wasn't, as women began challenging the status quo and demanded change.

As one decade folded into another, the feminist movement gained steam. The move for an Equal Rights Amendment to the Constitution slowly made its way through the process of acceptance or rejection state by state. "The Pill" became readily available in most states, allowing women to exercise their own reproductive rights. Finally, more and more women were participating in professional and political life.

A small number of women lawyers were invited to join law firms, even become judges at the local level, but most young women entering the law profession would turn to newly created public agencies designed to combat poverty and injustice for job opportunities. Although chased out of Florida, legal services agencies would provide the best opportunities for women lawyers like Jean.

Though short-lived, the experience that Frank and Jean shared in Florida, their exposure to abject poverty and the breadth of hidden injustice, had been searing and discouraging. But they also came away believing in the potential of the law to combat inequities, and with a deeper appreciation that there was a role for them in that fight. More than ever, they were committed to finding a way to do what they both felt they were supposed to do—shake things up. The question once again was where. The answer was not long in coming.

At the same time that the federal government was dismantling law reform efforts at the legal services agency in Delray Beach, it awarded a three-year funding grant to establish the first legal aid offices in Colorado. The new entity, Colorado Rural Legal Services (CRLS), would open its doors in Boulder, thirty miles northwest of Denver, within months. A separately funded legal clinic was also about to open at the University of Colorado (CU) law school, also in Boulder. Through a Georgetown Law School connection, Frank received an offer to work at the CU law clinic, and when that led to a job offer at the new legal services agency for Jean, they had found the "where". They packed up once again and headed west.

In the 1960s and 1970s, the Colorado familiar to most was the Colorado of western myth, a place with wide-open spaces and exquisite natural beauty that invited and welcomed newcomers. Explorers, cowboys, and mavericks were drawn to this yet-to-be-defined place, to hide out, or to make their mark. Frank and Jean felt sure that this place was the right place for them too, where home and people and work would mingle together and become the community they had been looking for.

Frank went on ahead to Colorado because his job started earlier than Jean's, and he began a search for their ideal house, the perfect match for who they were and what their life was about to become. That search took them to the hills above Boulder. This being Colorado, the house was not actually a house. It was a cabin.

"Frank had been there for a few months, so he had been looking. We had talked about what we wanted and when I got there, he took me for a drive," Jean said.

The drive took them up the canyon towards the town of Nederland. A few miles west of Boulder they made a sharp right-hand turn onto a narrow road that immediately began to climb out of the canyon, up and up, back on itself, and up and up again, one S-curve after another. They crept up and around rock outcroppings, through a set of old mining claims, with an occasional small cabin or a larger, newer house sprinkled about in this middle of nowhere. After ten minutes the road turned to dirt, the trees fell away and the hills and meadows in the distance came into view.

As they continued to climb, it opened up even more, with Boulder Falls and the snow-covered Indian Peaks mountain range in the near distance suddenly visible. It took Jean's breath away. "I loved it. It was exactly what I thought living in Colorado meant," she said. A quarter mile past a sign pointing to the Lost Angel Mine they turned onto a narrower dirt road, more cart path than road, which disappeared briefly into a clump of trees and then ended in front of a cabin near the top of Sugarloaf Mountain. The deed described the parcel as Wild Tiger Lode #4 claim, but it became known as Jean and Frank's first house in Colorado. It cost them $12,000 and the owners even threw in a horse.

Except for electricity, those who lived on Sugarloaf Mountain had to fend for themselves. For indoor plumbing, a septic tank would be needed. Heat and cooking would require either splitting logs or installing a ten-foot long propane tank in the front yard. Almost everyone had a dog, but few had the menagerie that the Dubofskys quickly acquired: two horses, a burro named "Strawberry", and a pregnant basset hound who proceeded to give birth to seven basset puppies.

Dream Canyon, a half-open, half-forested wilderness area located in the deep ravine just below the cabin, attracted another kind of menagerie: a constantly changing collection of Woodstock generation free spirits, flower children and wanderers akin to a group known as the Rainbow People. They lived off the land, camped out, sang songs, smoked dope, dropped acid, and made love, all in the clear mountain air. "It was hippiedom, that's for sure," Jean said. "We may have been the only people who lived on Sugarloaf who actually had jobs to go to."

Jean and Frank embraced the free spirit of their environment but not necessarily the lifestyle. Instead, they went to the office each day and worked among a different sort of free spirits, a group of recent law school graduates, mostly Ivy League educated, who also came to Colorado seeking opportunities unavailable at the stodgy Brahmin or large corporate law firms of Boston, New York City, and Washington. Some came to start their own practices or join small downtown firms, hoping to get in on the ground floor and help firms grow. Just as many came out of a desire to use the law as an instrument for social change, and they became innovators in a growing area of the law broadly described as public interest law.

This new breed of lawyer had cut their teeth on the civil rights campaigns, were often peaceniks, draft dodgers, former members of Students for a Democratic Society (SDS), or served as Vista and Peace Corps volunteers. The kind of law they wanted to practice took them to the criminal justice system, mostly serving as public defenders; to the political system, looking to elective, appointed or staff jobs; and to legal aid, civil rights, migrant's rights, and the new field of poverty law. There was an immediate connection among this idealistic group of young attorneys who moved to Colorado to find their place in the world.

When Jean joined the newly created Colorado Rural Legal Services (CRLS), she found herself among those same kindred spirits, including the brash and charismatic founding director of CRLS, Jonathan "Skip" Chase. With his long curly hair and dark beard, dressed in blue jeans and with beads around his neck, Chase looked and played the part of the prototypical radical lawyer/activist of the era.

As a law school professor, Chase spent a summer working in the fields and living in migrant camps, his way of preparing to teach a class on poverty law and migrant rights. As the director of CRLS, he did more than sit in his office and supervise other attorneys. When a partner organization near Fort Lupton staged a hunger strike to protest living conditions, what the organizers called a "live-in", Chase joined them. When migrant workers presented a list of demands to a farm owner for needed improvements in housing and healthcare, Chase was there to be the "or else": make the needed improvements or else CRLS would file a class action lawsuit that would shut the farmer down.

Jean met Chase while working for Mondale when Chase came to testify before a subcommittee hearing on migrant worker issues. In 1969, just as CRLS was hiring its first batch of lawyers, Chase and his CRLS cofounder, Bill Prakken, learned that Jean was looking for a job in Colorado and they felt lucky that Jean, with her legal services background and her prestigious job for Mondale, accepted their offer to come on board.

Bill Prakken made a similar daily trek up and down twisting-turning old mining roads to his cabin in Salina, another abandoned mining town just a few canyons away from Frank and Jean's cabin on Sugarloaf. Prakken was a "Reggie", a graduate of a fellowship program inspired by Reginald Heber Smith and his 1919 seminal work, *Justice and the Poor*. The Reggie program attracted some of the best and the brightest law school graduates to attend an elite training program introducing the concepts of a new kind of law practice called poverty law. The three-month program was primarily intended to prepare these attorneys to staff the newly created legal services agencies. There they would provide the most vulnerable and poorest citizens with legal representation on a host of mostly civil matters, from landlord/tenant disputes, to discrimination in jobs or housing, to accessing government health services. In addition to the skills needed to meet the many client-based needs, when these Reggies left their training program and were deployed to states across the country, they had something else in mind as well. Not only were they to use the law to make a difference in people's lives, their mission was also to change the laws, to "dream up test cases and class actions, launch legislative initiatives, and organize community action programs."[30] As Terry Kelly, a Denver lawyer and former Reggie later recounted: "We were pretty full of ourselves. We thought our job was to wake up in the morning, read the paper, and figure out who in the government we should sue."

Neither Jean Dubofsky nor Skip Chase were Reggies, but they fit the mold of activist lawyers looking beyond individual client cases to use the law to bring dramatic and broad changes to an unjust world. For many, including Jean, the early days at CRLS remained fixed in memory with an almost romantic quality, mostly because of Skip Chase. His leadership and his belief, conveyed and shared among his new recruits, that they were on a mission, that they could make a difference, that they were *the* difference for so many people who, without them, would be lost to injustice, was infectious. They all became true believers.

Chase was, Jean said, "the most memorable person I have ever met." She loved him for his convictions, for his passion, and for his commitment to the poor and the voiceless. And she loved him because of the way he treated her. In the legal profession at the time few women attorneys held the same status as their male colleagues. Even in legal aid and public defender arenas, where women lawyers were welcomed, not all men were comfortable or secure enough to treat women as professional equals. "I didn't fully appreciate back then how rare it was for someone to have the combination of qualities to be able to treat women as colleagues, as true equals," Jean said.

Almost everybody was smitten with Chase, much as the young, impression-able college students were smitten with Al Lowenstein. The two men were totally different personalities, but both were such committed, charismatic, and inspirational figures, that each in his own way drew others in and remained a pivotal figure in the lives of many.

Within a year or so of its founding, CRLS opened a half-dozen offices across Colorado's Eastern Plains, in the central San Luis Valley, and on the Western Slope. The lawyers, organizers, and staff from all these offices would usually gather one weekend each month for a staff meeting in Boulder. The commitment, energy, and youthful enthusiasm were a sight to see, except on the mornings after the inevitable Saturday night party. The parties were held at one or the other of the cabins sitting atop the canyons above Boulder, and by morning bodies in sleeping bags would be strewn across the cabin floors, a car or two often in need of rescue after having slipped off the edge of the driveway or a narrow road the night before.

In the summer of 1970, CRLS held its first statewide conference, a retreat of sorts, in a quiet isolated mining town in the southwest corner of Colorado, a five-hour drive from Denver. With only one road in and out most for the year, no paved streets, few hotels, and a one-person police force, Crested Butte was not yet the popular ski resort town of today, and the rowdy band of almost fifty legal aid lawyers, Vista volunteers, community organizers, and secretaries might have been a bit too much for the sleepy town. They stayed up late, wandered about with their dogs, and imbibed and ingested more than their fair share of assorted substances.

All hell broke loose when one of the dogs, named Free Huey Newton, went missing. ("Free Huey Newton" was a popular protest cry meant to register protest against the trial and imprisonment of Black Panther Huey Newton). In the search that ensued, the town's lone police officer arrested one CRLS employee for disturbing the peace. When word spread of the arrest, Jean and Frank and others soon gathered to protest outside an historic wooden structure that doubled as the police station, and the loud chanting of "Let us in. He's our client" woke the entire town. When Chase put his fist through a glass door in an attempt to free his client, he was also arrested.

While it was not their finest hour, some of the participants described that weekend as emblematic of their determination to utilize all the tools at their disposal, partnering when possible, cajoling when appropriate, threatening if necessary, to challenge even the most powerful forces if that is what it took to undo the injustices they saw around them.

CRLS attorneys focused mostly on issues brought to them by individual clients. Their job was sorting out their clients' grievances and advocating on their behalf. Chase tasked Jean with a different role, however. She was to head up what they called the Law Reform Unit, to take action when it was clear that instead of individual remedies, a broader approach was needed. Those broader actions often took the form of class action suits against local and state government or government agencies or the introduction of new laws. Jean spent a good portion of her time in courtrooms and at the state Capitol, working with policy makers and elected officials to change regulations or existing law or enact new laws, all to insure basic protections against injustice and equal access to needed services for their clients.

Jean's work on what became known as the "Hill-Burton" case likely had the greatest impact on the largest number of the poor, not only in Colorado at that time, but over time in the years since in states across the country.

After the Second World War, when the federal government ended wartime infusions of federal funds to state and local governments, U.S. Senators Lister Hill, D-Alabama, and Harold Burton, R-Ohio, co-sponsored a bill to continue the flow of a portion of those funds as federal subsidies for the construction of public hospitals.

A key purpose of the bill was to make sure that there would be health care services available for those who could not afford care at private hospitals. One critical provision required states and communities receiving these funds to provide care to those unable to pay. These requirements became known as the Hill-Burton community service and uncompensated care obligations, but while the requirement to serve the poor was written into the law, operating funds to cover the cost of caring for those who could not pay were not included.

Sick people, including many of the migrant farm worker clients served by CRLS, were often denied hospital services because they did not have the ability to pay. Despite many requests to accept these clients, the Weld County General Hospital, built with Hill-Burton funds, continued to refuse to provide health services to the children and farm workers working in the agricultural fields north of Boulder. Jean filed a lawsuit that wound its way all the way to the Tenth Circuit of the U.S. Court of Appeals, and that court ruled in favor of the migrant families. The decision opened the door for many similar lawsuits forcing hospitals across the country to provide the mandated healthcare service to the poor. "Largely as a result of the 1972 court ruling, hospitals today provide millions of dollars of free medical help annually to those who otherwise wouldn't get it."[31]

CRLS earned a reputation as a progressive champion of human rights, but it also earned one as an organization filled with hippies and radicals, a reputation that was only partially deserved. In addition to marching, striking, and protesting alongside their clients, the attorneys also sometimes wore blue jeans in the courtroom, exhibiting what others felt was disrespect for the courts, and they often displayed an attitude suggesting they were above the rules. Challenging the conventional rules was part of the CRLS mission because so many rules, procedures, and laws were the cause of so much injustice.

Battling the government and the established powerful interests could not help but contribute to the agency's outsider image. That Jean and other attorneys were involved with other organizations that also saw fit to challenge the establishment in other ways added to that outside-the-mainstream reputation. Jean was active in the woman's movement and was one of the original founders of the Colorado chapter of the American Civil Liberties Union. But it was some of the very public internal battles within CRLS that cemented a more radical image of the organization and its attorneys.

Behind the somewhat romantic image of Colorado as a place of freedom, independence, and reinvention was another Colorado, a place where smoldering resentments were fed by a long history of discrimination, bigotry, and injustice experienced for generations by migrant agricultural workers, mostly of Mexican descent. By the early 1970s, inspired by and working in conjunction with César Chavez and Dolores Huerta and the national farm worker movement, a younger generation of Latino leaders in Colorado began pushing beyond the tools of boycotts and strikes to bring attention to that injustice. The long history of unsettled grievances and still-tender wounds led young Chicanos to the same, more strident and militant place occupied by radical anti-war and black-power activists who saw guns and bombs and violence as necessary tools in their struggles.

"It was like what happens when you shake up a bottle of soda and you take your thumb off," according to Magdeleno Rose-Avila, a young CRLS organizer at the time. "When we began speaking out for the first time, it was like an explosion of emotions. For every job you didn't get, for every time you were called names and you didn't do anything, for every thing that was denied. And for every time we didn't fight back. All these pent up emotions; eventually it blows. Those of us who were young decided we were going to do something about it."

One action, on a very long list of all the things that these young Chicanos decided to do with their newly acquired activism, was to take over the statewide CRLS office located in Boulder. Literally take it over. A handful of the Chicano lawyers and activists employed by CRLS appeared at the office, accompanied with other companions as "reinforcements"—made evident through the weapons they were carrying—and announced that it was time for the privileged, out-of-town, Anglo do-gooder lawyers to leave. The following day they allowed Jean back into the offices briefly to retrieve some files, but the Chicano lawyers that took control that day became the leaders of the organization going forward, setting the agenda, managing the workload, and representing their own people. If not before, those tense takeover days cemented the image of CRLS as a hotbed of radical activity.

The forced takeover was a disappointing blow to the agency leadership, but not a surprise. Bill Prakken, one of the CRLS original founders who had moved on to start his own law firm, had been asked by Skip Chase to act as a negotiator with the Chicano lawyers who were demanding a greater leadership role at the agency. Chase and others recognized the validity of their desires but, as it turned out, did not act soon enough or directly enough to satisfy those demands.

With or without the takeover, the early, charmed days of CRLS were coming to an end. It would be just a matter of time before the agency would suffer the same fate as the South Florida Migrant Legal Services: funding for the aggressive legal challenges, the reform work, and the activism would be cut, and only the bare bones client work would remain intact.

9

The Political Game

The Legal Aid Society of Metropolitan Denver was the urban counterpart to the rural, farmworker-oriented, insurgent-led Colorado Rural Legal Services, with a similar focus on providing poverty law services to a broad clientele of the poor and powerless. The Denver organization was staffed by Reggies and many of the same kindred spirits who worked at CRLS, although the Denver operation had a much more buttoned-down establishment air about it, partly because that program evolved out of the more traditional legal aid model, with a community board to answer to and a United Way funding history.

Under the umbrella of that legal services agency, Jean was able to continue her work. Her clients and her mission remained the same, advancing the cause of justice and fairness for those left out, but as the agency's full-time legislative director, she expanded her reach and her influence. She became an expert on the dynamics of various legislative committees and the interests of the most influential legislators. When she wasn't working directly with state legislators or keeping track of bills being introduced, she spent time with state agency department heads and staff, especially those dealing with social services and healthcare, monitoring their monthly meetings, bringing issues of concern to the right people internally, and seeking collaborative solutions when possible. Litigation and legislation were familiar legal tools when all else failed, but just as often Jean found avenues to maneuver within the system to accomplish things quietly and behind the scenes. It didn't take very long for her to build deep relationships with a large swath of people engaged in matters of public importance.

She spent virtually all of her time at the state Capitol and other state office buildings, which placed her at the center of Colorado's political and governmental worlds. While it was a typical male-dominated environment, it was not a totally male environment. "There were some very knowledgeable, very active women, like Arie Taylor and Ruth Stockton, both state legislators. They were powerful women who were treated with great respect," former state representative Morgan Smith, a fellow legislator said. "And no one messed with them." For the first time, Jean worked with and among other women who were also engaged, smart, hard-working players with influence. Some served as staff aides, others as analysts or lobbyists, and a few were even elected state legislators.

Jean wasn't an elected official and did not have any direct power at all. Her power and influence came initially because of the knowledge and expertise that she acquired and shared. She was deft at helping legislators understand what a specific set of legal phrases might mean when inserted into or deleted from legislation during the drafting process. She could quickly identify potential problems with proposed legislation, ascertain if they might conflict with other laws or regulations already in place, then tip off legislators before they sponsored a bill that might end up embarrassing them. Soon she became recognized as one of the smartest legal minds at the Capitol, able to draft legislation more quickly and with more clarity and depth than the Office of Legislative Legal Services, whose responsibility it was.

She worked most closely with lawmakers who shared her social justice, progressive agenda, but often found a way to help Republican legislators with their bills too, cementing relationships in the unlikeliest of places and forging ties with many who did not necessarily share that agenda. As those ties and working relationships further developed, so too did her power and influence.

Jean came to have a bit of a fan club at the Capitol, and Wally Stealey, an influential lobbyist and later top aide to Governor Lamm, was one of those fans. "First of all, it was clear she was very smart. Her legal ability was beyond anybody sitting on the floor of the legislature. You should have seen her," Stealey mused many years later. "To master the place, you have to master each personality and you have to figure out how to put the puzzle together to get the votes you need. She could see each piece of the puzzle and had this uncanny analytical ability to get things done." Stealey remembered one particular time:

> She had this piece of legal aid legislation that had no chance of passing. And there was no legislator on the Democratic side who thought there was any chance they could get any Republican to carry the bill, so no one would volunteer to go over to the Republican Senate and even attempt to find a co-sponsor. But Jean said, 'I'll go.' So she went over to see the Senate president, Ted Strickland, a die-hard Republican who could not have been more diametrically opposed to just about everything Jean stood for. Yet through the power of her personality and the weight of her intellect, he agreed to carry her legal aid legislation. It passed the Republican controlled Senate, which was a big deal. She just always seemed to find the formula that was necessary to pass her bills.

In the political world, it is not easy to be sure about the motives of those providing analysis and advice. Yet Jean made friends quickly and, more importantly, became both respected and trusted. "To get help from someone I could trust implicitly was just so extraordinary," Morgan Smith remembered. "Jean would sometimes call me off the House floor when a bill was being discussed. I'd say, 'What have we got here?' And it might be some language for an amendment that I'd never seen before. I might not even have known there was an issue, but Jean would give me an amendment in the hallway and say, 'There's an issue but don't worry. You need to introduce this and you have to do it now.' And I would do it because I knew that she would be right." It didn't matter to Smith that he might not have known what the problem was or why the amendment was needed at that moment. What mattered was that he trusted her. And that was no small thing.

Jean loved her job. "Working for legal aid basically meant that you were hired to go out and find problems to solve. That's about as open ended as you could get. My clients were poor people and my job was to lobby for them. I was kind of my own boss; I had my little show and it was exciting for me to be in the middle of so many things." She was soon enveloped in the small but exhilarating world of Colorado politics. She was one of them, a player. A mostly unknown, quiet, behind-the-scenes player, but a player nonetheless. "It was exactly why we wanted to come to Colorado," Jean said. "Even not being from here, we could come and meet people and become involved and engaged easily, and feel like we were a part of the political community so quickly."

What mattered most, however, was the work and the accomplishments. And they added up. She took little credit for single-handedly changing the justice landscape. But over the course of her legal service years, in addition to the consequential Hill-Burton legal decision forcing hospitals to care for the indigent, Jean had her hand in a host of changes that did just that: changed the landscape for the poor and disenfranchised. She helped construct and pass a piece of legislation that created a basic "bill of rights" for residents of mobile home parks and later did the same for vulnerable nursing home patients. When Social Security regulations and Medicaid regulations conflicted, cutting clients off from medical coverage, she helped write new regulations that allowed coverage to be reinstated. She worked on a myriad of welfare and prison reform efforts that impacted thousands. When outdated old-age pension rules had the effect of leaving some deserving elderly ineligible for benefits, she helped institute changes in rules to provide those benefits. She successfully challenged the no-fault insurance industry to bar policies that discriminated based on age or sex or where people lived. She worked to construct new laws that for the first time gave women the right to have insurance, to establish credit to finance their homes or purchase a car, even to allow women to obtain credit cards in their own names. Only those closest to the inner workings of the Capitol were aware of Jean's hand in all of these issues and many other legislative and regulatory fixes that made the world a little bit fairer. None of these laws or regulations had Jean's name on them, and history would not record that Jean deserved credit for any of these things. And that was fine with Jean.

By 1973, the White House and the Congress had clearly lost their appetite to provide federal dollars in support of the kind of law reform work that had been jump started by President Johnson and his War on Poverty. As the Denver legal services grant cycle was nearing its end, many of the new breed of legal aid and poverty lawyers who had spent a few years ruffling political feathers, began to hatch alternative plans that would allow them to continue the work they had been doing.

Terry Kelly managed the legal services office in the Five Points section of Denver. Kelly and Jean had met at a protest march in Greeley, Colorado, not long after they both arrived in Colorado. "Those were the days of *real* civil rights marches," Kelly said. "It was a time when Corky Gonzales and the Crusade for Justice folks and all the lawyers from the Denver legal aid office and from CRLS would show up to protest something that was going on that wasn't right." Over the years, he and Jean became colleagues and friends, fellow warriors, trying to right the ills of the world. Kelly's two-year commitment as a Reggie had stretched to more than three years, and he was contemplating the possibility of stepping out on his own.

"It was a time when public interest firms were popping up around the country; the most famous was the Southern Poverty Law Center. It was a model that was idealized. Such a wonderful idea! We would initiate civil right cases or class action suits and we wouldn't have to worry about the federal bureaucracy; we could just do the work," Kelly said. When Jean expressed an interest in doing the same, a partnership was born. "I was smart enough to know that Jean was pretty special. She was committed on a real basis to these people and to this work. She was someone who didn't have an ego, and was a wonderful person, very easy to get along with. I said 'Let's do it'. And we did."

In 1973, they rented a small two-room office suite, acquired a Dictaphone and a secretary to share, and launched the public interest law firm of Kelly & Dubofsky. Jean's private office doubled as the break and copy room, with a small refrigerator and a copier nudged into the corner of a room the size of a large closet.

Their vision was to create a firm that could continue the legal reform and justice work they both were committed to. If success was measured in the number and range of cases that came their way, their first year was a great success. Their friends in legal services, at the public defenders' offices, and at the ACLU gladly sent over a variety of challenging social justice cases that those agencies were not able to take because a client's income made them ineligible for their services. The clients who arrived on their firm's doorstep made for great cases that fed their souls, but with clients usually unable to pay or pay very much, seldom fed their pocketbooks.

One of those cases referred by the local ACLU office was that of Ann-Marie Sandquist, a nine-year-old Denver girl who wanted to play baseball. She signed up to play for the Most Precious Blood Tigers, a team of the Catholic Youth Recreation League (CYRA), a boys-only baseball league. The Tigers' coach welcomed Ann-Marie to the team, but when other parents and coaches complained that no girls were allowed, the league officials fired the coach, banned Ann-Marie from the field, and then made the Tigers forfeit the two wins in games she had already played in.

Even before the coach was fired and before Ann-Marie was banned from the field, things had started to get nasty. Often when she stepped on deck getting ready for her turn at the plate, or when she straightened her cap, picked up her glove, and jogged out onto the field, there would be taunts and jeers from the sidelines. "Getting up to bat and people booing, or a ball coming to me and people booing, and striking out and hearing cheers [made it] not all that pleasant an experience," Ann-Marie said.[32]

Sometimes league officials charged out onto the field and beckoned the two coaches to join them so that they could explain that if Ann-Marie stayed on the field and played, the Tigers would have to forfeit that game too. Sometimes her father would jog out to argue that this was ridiculous and she should just be allowed to play. One opposing coach wouldn't let his team take the field if Ann-Marie was going to play. Word traveled fast that something was brewing with the Most Precious Blood Tigers. Television crews started to cover the games. Stories began to appear in newspapers. Eventually, over a hundred onlookers appeared at one game to see what all the fuss was about. This was a league for nine-year-olds, with volunteer coaches and volunteer umpires, most of whom were parents of the children on the teams. Children like Ann-Marie who just wanted to play summer baseball.

Pat Oliphant, the Pulitzer Prizing-winning cartoonist who made the *Denver Post* his home back then, captured the drama and silliness of the whole girl/boy drama with a four-column-wide cartoon. In a rag-tag built tree house set high above the ground, eight boys lounged around as a curly-haired woman wearing glasses, dressed in high heels, and carrying a small briefcase under her arm shimmied up a rope to the tree house. One of the boys, axe raised above his head, was set to slash the rope before she could arrive. The sign above the door of the tree house read "Strictly NO Girls". The caption below read: "I'm from the American Civil Liberties Union, and We've had a Complaint..."[33]

Inevitably, when neither Ann-Marie and her parents nor the league officials would back down, lawyers were called in. Ann-Marie's parents insisted they were not looking for a fight or seeking to lead a cause. They simply wanted their daughter to be able to play baseball. Jean Dubofsky listened to Ann-Marie's story and quickly calculated that this had all the makings of an equal rights and sex discrimination case. The issue had been addressed at the federal level two years earlier when Title IX was enacted, requiring equal opportunity for girls to participate in sports wherever federal dollars were involved. It may have been a stretch technically, because the CYRA did not receive federal funds. But they played in Denver's public parks, and the city of Denver received federal dollars. Denying a girl the right to play in the city's public park because of her gender would be illegal, Jean told them, either on constitutional grounds or under the Denver City Charter, since both prohibited discrimination on the basis of gender.

Jean filed a lawsuit asking that the CYRA be barred from using city-owned fields unless it allowed Ann-Marie to play. A district court judge issued an injunction that required the league to let Ann-Marie play until the whole legal matter could be sorted out.

The league and its officials were just a group of volunteer dads who wanted their sons to play sports and they never really stood a chance when faced with a constitutional challenge. "The plaintiffs appear to be…ready to go all the way to the Supreme Court if necessary,"[34] the attorney advising the league said, but the league had neither the money nor the desire to be drawn into a long sex discrimination legal battle. And so the league agreed to allow Ann-Marie to play baseball with the boys.

This was the first case in Colorado and one of the first in the country to challenge boys-only sports leagues. It served as precedent for future challenges that led the way to more opportunities for girls everywhere to participate in sports.

Being public interest lawyers out on their own was exhilarating for Jean and Terry Kelly, but it did not pay the firm's bills. Their steadiest income came from a small contract with the Denver legal services office, but with minimal additional income coming in the door, it was clear that they would have to develop a broader legal practice to survive financially. Kelly dug in and began taking paying clients, mostly divorce work at first. Jean was not greatly enthused about doing the same. Her affinity for broader public issues and ties to former legislative colleagues had her paying attention to what was happening under the statehouse dome. A Democratic state representative, Dick Lamm, was running for governor and a former state senator, J. D. MacFarlane, also a Democrat, was in the middle of his own campaign for attorney general.

Unlike most of the young liberal activist lawyers-turned-politicians who had flocked to Colorado from places far and wide, MacFarlane was a Colorado native from tough, gritty, blue-collar Pueblo, a mining, manufacturing, and steel town. He was plenty smart. After graduating from Harvard, he went on to law school at Stanford, making law review.

And, unlike most of the newcomer lawyers, he also found time for a stint in the army, and then spent two years working in Washington as a government systems analyst. When he returned home to Colorado in the early sixties, he took a job in the local district attorney's office.

His loved his job as a prosecutor but found one aspect of it unnerving. "I was appalled at the total lack of legal representation for the indigent," he said. "There was no legal aid then, no public defenders, nothing like we have today." When one of the new War on Poverty agencies allocated significant dollars to provide such needed services, MacFarlane applied for and received a grant, making Pueblo County the first county in the country to provide public defenders to those without the ability to pay for lawyers. He became active in the Young Democrat group and was noticed by local party leaders as an up-and-comer. The party leaders eventually recruited him to run for local office.

By 1965 MacFarlane was on his way to Denver as an elected member of the state legislature and from the beginning he stood out. Some remember him as refreshing, down to earth, and brilliant, a man full of ideas and ideals, passionate about doing the right thing, someone who never forgot his roots and was unafraid of rocking the boat. Others remember him as quirky, a little unpolished, and a little too "Colorado", meaning unsophisticated. He was a character, to be sure.

MacFarlane soon won election to the Colorado State Senate and moved up to hold the chairmanship of the powerful Joint Budget Committee (JBC). That is where he and Jean met. At the time, Jean was at the Capitol lobbying on the whole range of things that MacFarlane himself advocated. MacFarlane later said he was always happy to see Jean coming.

They saw a lot more of each other after MacFarlane left the Senate and began lobbying on behalf of the creation of a statewide public defender system. "We cared about the same things. When I was on the JBC, I funded the things that Jean pushed for. I respected what legal services was doing," MacFarlane said, "and I knew her as an extremely smart lawyer. She just knew a whole lot about a whole lot of areas of the law and that just impressed me."

Which is why, when MacFarlane decided to run for attorney general, he asked Jean to become his campaign manager. Jean was a bit bewildered at his proposal. She had never managed a political campaign and, although they knew enough of each other to be drawn to each other's side at the state Capitol, spending their days fighting for the same things, doing battle together, she and McFarlane weren't necessarily personally very close. They did have another thing in common, however. They both had ties to and great affection for a mutual friend, Wally Stealey, whose advice and counsel MacFarlane greatly relied upon.

Jean volunteered to take on the campaign job, on top of her work at the law firm, downplaying the title of campaign manager. "I told Wally that I wasn't all that experienced in politics and he said, 'Don't worry, I can take care of that.' I had the title and my name was on the brochure as campaign manager," Jean said, "but nobody really managed J.D. He just did his own thing. And Wally took care of the rest of the politics."

Political change was in the air all around Colorado. The Republicans were on the run and the Democrats, in the guise of the new "young Turks", were ascendant. Pat Schroeder, a woman lawyer from Denver, was elected to Congress in 1972. Gary Hart, presidential candidate George McGovern's 1972 campaign manager, was about to be elected to his first term in the U.S. Senate. And any campaign with an "out with the old guard, in with the new" theme fit the times. So it was not a huge surprise that in November of 1974, Dick Lamm was elected governor and J. D. MacFarlane was elected attorney general.

The first decision MacFarlane made after he won was to appoint Jean to be his deputy. Although she must have contemplated the possibility that MacFarlane might win and his win might mean new opportunities for her, Jean professed surprise. "I'm sure I wasn't really thinking that far ahead," Jean said. "And we didn't really know if he'd win."

MacFarlane *had* been thinking that far ahead, however. When Stealey and MacFarlane approached Jean initially to become campaign manager, they did so because they held her in high esteem for her intelligence and her ability to get things done. When the campaign was over, the real work would begin. "J.D. thought so highly of her and he had already made his decision to ask her to be in the attorney general's office long before he won," Stealey said later. "By the time we all went out to dinner election night, he had already asked her."

"She was probably the smartest lawyer I ever knew and that's why I wanted her there," MacFarlane said. "She was on the right side of things, or I guess I should really say the 'left' side of things, which is where I was. I also really liked her." MacFarlane's decision to appoint her as deputy attorney general wasn't simply about Jean and her fine qualities, however. It was also about his own sister.

"I had a sister six years older than I," he explained many years later. "She'd been high school valedictorian, she'd gone to CU, then Columbia Law School. I knew what was going on with women lawyers, the way they were treated." His sister eventually had a rich and rewarding career but early on no law firm would hire her. Eventually, when she was hired by one of the big corporate law firms, the only thing they would let her work on were wills and estates, the traditional role for the few women lawyers who could even get jobs at those firms. "It burned me up at the way my sister was treated, especially since a lot of the women, including my sister, were a whole lot smarter than the men who were treating them that way."

"I wanted Jean. But I also wanted to make the point, the major point, that women lawyers were just as good as men. Some better." Colorado had never had a woman deputy attorney general. MacFarlane was determined to appoint the first woman to that job.

There were, however, two potential complications. The Kelly & Dubofsky law firm was barely off the ground. Jean and Terry Kelly had made a commitment to one another and, mostly out of loyalty to Kelly, Jean was torn about walking away from the firm.

Although Kelly confessed to "feelings of abandonment," he made it easy for Jean to accept the appointment. "I thought it was great that she would be in the middle of the action again. It was like she had captured government, for Chrissake," Kelly said. "For one of us to be able to be inside and influence the very important work of that office was something special." In some ways Kelly was almost as thrilled as Jean at the job offer, maybe more. Being a practical sort, Kelly calculated a direct benefit to the firm. "It didn't hurt me or my reputation to have Jean in the attorney general's office. It enhanced it, made me and the firm more legitimate," he said.

The second potential complication was personal. Jean was pregnant.

She and Frank had wanted children, looked forward to having a family. Jean had a favorite aunt who had never been able to have children and, after almost six years of marriage, Jean had begun to wonder if that was going to be her fate as well. But by the time of the November election and the job offer from MacFarlane, Jean was a few months into her first pregnancy. There was no rulebook to guide this new generation of professional women on the subject of pregnancy. In the past, women knew what to do. You got married, had a baby, and then stayed home and cooked and cleaned and took care of the kids. Having a baby and working was relatively new ground.

In 1974 it was still quite common for employers to steer clear of hiring women if they knew they were pregnant; it was also quite common for women to leave their jobs or be asked to leave once their pregnancy became obvious. It wasn't so much that Jean wondered if she would be able to handle being the new deputy attorney general and a mother at the same time. But she wondered what MacFarlane's view of the situation might be.

This complication turned out, however, not to be a complication at all for the new attorney general. This time it was not about MacFarlane's sister; it was about his wife. She was a lawyer too. And women lawyers like his wife and like Jean were bound to do what most married women of a certain age did. They had babies. According to Jean, MacFarlane's reaction when she told him she was pregnant was "So you'll have a baby, and you'll figure it out." MacFarlane would not only appoint the first woman deputy attorney general; it would be a woman about to have a baby.

Whatever apprehension or second-guessing Jean might have had about the job, Frank Dubofsky never doubted for a moment that she would take the job. "In a way Jean got rescued by J.D.," Frank said, "rescued from having to take the domestic cases to pay the bills if she had continued with the law firm."

Jean packed up her boxes once again, said goodbye to her friend and partner Terry Kelly, searched for the rare maternity dress appropriate for a public executive, and moved over to the attorney general's office.

10

First Woman
Deputy Attorney General

Jean Dubofsky and J.D. MacFarlane proved to be a good match. Each had a deep and abiding commitment to the disadvantaged and those without a voice, were known for their intellects and their integrity, and they had great respect for one another. But being a good match had as much to do with their differences as it did with what they had in common.

"J.D. was a guy just bursting with ideas, but he was always going off on one idea or another. Jean was a lot more practical and was the person who held things together," according to Morgan Smith, who knew MacFarlane and Jean since their days at the state Capitol. "He was also a very, very partisan guy, a political guy who would go after people and he could have gotten himself in a lot of trouble. To have someone like Jean, who was not seen as a threat and could calm things down, was probably very important, more than we thought at the time. Sometimes he'd push the edge of what he wanted to do, and Jean would pull him back."

Frank also thought Jean and MacFarlane were compatible, but for a different reason. "J.D. MacFarlane was a J.D. Salinger type. He was a quiet person, not particularly talkative, and Jean was fairly comfortable with people who didn't talk all that much. Because her father was like that."

Even before Jean had settled into the day-to-day job inside of government, she quickly discovered that a public role outside of the bureaucracy was very much a part of the job. More than many other states, Colorado had a history of being more open to having women involved in the political system, but they were still an oddity in positions of influence and power, which is why Jean immediately received her share of public attention.

Jean was a well-known activist in Colorado's burgeoning feminist circles, supporting both a Colorado Equal Rights Amendment and the national Equal Rights Amendment (ERA), working collaboratively with a range of groups on issues of particular concern to women, and eventually serving on the Colorado Commission on the Status of Women. But with her new role, she soon became one of the most prominent and visible women in state government. In early April of 1975 she was featured in the Living Section of the *Denver Post*[35] and in the *Daily Camera*.[36] In the *Camera*, she was the subject of two stories on the same day, appearing in the Sunday women's section. The first story focused on Jean's views regarding one of the most controversial issues of the day, the ratification of the ERA; the second featured Jean's work as a public interest lawyer and the life of a woman attorney. Two photos accompanying the stories showed Jean in a dark jumper. A petite woman, she appeared to be carrying more than her usual weight. Seven weeks later, she gave birth to their first son, Josh.

Jean did not have the luxury of waiting until after Josh was born before she took on the heavy workload inside the AG's office. MacFarlane ran on a campaign platform of consumer rights with a particular focus on changing the way the Public Utilities Commission (PUC) operated. But ideas about fundamental changes to the structure of the attorney general's office had also been percolating in his head since his days on the Joint Budget Committee. He had a plan in mind that amounted to a total reinvention of the office. One of the biggest and most controversial changes he envisioned would end the practice of staff attorneys being allowed to maintain a private law practice with outside paying clients. It was a well-entrenched custom that MacFarlane strongly felt opened the door to conflicts of interests and the potential for corruption. "You had the state's water law attorneys who had other water law clients," MacFarlane argued. "It was a clear conflict of interest and that is just one example. The same thing was happening in almost every department."

During his campaign, MacFarlane made clear that he would end the policy that allowed the state's legal staff to have a separate outside law practice as well. Many of those attorneys were stunned, however, when, after he was elected, he actually did what he said he was going to do.

"I had a big meeting after the election with the staff before I was sworn in and I told them flat out, 'If you don't want to stay with what you get paid here by the state, then you might want to look for another job because I'm not going to allow any outside compensation. From now on, you have only one client, the state. If you want your private clients, you have to leave.'"

He would also upend the practice that allowed each state agency and department to hire its own attorneys, who would work at the agency under the auspices of each agency head and have little supervision from or accountability to their supposed boss, the attorney general. From now on, MacFarlane told them, everybody would work for him, not separate agency heads. And everyone would move into a central office next to the Capitol just as soon as a space could be made ready to have everybody under one roof. The protests were swift and loud but had no effect on MacFarlane's plan. When the attorneys saw that MacFarlane meant what he said, within a week twenty-five attorneys had resigned, and within months more would follow.

MacFarlane had a plan to reorganize and restructure the office, and hiring new attorneys was at the center of that plan. "I think the idea I had in my head was to create divisions and have each one headed up by the smartest lawyer I could find." What he really meant, however, was the smartest lawyer that *Jean* could find. Jean was given the responsibility for implementing all of the dramatic changes he envisioned, especially the hiring and then supervising of the huge influx of new attorneys.

"I told her we were going to break this nonsense up and I preferred she do all the hiring," MacFarlane said. "And because I was a big proponent of women, I wanted her to bring other women too. I respected her judgment and knew she'd figure it out."

Mary Mullarkey was one of the first attorneys hired. She had been in the class behind Jean at Harvard Law, but they only met after Mullarkey moved to Denver for a job at the newly established office of the Equal Employment Opportunity Commission, a federal agency. That job turned out to be "horrible", according to Mullarkey, too bureaucratic and filled with day-to-day drudgery. Soon she began actively looking for another opportunity in Denver. She was not politically active; she couldn't be because of the Hatch Act which forbade federal employees from political involvement. But Denver had become a hotbed of progressive activism, and she gravitated towards the broad circle of young, progressive, activist lawyers who were all very engaged in Colorado politics. The sea change of Democrats taking over powerful positions in public life continued when Lamm was elected governor and MacFarlane attorney general. Mullarkey hoped this new generation of political leadership would lead to job opportunities for someone like her.

"When J.D. got elected, I thought that might be my salvation, so I decided to apply for a job with him. They were setting up a new office and he had really big ideas about changing the attorney general's office," Mullarkey said. "I thought, this guy is exciting, he'll need all these new lawyers, so I applied for a staff job, doing something in employment law or human resources, because that was my background and experience."

Jean did not know Mullarkey well but they had friends in common; Terry and Alice Kelly lived across the alley from Mullarkey. Jean quickly recognized that she was exactly the kind of lawyer J.D. had in mind. The first hires were not going to be staff lawyers, however; they were going to be division heads. Much to Mullarkey's surprise, the job they offered her was division chief of the appellate section.

"You want me to do what?" Mullarkey remembered asking. "The appellate section was mostly criminal appeals. I said, 'You realize I've never done criminal law?'" MacFarlane's response was classic J.D. "Well, you took it in law school, didn't you? You'll be fine."

Both J.D. and Jean told Mullarkey they wanted to change the culture in the AG's office. "They said they were looking for smart people to change things, and they wanted women in supervisory positions. It was so exciting. So, of course, I said yes."

For Jean, working with legislators and with the governor's staff and continuing to be a player in the wider political and governing circle were all pieces of the job that were very familiar. But she was also starting fresh in a way, taking on a very different set of responsibilities. A large and consuming part of her job was human resources: recruiting, hiring, deploying, and supervising scores of new lawyers throughout state government, all within a new management structure. She was also responsible for untangling the thicket of an unwieldy legal system that had grown up over decades. Her clients were no longer the poor or the disadvantaged or those left behind. Her job was not advocacy or lobbying or identifying issues of injustice and finding ways to resolve those issues. Her job was essentially to build a huge new multi-dimensional law firm capable of representing state officials and agencies and the people and interests of the state of Colorado.

And so that's how Jean began her new job, by hiring smart people, including smart women, and sending those smart people out to explain the new way lawyers would be doing business in state government. She experienced her share of internal battles with the old-timers—all men, of course—who were used to doing things their own way and resentful that they had to take orders from the new regime, especially this young woman who was now their boss. But J.D. and Jean persisted, and before long the attorney general's office was filled with new energy and new faces and some of the best and the brightest young attorneys in the state. Many of their new hires would later go on to be judges at both the district court and appellate levels, and would be the founders and partners in some of the most prestigious law firms in Denver. "The attorney general's office became one of the great gatherings of legal talents you could ever imagine," Morgan Smith said.

Jean flourished in her day-to-day job and in the new public role that came with the job. She found it exhilarating, challenging, and a great learning experience. The daily bureaucratic, management, and personnel issues were all consuming, however, and she began to miss two important things. She missed the sense that she was contributing to the justice equation. And she worried that she was missing out on another role that she was equally enthused about—being a mother. After almost a decade of progress that opened the doors for women in professional and public life, Jean experienced emotions particular to this new generation of women: how to be both a mother and the professional she had worked so hard to become.

Frank and Jean had moved down from their Sugarloaf cabin and into Boulder's leafy Mapleton neighborhood, just a few blocks from downtown, which shortened Jean's commute to and from Denver by twenty minutes each way. Yet she still had to leave the house early each morning, in the dark during the winter, to catch the bus to Denver. She returned home in time to fix dinner and put Josh to bed. The Dubofskys had a nanny who came to the house and Frank's law office was close by, so he was available to care for Josh in the mornings until the babysitter arrived. But the commute, the long work hours, and Jean's stressful job were hard on everybody. "I felt a lot of the tug with a baby at home and leaving every day," Jean said. "And Josh was not an easy baby. He was intense and he would just cry and cry. It didn't seem like there was anything we could do to comfort him. So it was hard."

Jean never discussed it with friends, never really admitted to herself or to others that anything was other than perfectly fine, but exhaustion and pangs of guilt were ever present during her two years as deputy attorney general. Years later when asked if she had any regrets about her career, Jean mentioned only one. She wished she had spent more time at home with Josh after he was born. "We were lucky. We had lots of help, but I felt as though I had not given Josh the attention he deserved."

In the spring of 1977, Jean learned that her life was about to give new meaning to the word exhaustion. She was pregnant again and their second son would be arriving in the fall. "When I found I was pregnant with Matthew, I knew that what I wanted to do was to spend more time at home." The restructuring of the AG's office had been successful and it all was running smoothly. Jean was confident that others could now easily take her place. "I felt it wouldn't be fair to Josh if I just waited and came home with a new baby, so I stopped working at the beginning of the summer, giving me some time alone with Josh before Matthew arrived."

Over the next couple of years, Jean was mostly a stay-at-home mother, enjoying her time with Matthew and Josh as they toddled their way into little boyhood. She was able to engage more in the Boulder community and spend time with other mothers raising their kids and with friends she had met through election campaigns and other civic activities. A few days a month she drove into Denver and did a little legal work at the old Kelly & Dubofsky firm, but mostly she was happy to be home with her boys.

Being happy at home with the boys did not translate into being content to put her career on hold forever, however. The pull to do something more, to be back contributing on issues that mattered, remained strong. As one year at home turned into two, she and Frank began talking about what might be next for her.

PART THREE

11

The Witch Hunt

Jean loved being a lawyer and had enjoyed the range of professional opportunities that the law had allowed her to pursue. Her legal aid experience, her years of advocacy work in the political and government arena, and even building her own law firm had all fueled her passion, challenged her intellectually, and been stimulating learning experiences. With all of that, there was one piece of the legal landscape that she had not experienced, and that was the judiciary.

The newly constructed state justice center was located just a block from the Capitol. It was a unique marvel of architecture that came to be known as the Toaster Building because, to most, it looked like a toaster. Passers-by routinely stopped to gaze at this strange looking edifice that housed the state appeals courts and the state supreme court.

"The first time being a judge crossed my mind was while I was working at the attorney general's office. I was on the sidewalk one day looking up at the brand new Toaster building." She began to wonder, she said, if she would ever have the chance to work in that peculiar building; ever have the opportunity to be an appeals court judge. Jean had overseen some the state's appeals while in the attorney general's office and was intrigued by the role that those judges played. And while she thought being an appellate judge might be a good fit for her, she also presumed it would take some years gaining experience in lower courts before she would be considered for such an appointment.

The first chance Jean had to ponder a real possibility that she might have the opportunity to work in the Toaster Building came in late 1978, two years after she had left the attorney general's office. A colleague from her days working at the statehouse called to tell Jean about an opening on the Colorado Supreme Court with the strong suggestion that Jean apply for the appointment. Jean was taken aback at first. Supreme court justices were the highest level in the judicial system. She had never been a judge on any of the lower level courts. How could she expect to even be considered, never mind be appointed? And she was a woman. There had never before been a woman on the Colorado high court.

Jean assumed that the "never before had there been a woman" factor was a drawback. It was, in actuality, a factor in her favor. Jean began to hear from a number of friends and former associates at the Capitol that she was on Governor Lamm's radar as a possible replacement for a retiring justice on the supreme court. Lamm very much wanted to appoint a woman to the supreme court and the appointment was his to make.

Jean was skeptical. She focused on the obvious reasons why she did not think an appointment was within the realm of possibility. She had never been a judge. She had been mostly home for the last two years, a stay-at-home mother. She and the governor were not that close. Rumors and gossip that circulated around the Capitol were only that, rumors and gossip. Her skepticism made her reluctant to apply mostly because of her fear that she would simply be rejected. It would be an embarrassment. When friends would call to check in on what she was thinking, she mostly demurred. Oh, I don't know, she would say. I don't really think I have a chance.

But as Jean mulled it over, she recognized that despite the obvious disadvantages, it might not be totally preposterous to think she might be given consideration. Although she and the governor were not close personal friends, their paths had often crossed. They had known each other when Lamm was a legislator during Jean's days with legal aid, and Lamm was governor during her time in the attorney general's office. Lamm knew Jean well enough and appreciated her abilities enough that, earlier that year, he had appointed her to the Insurance Commission, an important new regulatory board. Still, she had her doubts about the likelihood of a supreme court appointment, especially given the complexities involved in such appointments.

When the state court system was first established, Colorado was still very much a part of the Wild West, and all judges, including those on the supreme court, were elected by the voters, not appointed by the governor. This raised all sorts of justifiable suspicions that political shenanigans occasionally occurred in the courtroom. In 1966, Colorado abandoned the election of judges and moved to an appointment process designed to take politics out of the courts and lessen the opportunity for biased decisions. The new process for selecting supreme court justices gave the governor the power to make the appointment, but only after another body provided the governor a list of names.

First, the governor had to name an eleven-member panel of lawyers and citizens tasked with reviewing applications. This panel, the Judicial Selection Commission, then selected three people they judged to be most qualified, and the governor was then free to select any one of the three to be the next justice of the Colorado Supreme Court.

By the late 1970s women activists were increasingly flexing their muscles, their voices, and their votes and, in Colorado, were advocating forcefully for women to occupy more seats at the state leadership table. The appointment of a woman to the supreme court was at the top of their list. Governor Lamm had made a commitment, during his first campaign for governor and during his recent reelection campaign, to increase the number of women and minorities serving in high office. He often spoke specifically about his commitment to appoint more women judges, including, and especially, to the supreme court. If Jean needed one more reason to believe there was a chance she would be given full consideration, it was the growing political pressure to appoint a woman to the high court.

Lamm's first opportunity to make a supreme court appointment came in 1976, early in his first term. Much to the chagrin of women activists and supporters who had helped elect him, his pick was not a woman. In addition to the increased public pressure from women activists, disappointed that he had not made good on his promise, Dick Lamm had to come home each night to his wife Dottie, a well-known and well-respected women's advocate in her own right. Lamm continued to make reassurances at home and in public that he would keep his commitment and place a woman on the high court, but, as he often reminded critics, the selection committee had to first do its job and include women on the lists that they forwarded to him. Finding qualified women to serve on the court was not an easy task, however, especially if guided by the long-established, traditional criteria: years of experience in a distinguished law firm, followed by years of service as a lower court judge. Women had only recently been welcomed into the profession; law firms had only barely begun hiring women lawyers into senior roles; and only a handful of women served as judges in the lower courts.

After his reelection in November, and about to begin his second term, Lamm knew that, due to mandatory retirements, within a year he would make two new appointments to the supreme court. If the selection committee gave the governor the opportunity, it seemed certain that Lamm would make that historic appointment. The only questions were who and when.

When the selection committee began reviewing applications in late 1978, Jean's was among them. Like all top candidates, she had been invited to appear before the group for a formal interview. When the selection committee sent the governor the list with the required three names, it provided the governor what he had been pressing for: one of the names on the list of three was a woman.

"I was under a lot of pressure to appoint a woman and I wanted to appoint a woman," Lamm said. "But when I got the three names, I didn't really know anything about the one woman on the list." Her name was Brooke Wunnicke. She was a respected, but little known, deputy district attorney in Denver, and a Republican.

Lamm was most familiar with another name on the list: Luis Rovira. Rovira was a prominent member and former president of the Colorado Bar Association and considered to be one of the finest attorneys in the state. He was someone Lamm knew well, someone Lamm had great respect for. "Luis had just spent an incredible amount of his own time and energy contributing in so many different ways. I had served with him on the Colorado Mental Health board and I just so admired him. I had nothing against Brooke Wunnicke, but I didn't know her at all. I knew Luis and he was so outstanding, was such a fine and honorable man, that he had to be my pick."

Lamm's appointment of Rovira was also an historic first. Rovira was the first person of color and the first Hispanic to serve the Colorado Supreme Court. Lamm would not receive any plaudits or political credit among Latinos for this pick, however, because Rovira was a Republican, was not of Mexican descent, and was not an active member of the state's Hispanic leadership. And the women were still waiting.

Rumors that a woman's name appeared on the list of three given to the governor began circulating, but since the entire selection process was secret and the names of the applicants and the three selected were never made public, no one knew for sure. Still, the rumors swirled, and by the time the selection process began again a few months later, the pressure to name a woman to the high court was at a boiling point.

"I was feeling the pressure to appoint a women but I wanted to appoint the right woman, not just any woman. When I appointed Luis I knew we had another appointment to make soon. We were looking ahead and I had every anticipation that we would get a better choice of a woman soon," Lamm said. His anticipation that a better choice was coming was not just wishful thinking. It was due to changes in the composition of the selection committee that had occurred in the few months since the last appointment.

In the interim, the terms of three of the members had expired and the governor appointed new members to fill those seats. Lamm made his picks for the selection committee carefully and in accordance with the guidelines for balancing political parties, geography, and professions. But he had very explicit instructions for each of them. "When you send me the three names, you need to include the name of a qualified woman," Lamm instructed. "I told them: Find me a woman for the supreme court!"

When the time came for Justice Pringle to retire, the committee began its selection process again. Jean did not want to re-apply, fearing the same thing would happen: she would be passed over again. A second rejection would be too much to bear.

But calls of encouragement began once more. Although the names of the three were not disclosed, word did eventually leak out that Brooke Wunnicke had been the woman on the last list sent to the governor. But another name leaked out as well. The rumor circulating at the Capitol was that when the voting of the selection committee concluded last time, Jean had been fourth on the list. The process was secret, so no one could know for sure. But Jean had worked at the Capitol for years and knew many of the players who were supposedly the sources of these rumors. She knew that it was possible, maybe even likely, that the rumors and speculation passed on to her were true. If you apply again this time, she was told, you would be an obvious choice. Especially with the three new members on the committee.

Jean reactivated her application, and in early June she rode the bus down to Denver for her second interview before the eleven-person Judicial Selection Commission, and the wheels of the process turned again. Justice Pringle wasn't scheduled to retire until mid-July, and even if the committee did select Jean as one of the three names to go to the governor, she would then have to interview with him, and then more time would pass before he announced a decision. So Jean wasn't exactly waiting by the phone.

Yet, on that Friday afternoon, just days after the selection committee interview, Jean was in the laundry room preparing to move the wet clothes from the washer to the dryer when her phone rang. It was Governor Dick Lamm. The conversation was short and, for Jean, very sweet. "I'm appointing you," Lamm said. "We'll have a press conference tomorrow morning." And that was that. For the second consecutive time a woman's name was on the list sent to the governor. But this time it was a woman the governor knew well. He didn't need to interview Jean, he said, and he had nothing to gain by interviewing the others. "I didn't feel the need to go through the motions of pretending that I didn't know what I was going to do. It was time to just get on with it," Lamm said. "I knew who I wanted."

On that Friday in 1979, when the U.S. Supreme Court was still a male only club, Jean Dubofsky had just learned that she was to become the first woman in 103 years of Colorado history to be appointed to that state's supreme court. She was home alone and Frank didn't answer his office phone, but Jean needed someone to tell, so she ran down the street to tell one of her neighbors. Then just as quickly she ran back home to get on the phone again. She needed to find Frank. And she needed to find a babysitter for the next day's press conference. And she still needed to move the wet clothes from the washer to the dryer.

The following morning Jean hugged the boys goodbye, and she and Frank drove down to Denver for the press conference. She took her place at the microphone in front of the gaggle of cameras and reporters. If it hadn't dawned on her before just how newsworthy her appointment would be, or just how different she would feel to be the one standing in front of the cameras instead of behind or to the side, it was clear to her that she had just taken a step into a new dimension. Then, as she glanced down, in a moment of shyness perhaps, she noticed a big chocolate smudge on her beautiful silk scarf. *Ahh*, she thought, *the Fudgsicles!* In order to distract Josh and Matthew before running out the door, Jean had given the boys Fudgsicles as a treat. When Jean gave the boys a quick hug, a bit of the chocolate found its way onto her scarf. Jean smiled to herself, flipped over the scarf, and turned back to the waiting members of the media.

Jean could not help but be caught up in all the excitement. The prospect of a new professional challenge was obviously a huge part of her excitement. But the historic "first" was part of it as well, and that was the part that captured all the attention.

"Jean E. Dubofsky, 37, a Denver attorney who considers herself a feminist, was appointed as the first woman justice in the state's history," was the lead sentence in the *Denver Post* story the following day.[37] The details that followed referred to her service on the Commission on the Status of Women, an award from the National Organization for Women, and her work advancing women's rights as key credentials.

While the call from the governor came much more swiftly than expected, the swearing in ceremony had to wait until Justice Pringle's retirement became official three weeks later. At first, those weeks were extraordinary. Flattering profiles appeared in the daily papers, and the phone rang off the hook as people from so many parts of her life called with congratulations and well wishes.

That feeling of hopefulness, that glow of great possibility, did not last, however. Before Jean was formally sworn into office, her selection became the focal point of relentless political attacks, mostly deeply partisan and personal. The assault began after a Republican state senator and longtime Republican nemesis of the governor, Ralph Cole, held a press conference. He accused the governor of illegally tampering with the judicial selection process and called for a formal investigation.

Soon after the Cole press conference, Otto Moore, a former chief justice of the Colorado Supreme Court during the time when justices were elected, not appointed, followed up with colorful language of his own. Moore called the whole selection process a "Star Chamber" proceeding, a "sham and a pretext."[38] Dubofsky was less qualified, had less experience, and would never have been on the list sent to the governor unless the process had somehow been rigged, Cole and Moore charged. Governor Lamm and his staff had somehow gotten to the Judicial Selection Commission and manipulated their choices so that the governor could appoint his political friend, Jean Dubofsky. Within weeks, three separate investigations were launched and months of headlines and newspaper stories followed, all suggesting some kind of chicanery behind the governor's choice of Jean Dubofsky to become the first woman on the Colorado Supreme Court.

Not only did Jean need to find babysitters, buy herself some new clothes suitable for being a justice, learn a new job, hire a law clerk, and begin immediately to focus on a large number of very complex judicial cases, she had to do so under a cloud of accusations and suspicion, and in the midst of a series of very public investigations.

Jean called that whole period the witch hunt. It went on and on for months. The most attention grabbing investigation was conducted by the state legislature. It formed a special investigative committee and began holding a series of headline-provoking hearings that one long-time state legislator called the most abusive and unfair set of hearings he had ever seen.[39]

When the committee called witnesses who made claims of executive privilege or secrecy oaths and refused to testify, it issued subpoenas. Eventually, selection committee members and key members of the governor's staff were all forced to testify, as were colleagues and friends of Jean. Many felt the need to hire attorneys. All were asked to reveal who they may have spoken with, asked to describe what pressure they may have tried to exert or that was exerted on them. All of the questioning was heavily laden with innuendos of wrongdoing and illegality, leaving many feeling that their integrity had been impugned.

One by one, each member of the selection commission testified to the same thing: neither the governor nor anyone one in the governor's office had contacted them about Dubofsky or had tried in any way to influence their process. One commissioner who worked as a lobbyist at the Capitol said that she had heard the rumors that Dubofsky would likely be the governor's pick, but referred to the general gossip around the Capitol as double and triple hearsay, and not the same thing as arm twisting or political pressure.

Brooke Wunnicke, who had been passed over by the governor and was thought to be colluding with Cole and Moore in their attempt to cast doubt on the nominating process, testified that she had heard rumors that Jean was the governor's pick even before the selection committee met. She was reluctant to reveal confidential conversations and refused to name names, she told the committee, because all she learned was based on second or third-hand information. Others testified that although they had no specific knowledge of any attempt to influence the selection committee, it was "the worst kept secret in town" that Lamm wanted Dubofsky on the bench.[40]

Jean refused to be intimidated by the accusations and investigations, but she was not totally immune to the barrage of negative innuendo. Even if some of the accusers went out of their way to stipulate that they meant no disrespect to Jean, it was a damning of faint praise, tinged with some reference to her inexperience or her age or her political connections or her admitted feminism. They left no doubt they were questioning her credentials and qualifications and her right to don that long black robe.

"They were going to jump up and down, maybe thinking it would make me resign or maybe so they could make sure there wouldn't be anyone like me to come along again any time soon," Jean said. "That's what they were after, I suppose. But resigning never ever occurred to me. It was just not in my make-up."

During the investigation, Jean started a folder labeled witch hunt. Each time a newspaper article appeared, or a report was issued, or a note arrived from a friend who had been called to testify, Jean would simply file it away into that manila folder and then get on with her work at the court. She tried to disconnect herself from the controversy. She'd been in the middle of state politics long enough to know that the accusations about political influence in her selection were proxies for long-standing simmering political animus between some of the Republican "crazies", as they became known, and the Democratic governor. There was nothing she could do about the political circus that swirled around her appointment, Jean decided. All she could do was stay focused on doing her new job.

12

The First Woman Justice

Critics of Jean's appointment were correct about one thing: she did not look like a supreme court justice. Not only was Jean the first woman appointed to the Colorado Supreme Court, she was also the youngest justice ever to serve. She was thirty-seven years old, but with her slight build, short pixie haircut, and fashionable oversized eyeglasses, she could have passed as a college student. The colleagues she joined were almost all twenty years her senior.

Under fire from investigations and accusations about her appointment, she anticipated that her first and most difficult challenge might be demonstrating to her fellow justices that she belonged. Much to her surprise, they telegraphed immediately that she had nothing to prove to them. Her new colleagues quietly wrapped their fatherly arms around her, welcoming her to the court. She was one of them now, and the justices responded as if attacks on her were attacks on all of them, and on the court itself.

"It was as if all of a sudden I had six new best friends," Jean said. "The uproar over my appointment probably brought us together more quickly than might have happened otherwise."

It also helped that Chief Justice Paul Hodges had the wisdom not to try to ease her in slowly but instead immediately piled on the work, assigning Jean most of the new opinions so that her caseload would quickly equal that of the other justices. Before she had even hired her first law clerk, she had been assigned a dozen opinions to write, and a two-foot tall pile of petitions in need of review was stacked on a corner of her desk, her share of the thousand that arrived each year. If Jean was to become one of them, Hodges concluded, it would start with the workload. From the very beginning, it was the work, one case or one legal issue after another, that made Jean feel most at home.

Jean had worked hard her entire life, but during those first months on the court she worked especially hard, was more focused, more determined. She took particular care to read every brief thoroughly, to write and rewrite every opinion until it was polished and perfect. She stayed up late, woke before dawn, and took stacks of material with her so she could work on the bus, all to make sure no one—not her colleagues, not the lawyers who appeared before her—would have any doubt that she belonged in that long black robe. She was the first woman and felt the weight that came with that distinction. "Even more than before," she said, "I had to make sure I did not make any mistakes."

In many ways, life as a justice resembled that of a scholar, an academic, or philosopher: researching, analyzing, and publishing conclusions. New assignments came along each week, so that even as the justices completed one case and sent it out the door, there would be another one waiting to come in. All of this suited Jean's more cerebral and analytical nature, and allowed those pieces of who she was to blossom more fully.

Jean brought all of her skills and interests and experience to the court, but not her advocacy. She had a keen sense that in this new role, her obligation was not to change the law but to ensure the law was followed, a very different proposition from her activist days. Much to the surprise of some of her early critics, who assumed she would use her position to advocate for radical notions, Jean did not think it proper to use the cases before the court to push a liberal agenda. Part of it was her respect for the court's role to decide cases based on the facts, and not attempt to use cases to accomplish other political goals. Part of it was the practicality of needing to gain and hold the three other votes necessary for a decision. Going it alone was not an option. She earned a reputation as someone writing to the middle of the political spectrum.

Jean's lack of previous judicial experience was cited by critics as evidence that it would be difficult for her to serve successfully; on the contrary, it may have been advantageous. Former judges had to make the difficult switch from having the sole power to decide each case as they saw fit, without the need to persuade three other justices to join them in an opinion. But persuading others had been a large part of Jean's professional life. Her days at the Capitol were spent looking for a middle ground that would be acceptable, as she did when seeking compromises to get bills passed, or pushing for new policies and regulations. To forge a majority on the court, each justice was required to take into account colleagues' concerns and craft legal arguments to cobble together agreement among differing points of view. Jean had years of practice doing just that.

The trappings that came with being a justice were a less comfortable fit for Jean than the court's analytical and substantive work. Unlike some justices who gave off airs of expecting to be deferred to, when Jean slipped on her black robe she did not suddenly transform into the royal "Justice Dubofsky". Jean remained Jean, her life and her sense of herself defined not by her title or robe or high status, but by who she had always been. Her office and her style of management and leadership did not take on imperial airs either. The clerks popped in and out of her office regularly with questions or thoughts or simply to avoid tramping down the hall to the staff bathroom.

"I remember my interview with her when I applied for a job," one former clerk said. "Here I was in the office of a supreme court justice and I was a little intimidated. I couldn't believe it when someone just walked through her office, right by us, to use her private bathroom."

Although her clerks insisted on calling her Justice Dubofsky, not Jean, as she invited them to, she regarded and treated them as colleagues. They discussed cases, the law, and the work that needed to be done. Jean and her staff were a team and she treated each person with as much respect as they showed toward her. She provided clear direction and undisputed legal guidance, but she welcomed the opinions of the clerks and invited them to make their case when they felt there was a different or opposing argument that needed to be made. They did not hesitate to spar with her when the occasion arose, but she was often way ahead of them with explanations for why she had already considered their counter arguments and found them wanting.

Her court nuclear family was small; it consisted of a law clerk or two and a loyal and trusted secretary, Livy Filipek, who had followed Jean from the legal services office, to Kelly & Dubofsky, then to the attorney general's office, and, finally, to the court. Her extended court family was not much larger: six other justices, their small staff, and less than another dozen support staff in the clerk's office. Personnel changes were constant as most law clerks served for a year and then moved on, replaced by new clerks.

An ever-present part of the court's daily workload was sifting through hundreds of cases that poured in from the lower courts, seeking "certiorari", the supreme court's agreement to accept the case for review. During Jean's years on the court, more than a thousand requests arrived each year; only a few hundred cases were accepted for appeal. When each new batch of law clerks arrived in the fall for their first day of work, they generally found a very tall stack of papers on their desks—the "cert" pile. These fresh-out-of-law-school attorneys were central to managing these requests. Their primary responsibility was to review all cert petitions and then prepare an initial memo providing a recommendation and rationale for why each case should or should not be accepted by the court for review.

The clerks also assisted in the writing of opinions, although few justices granted them a free hand. While Jean occasionally gave clerks the opportunity to do a first draft, it was rare for a clerk's draft opinion to survive intact once Jean took a hand to it. She edited. She moved sections. She added and subtracted arguments. She rewrote every paragraph. She asked for additional case support. She polished. "Jean would totally make our drafts her own," one clerk said. It was a proud moment for any clerk to read one of Jean's final opinions and find that a phrase or a sentence from the draft they had initially provided remained.

More often, however, Jean drafted her own opinions, laying out her basic arguments, then fleshing them out with case law before passing the draft to a clerk for reading, editing suggestions, further research, and case backup. She was a precise and meticulous legal writer. "Jean taught me a lot about legal writing. Still today, almost thirty years later, if ever I see something in passive voice, I hear Jean's voice of criticism and out it goes," said one clerk. "Every time I drafted an opinion," said another, "Jean would go through it and take out all the adverbs and adjectives. We learned to appreciate her 'death to adjectives' approach and often laughed at all the words she would eliminate."

A few of the other justices permitted their clerks to do the opinion writing, but Jean and most of the justices shared Justice Joseph Quinn's view that opinion writing was not a proper role for a clerk. "Even if the clerks are very smart and even if they may know what the law is, they don't yet understand the significance of things," he said. "Understanding what is significant and what is not significant, you can only learn by experience. So I never thought justices should simply let their clerks write the opinions. That was the job of the justice."

There may have been questions about Jean's youth or judicial inexperience when she was appointed to the court, but it did not take long before her colleagues concluded that those questions were unfounded. She brought to the court an exceptional and sophisticated understanding of the law and a work ethic befitting the role of a justice. That Jean showed she belonged among this group considered to have the best legal minds in the state was no small hurdle to overcome. But it wasn't just about belonging; soon it was about leading, especially after a nucleus of four younger justices—Rovira, Quinn, Lohr and Dubofsky—sparked a shift, at first subtle, then more noticeable, in how the legal community regarded the court.

Justice Luis Rovira arrived at the court five months before Jean, and two other new and younger members, Justice George Lohr and Justice Joseph Quinn, joined the court within a year of Jean's appointment. The newer justices were closer to her age than the older justices who had been ensconced on the court for more than a decade. The arrival of Rovira, Quinn, Lohr, and Dubofsky made for a very different-looking new court, drastically reducing the average age of the justices and bringing different sets of experiences along with them. They appreciated each other's intellect and seriousness and genuinely enjoyed each other's company. Their workloads were heavy; their days were long. Most simply ate lunch alone at their desks, and their one-on-one conversations were almost always about cases and legal issues that needed resolving to ensure consensus. They became friends; not the social friendship of Saturday nights on the town, but the kind of collegial professional friendship that brightened the days.

Court watchers began to notice that the new justices tended to write lengthier opinions, to deal with not just some, but all of the legal arguments presented by the briefs, and do so more completely, with a more detailed analysis and a more thorough rendering of how they weighed the complexities of the case. While some in the legal community groused about the new, lengthier opinions, most appreciated the improvement in the quality of the court's opinions. Respect for the court and its work grew.

"Before this new group arrived, I think Colorado was viewed as a backwater of judging and jurisprudence, with opinions that tended to be very terse and very short. Often you couldn't divine what reason got them from here to there, and the opinions were not respected," according to Lori Potter, a well regarded Denver attorney and one of Jean's former clerks. "But the new justices shared a commitment to being thoughtful and complete in their writing, and it elevated the reputation of the court. Lawyers from other regions began to look to decisions of the Colorado Supreme Court for guidance and reasoning on legal issues."

Unlike the U.S. Supreme Court, where ideological divisions have tended to be determinant, justices at the state supreme court level were generally much less visibly ideological, perhaps partly because the cases that come before such courts revolve around mistakes in the law or the sorting out of complexities of competing laws. Even when dealing with constitutional questions, ideologically based differences played a minimal role in decisions most of the time.

Yet, state justices did not arrive at the high court devoid of their own philosophical, ideological, and political biases. Even when the focus is on the facts of a case, in the end where a justice stands in a case "often came down to a basic philosophical difference about the fundamental purpose of the U.S. Constitution and the Bill of Rights," according to Justice Quinn. He used the example of the exclusionary rule, often at issue in cases before the court. "When you are trying to decide what testimony or evidence should be allowed and what should be excluded, the side you come down on is primarily a function of whether your basic philosophy is that the primary function of the law is to protect people, or the primary function of the law is to protect the government as it exercises its power. Is the purpose of the Constitution to protect society from antisocial behavior or to protect individuals from the government or government overreach? This is a fundamental underlying philosophical difference and when people disagree there it's bound to affect their legal interpretations and decisions."

Differences among the justices also sprang from their life's experience. Quinn cited Jean in particular as coming to the court with a different point of view from most other justices because of her legal aid work and advocacy for the rights of the poor. But he could have been speaking for himself as well. As a young attorney he spent four or five years working as a public defender.

"You don't leave behind what you are. You bring all of it to the court with you," Quinn said. "Many judges can't relate to the needs of people because they spent their careers helping big corporations or commercial interests, and so they think the law exists for business or big commercial interests, or for social control by the government. Jean worked with ordinary people and she could relate to those people and understood the role of the law for ordinary people." Quinn and Lohr shared Jean's view of the critical role the law played in protecting the rights of individuals and were often were on the same side in difficult cases.

Criminal cases made their way up through the levels of appeal to the supreme court more than civil cases, primarily because most criminal defendants have public defenders and, because they are not personally paying the legal bills, they have essentially nothing to lose by continuing one appeal after another. The criminal cases that the court accepts for review are cases that raise fundamental constitutional questions, such as the right to a speedy or fair trial, the right to a jury of one's peers, or the right to an adequate defense. These and other equal rights, privacy protections, and due process concerns were often at the heart of probable cause, evidence suppression or admissibility, and the search and seizure questions that regularly came before the justices.

For Jean, memorable cases were often framed by a vivid image and a specific question. If a policeman walks up to a house and the blinds are half open and he looks through and sees someone with heroin packages, is that a constitutionally legal search or not? Should a confession made by a person who hears voices, is paranoid and irrational, and is determined by psychiatric evaluations to be severely mentally ill be considered voluntary or not, given that the legal definition of voluntary includes the criteria that the statement be "rational"? Should the testimony of a witness saying she heard screams be allowed or overruled as hearsay? If a detective asks a suspect in custody if he knows why he's being arrested and he says yes, is that a Miranda violation or not?

For Jean, the most unforgettable cases were not necessarily the criminal cases. She was drawn most to cases where, because of changes in society not envisioned when laws were written, or because different laws passed over time provided conflicting guidance, there was what Jean called "unsettled law that needed settling." For instance, in one of her first child custody cases, she argued in her written opinion that the times had changed and judges could not simply decide a custody case based on the reading of a legal custody agreement made years before shared custody agreements had become commonplace.

She was also drawn to cases that were challenging and complex on a very human level. A father asking that he be relieved of the legal responsibility to support his child because he had wanted the mother to have an abortion. A blood bank seeking relief from liability over blood donations. A custody dispute when one parent moved a child to a far away new school system without agreement from the other parent. A firefighter's widow appealing the denial of retirement benefits because she married the firefighter after he retired. Parents seeking the right to authorize a hysterectomy for their retarded fifteen-year-old daughter because they feared she would become pregnant.

Jean loved to be challenged by cases that required her to master a new subject and demanded a detailed understanding of the facts of the case before she began weighing the nuances of case law, or statutes, or state and federal constitutional issues. It might take Jean six or eight months to work her way through these cases.

A water case, *Alamosa-La Jara Water Users Protection Association v. Gould,* was one of those cases, and may have been Jean's most complex and most important case. It was the only water law opinion Jean was assigned to write because most water law cases were assigned to justices with water law expertise. Water use holds such a place of importance in the West that special state water courts were established in the late 1960s to sort out the battles—battles that sometimes traced back to territorial days—over rights to the limited water that flows in and out of Colorado. New Mexico, Texas, Arizona, California, Nebraska, and Kansas are all dependent on decisions over rights to water flowing from Colorado. Any water case that makes it to the Colorado Supreme Court becomes critically important far beyond the state's borders.

"Rules for water law were developed before Colorado even became a state. I loved the history and having to sort out the rules that developed and changed and why they should change," Jean said. For her water case, she had to reach back into the historic compacts and rules about water flow from branches of the various creeks and rivers (including the Alamosa River and La Jara Creek) and sort out rules going forward regarding decisions of state water engineers about the flow of surface water and underground diversions. In the *Alamosa-La Jara* opinion, Jean introduced the important concept of the "public interest" into the legal equation, ruling that it was not just the arguments and historic legal claims of the competing sides in a dispute that must be weighed by the court, but the interests of the public must also be weighed. The *Alamosa-La Jara* opinion was later included in law textbooks as a pivotal case that opened the door to considering not simply the rights of compact holders but the public's broader interest as well.

Only a small percentage of Jean's cases became textbook cases but most were weighty and multi-layered; a few caught the attention of the press. One such case was a libel case that morphed into a freedom of the press case.[41] It pitted a group of city officials against their hometown newspaper, the *Greeley Tribune*, when the officials sued the paper for libel. The district court found the paper and the reporter were guilty of libel, but the Colorado Court of Appeals reversed the decision, throwing out the finding of libel. That court relied substantially on *N.Y. Times v. Sullivan*, the landmark U.S. Supreme Court case regarding libel standards, when it came to reporting about the actions of public officials.

When the case finally arrived at the Colorado Supreme Court, Jean's opinion also relied on *N.Y. Times v. Sullivan*, yet she found the opposite, that the newspaper did indeed libel the city workers. Jean's habit of thoroughly reading the transcript of the original case revealed a set of facts that led her to that different conclusion. Few appeals court judges had the time or inclination to read the entire record. But Jean always felt that reading the entire record was the only way to truly follow a case's legal theory and its arguments.

In addition to writing opinions when assigned to, Jean occasionally would commit a significant amount of time and effort on a dissent. She was not an aggressive writer of dissents and wrote them for only two reasons: when a group of her colleagues felt it important to record their objections, or when Jean felt a serious misinterpretation or misreading of the law or the Constitution had occurred. *Lujan v. Colorado State Board of Education* provided both reasons.

Dissents rarely presented the challenge or complexity of the majority opinions justices were responsible for writing, but *Lujan* was an exception. It was the most important challenge to the state's system of financing public education in Colorado history. When the majority overturned a lower court ruling issued years earlier by Justice Quinn while he was a district court judge, Jean took on the dissent as if it were one of the most important opinions she would ever write. (Quinn, of course, had to recuse himself in the case when it came before the supreme court.)

As a district court judge, Quinn had ruled that the wide disparity in funding for education in towns across the state deprived students of equal educational opportunity, the standard required by federal and state constitutions. Jean's powerful and detailed dissent supported Quinn's original finding that the state's limited educational funding *did* violate equal protection guarantees of the U.S. Constitution *and* also violated the Colorado Constitution's guarantee of a "thorough and uniform system of free public schools." Neither the majority opinion nor the dissent in *Lujan* fully settled the complicated issue of Colorado's funding of public education, however, and the debate over what constitutes an equal education continues to this day.

13

Storm Clouds Inside the Court

In many ways Jean was suited to her role as a justice. But there were challenges and aspects of the life of a justice that were less comfortable, sometimes even difficult. The most obvious and understandable challenge was not a new one. Jean was still the mother to two small boys, still living in Boulder and commuting daily to Denver, still doing her best to manage the household, pack the school lunches, and be fully present at home, all while serving in a very demanding, high-profile public position.

As often as she could, she caught the four-thirty afternoon bus and would walk through the back door and into the Dubofsky kitchen by six o'clock. The next three hours would be all about the family. She'd cook, they'd have dinner, do homework, read stories, and take the dog for a walk. Once the boys were tucked in, Jean would fall into her own bed and sleep until four o'clock. She would then rise and attempt to fit in a couple of hours of work before the morning ritual of getting the kids up and dressed, making breakfast, and sometimes helping young Matt, who liked to sneak downstairs at five-thirty to do his homework with his mother before she left for work. She was often out the door by six-thirty. It was a grueling schedule but, unlike most working mothers, especially mothers raising their kids alone, Jean had the financial resources to make it work.

"At one point I think I hired half of Boulder," Jean said. They would watch the boys, clean the house, mow the lawn, and prepare meals on occasion. "And I had Frank." Frank had his own busy and demanding legal practice but his office was in Boulder and he was there to take the boys to school and was just a few minutes away when after school or early evening activities called for a parental presence. When Jean accepted the appointment, she knew what to expect. She understood what it would take to manage her family life, because she had done it before. "I had a system," she said, "On my next day off I would get things ready for the coming week. And it seemed to work."

There was one aspect of the life of a justice that she hadn't expected, however. In striking contrast to Jean's previous interactive, very public, and outwardly focused roles, in becoming a supreme court justice it was as if she had entered a convent. Once she donned the black ankle-length robe, her life became a cloistered existence. Just as nuns spent their days in seclusion and contemplation, so, too, did Jean and her colleagues on the court.

"The whole atmosphere resembled a fortress and monastery. It was a very quiet and monastic existence," said one of Jean's clerks. It wasn't just the solitary, academic life style of studying, research, and writing that was so isolating; it was also the absence of daily interactions with the outside world. Most justices served on a few committees that took them outside the courthouse, but Jean's days with a calendar crowded with meetings with colleagues, clients, or community members, were gone. Occasionally visitors found their way into the judicial building and onto the elevators, but once arriving on the fifth floor, they were met by a counter and a set of desks that housed the office of the clerk of court. Few were allowed beyond that point.

The court's inner sanctum consisted of a separate office for each justice, located on either side of a long hallway. A small anteroom, little more than a windowless cubbyhole, housed the secretary and clerks, and behind it was the justice's own spacious private office—

with windows and a private bathroom. The justices and their staff spent the bulk of their hours in their own little world, researching, reading, writing, typing and retyping, with little contact with others, even those along the same hallway. It was as if seven separate mini law firms existed under one roof. "Every judge's office was an island," was how one court insider described it. The fifth floor was a sea of islands, floating off shore from the world at large.

Another facet of the isolation was how friendships changed. The demands of Jean's job meant less time for casual lunches and social gatherings. Many of Jean's friends were attorneys and public officials. And much of the court's business intertwined with cases or issues they might be involved with, which posed potential conflict situations. Once she became a justice, Jean and her friends found they were becoming careful with each other, tempering their conversations, mindful of what could be said or not said. Jean missed the easy banter about the law or public issues. It wasn't the same anymore.

Most of Jean's court colleagues were quiet, solitary figures, each with personalities and quirks that earned them various degrees of affection, or lack thereof, from those around them. As friendships became more distant outside of the court, a strained relationship inside the court emerged and became the most troubling and difficult aspects of her life as a justice. While sitting on the bench during oral arguments or in other public settings, and in dealings with staff and colleagues on the fifth floor, the justices generally exhibited courtesy, proper decorum, and good manners toward one another. If there were any deep disagreements or any animus between any two justices, it was not obvious in the day-to-day workings of the court. Behind the closed doors of the weekly Conference, however, it was an entirely different story.

Thursday Conference was the time each week when justices gathered—alone, without staff—to make decisions about which appeals to accept or reject, discuss cases after hearing oral arguments, take votes, assign cases, and vote again prior to releasing opinions. It was the time and place to air disagreements and debate conflicting interpretations of the law or the facts. Exchanges would occasionally become heated, mostly the result of a professional or legal dispute. But these differences were easily set aside as they moved on to a next case, where dissenting colleagues might suddenly find themselves on the same side.

On many occasions during Jean's time on the court, however, once the Conference room door closed, the atmosphere of mutual respect, civility, and collegiality devolved into pettiness and personal disrespect. The degree of discord that bubbled up, one justice said, never rose to the level of what happened in Illinois, where judges infamously came to physical blows on more than one occasion. A court tradition of never discussing the details of the goings-on behind the Conference doors limited the willingness or enthusiasm of most justices to provide details, even thirty years later. Yet, all the justices interviewed by the author conceded that there were some very troubling relationships at times and they mostly had to do with what one justice called "the bad behavior of Bill Erickson". Jean, in particular, was often on the receiving end of that behavior.

Justice William Erickson had a colorful career as a trial lawyer, including famously representing the man convicted of the 1961 headline-grabbing kidnapping and murder of Adolph Coors III, heir to the Coors beer empire. Erickson was a towering figure in Colorado and national legal circles and within the Republican Party. His career was dotted with several "almost" moments: he was a finalist for the special prosecutor position that went to Archibald Cox during Watergate, and was once nominated, but not confirmed, for an appointment to the federal bench.

An old-fashioned straight arrow with a burr haircut—what Erickson once described as the last World War II haircut left in Colorado—he had a fine legal mind, was a hard worker, and was revered by many of his law clerks. But often he could be a difficult, demanding, and exacting justice. "He rode his clerks really hard," according to one justice who served on the court with him. "He was a tyrant."

He also had a competitive streak. He insisted that regular reports be issued detailing how long each justice took to write opinions, and he enjoyed regularly pointing out how unproductive some of his colleagues were compared to him.

That competitiveness even extended to inconsequential matters, such as arrival time at the office. He was determined to be the first at his desk each day, before any of his colleagues and before any staff.

A possibly apocryphal (but likely true) story has been passed along from one class of law clerks to another for decades. It seems that one day the always-early Justice Erickson arrived at the office to find one of his new clerks already at his desk. Miffed, the next day Erickson arrived thirty minutes earlier, successfully beating the clerk to the office that day. But the clerk, ever eager to impress, decided to report for work even earlier the following morning. When Erickson came through the door and found the clerk already at his desk, he exploded. The clerk was ordered to never again come to work before eight o'clock.

Erickson's verbal communication style was in keeping with his opinion writing: terse, short, conclusory. Erickson thought it unnecessary to elaborate on how he arrived at his opinions and was often abrupt when asked by a colleague to do so. "I've said all I had to say," was his standard response. His unnecessarily sharp, sometimes dismissive and demeaning comments, especially toward a particular colleague who seemed not to be in his good graces at the moment, made everyone uncomfortable, although most justices professed to being unfazed by his behavior and simply tried to ignore it. As one justice said, "Bill was just who he was. It was just his way."

When Jean first came on the court, Erickson went out of his way to befriend her, being solicitous and overly complimentary in an almost courting manner. But when Erickson became chief justice, the courtship ended and the friend became the enemy. The change from friend to foe occurred on the day that Erickson was elected by his peers to become the chief justice.

Each year the justices elect one of the group to serve as chief justice for the coming year; in reality, however, once elected chief justice, most go on to serve year after year, the annual election a mere formality. A few days before the scheduled vote in 1983, Erickson came to Jean's office. He told Jean that Chief Justice Paul Hodges was planning to step down. Erickson thought himself to be the logical choice to succeed Hodges, given his long and distinguished career on the court. He asked for Jean's support and for two additional favors: Would Jean be the one to nominate him? And would she serve as his deputy chief justice?

Without a great deal of thought, Jean agreed to Erickson's requests. Paul Hodges had been chief justice for six years and had occasionally hinted at future retirement plans, and Erickson had been very solicitous and helpful to Jean and seemed like a logical choice to succeed Hodges. At the next Conference, the day for the annual election of chief justice, Jean moved the nomination of William Erickson to be the next chief justice. As soon as she spoke the words, it was as if the molecules in the room had rearranged themselves and all the air had been sucked out of the room. The dead silence that followed and the look of shock and hurt on Hodges' face made it evident that he had not been informed of his own imminent replacement as chief justice. The vote proceeded and Erickson was elected chief justice.

"I did as Bill asked and I nominated him, but I could tell by Paul's face that he knew nothing about that," Jean remembered, still pained many years later at what she had been a part of. "Bill used me in a way that was pretty ugly. Trusting him was such a huge mistake on my part."

It was a terrible blunder. That Jean would unwittingly be a part of such a gambit was inexplicable. Jean was disappointed in herself, heartsick about her role, and angry about being used.

"I confronted Erickson about not telling the truth about Paul Hodges and from then on our relationship did not do well." From then on, Jean began to feel a little bit like she had returned to Professor Casner's class at Harvard Law School. Erickson regularly made disparaging or derisive comments or would shoot a look of disdain in her direction. He would raise his eyebrows in a way that could only signal dismissiveness, and his tone would drip with unmistakable condescension or contempt. The sexism and chauvinism Erickson showed was not as flagrant or blatant as Jean's Harvard professors, yet, in some ways, that made it even more difficult to address.

Erickson wielded another weapon to get under the skin of other justices: writing biting dissents when there was no reason to do so. When Jean first came on the court, Chief Justice Hodges told her of the tradition among the justices to avoid writing more than one dissent each year directed at the same colleague unless there was a compelling need to do so. It was a way to encourage comity and foster respectful working relationships. Bill Erickson did not adhere to that tradition. Once a fellow justice made his enemies list—and Jean was not the only justice subject to Erickson's enmity—he or she could expect a piercing dissent almost every time that justice authored an opinion that he did not join.

The discomfort caused by the occasional poor treatment of a few justices by Erickson each Thursday did not elicit great concern on the part of most of his colleagues. Partly it was because the volume of work, the daily pressures—to read and research, to prepare for oral arguments, to write—were all-consuming, and partly because there was no appetite to directly confront such issues within the group. But when an increasing number of administrative matters within the purview of the office of the chief justice began to surface as problems that needed to be dealt with, concerns about Erickson's overall leadership became harder to ignore.

In addition to leading the high court, the chief justice was the executive administrator of the state judicial system and responsible for office space and supplies, the size of caseloads in the lower courts, legislative affairs, salary levels for judges, and a host of other personnel and management matters. As in any bureaucracy, when the response from above is lacking, sometimes even petty concerns and issues fester and morale falls. Erickson neglected the relationship between the chief justice and the state legislature, ignored minor pleas for adequate office supplies or mileage reimbursements, and failed to advocate for much needed reforms, including long-awaited promises of pay increases for judges and staff.

Occasionally Jean would hear of those concerns and raise them with her colleagues, but they would often wave her off. You're not going to change anything, they would say. Or they would deliberate amongst themselves about strategies or fixes that could be employed to address some of the most troubling matters and take them to Jean with the expectation that Jean, who had the most administrative experience, would implement some of the needed fixes. As progress on overdue reforms stalled and complaints mounted, more of the justices reluctantly began to appreciate that they needed to address the broader concerns of Erickson's leadership.

Eventually, the corrosive combination of Erickson's needless, biting dissents, his personal slights, and the growing administrative woes led even the justices who preferred to avoid dealing with the issues to concur that change was needed. When it came time for the annual election of a chief justice, the justices took the unusual step of voting to replace Bill Erickson. Justice Joe Quinn became the new chief justice.

As chief, Quinn quickly addressed many of the administrative and management issues, but the personal dynamics behind the scenes changed little. Bill Erickson's derisive behavior at Conference and his continued unnecessary dissents wore on Jean, even more so when Erickson began singling out two other justices for the same kind of dismissive treatment he often directed at her. Occasionally she would confide in Frank or close friends that the continuing interpersonal discord left her contemplating how much longer she wanted to remain on the court.

Jean did not have a specific timeline for leaving, nor had she made any clear decision that an end was in sight. But after serving on the court for more than six years, she occasionally would find herself wondering what might come next. Still, she had no inkling that the need to begin planning for what might come next would arrive much sooner than she had anticipated.

14

The Accusation

People who knew the Dubofskys often scratched their heads at what an unlikely couple they seemed to be. Jean was quiet, shy, demure; Frank was ebullient, loud, sometimes brash, often a jokester. Those who knew them well, however, appreciated that despite their seemingly contradictory personalities, they were very much alike. They adored their boys and made them the center of their lives. They were drawn to the cause of injustice at the same time and in the same place. They shared the same personal and professional values, sought similar experiences as public defenders and legal aid lawyers, and were both infused with the same fierce commitment to advocacy on behalf of the poor and the powerless.

Their careers, however, took different paths. Frank eventually moved into private practice as a plaintiff's attorney while Jean remained mostly in the public sector. Their separate busy professional lives seldom intersected and, trying to balance those careers with being good parents, their time together was rarely spent discussing their respective legal cases. Until one day, unexpectedly, a case came along that bound their legal and professional lives together.

In Boulder and in Colorado legal circles, Frank Dubofsky was as well known and well regarded as Jean. He was past president of the Boulder Bar Association, earning a laudable reputation as a plaintiff's attorney, with medical malpractice a specialty. It was no surprise then when a young mother who thought her birth control pills might have been responsible for destroying her health, contacted Frank in late 1979.

In the late 1960s and early 1970s, birth control pills became the contraceptive method of choice for young women. Ortho Pharmaceutical was one of the first drug companies to develop and bring the pill to market. Its product, Ortho Novum 50, became the most prescribed oral contraceptive. Despite unanswered questions about potential side effects of these estrogen-based pills, especially over the long term or when taken in higher doses, in 1960 the FDA deemed the pill safe and its use soared over the next decades.

When Jo Ellen Heath came to see Frank, she was thirty-three years old and, until recent years, she had been a healthy, active young mother. Before her daughter was born Heath had taken Ortho Novum 50 and she resumed taking the pill when her daughter was just under a year old. Soon after, however, she experienced occasional breakthrough bleeding. Her doctor recommended a change to a higher dose estrogen pill, Ortho Novum 80 (the 50 and 80 refer to the number of milligrams of estrogen). Heath switched to that higher dose pill and her breakthrough bleeding disappeared.

She continued taking Ortho Novum 80 until she began to experience a series of health problems that quickly escalated, eventually leading to acute kidney failure, a kidney transplant, and serious complications to her immune system. This very ill young woman, her body ravaged by one medical crisis after another, learned that a likely trigger for her downward slide was the ingestion of high estrogen dose birth control pills. With Frank's help, Heath sued the manufacturer.

Three years later, despite many attempts at a settlement and after a lengthy district court trial, a jury eventually agreed that Ortho Pharmaceutical was liable for Ms. Heath's kidney failure. In March 1983 Heath was awarded $1.5 million dollars. Not surprisingly, Ortho Pharmaceutical appealed, and the wheels of justice began to turn once again. Eventually, in 1985, after a ruling by the Colorado appeals court, Ortho Pharmaceutical appealed again and the case arrived at the Colorado Supreme Court.

As the legal process wore on over the years, Heath became increasingly fearful that the case would be reversed or sent back for retrial and that she would never see any of that money. At different points along the way, she pressured her attorneys to settle the case. She lived in very precarious financial circumstances and believed that a smaller payment was better than nothing. Her attorneys, though, consistently reassured her that eventually the award would be upheld. They counseled patience but, at her insistence, the attorneys began settlement talks once again in 1985. Those talks also did not lead to an agreement and the case continued to oral arguments before the Colorado Supreme Court.

By the spring of 1986, a full year after oral arguments had been heard at the court, and over a decade since her kidneys began to fail, Ms. Heath, feeling desperate due to increasing financial pressures, urged her attorneys to seek a settlement once again. By now, her attorneys were apprehensive about the court's lack of action. Even the most complex cases before the supreme court were normally decided within six to eight months of oral arguments. Now, a full year had passed since oral arguments. *Ortho Pharmaceutical v. Heath* was by then the oldest pending case of the term and the delay was inexplicable. The uncertainty simply became too much for Heath. Please, just settle this, she told her lawyers. I can't take this anymore.

In June 1986, Ortho Pharmaceutical and the lawyers at the Dubofsky firm entered into yet another round of settlement talks. Offers and counter-offers began again, and eventually the two sides reached an understanding that $800,000 was the figure that each side could agree to. While her attorneys continued to advise Heath that waiting for the court's decision might be the better option, she decided to accept the

$800,000 offer. The legal settlement was formally agreed to on July 3, 1986, a Thursday.

Thursday was Conference day at the Colorado Supreme Court. As they did every Thursday, the justices met in the morning. And this day they voted to issue opinions in a half-dozen pending cases. One of the cases on the docket was *Ortho Pharmaceutical v. Heath*.[42] The decision, written by the newest justice, Anthony Vollack, was a non-decision. Citing a judicial error regarding jury instruction, the majority voted to send the case back to the lower court for retrial. The vote was four to two. Only six justices participated in this case because the seventh justice, Justice Dubofsky, was married to the plaintiff's attorney and could not participate in a case that involved her husband.

From time to time, each of the justices had cause to recuse themselves from participating in a decision. Sometimes it was because they were familiar with or had been party to the case while serving on a lower court. Other times it was because they had a personal relationship with one of the participants in the case or a personal interest in the outcome of the case. Whatever the reason, once justices recused themselves, they followed a set of standard procedures. They didn't read the briefs. They didn't sit at oral arguments. They absented themselves at Conference whenever the case was being discussed. They didn't read any opinions or dissents that were circulated during the opinion-writing process. They didn't have conversations with other justices about the case. Those cases were simply out of the sight of the recused justice.

Jean did not know why there had been such a long delay in issuing the opinion or what the issues were, but she was aware that something had been going on with the *Ortho* case, especially because for the previous five or six weeks it had been on the court's Conference agenda and she'd had to absent herself from those discussions. Near the end of that third of July Thursday, just before the holiday weekend,

Jean saw the list of the opinions to be released the following Monday and Ortho was finally on the list. She would, however, not be privy to the outcome of the decision until it was made public the following Monday.

When Frank called Jean that afternoon to clarify some plans for the kids and dinner that evening, he let her know that he had finally acceded to his client's wishes in the *Ortho Pharmaceutical* case and they had reached a settlement. Since Jean had seen the announcement sheet containing the list of opinions ready to go forward, she informed the clerk of court and the chief justice's office that Frank had called with news of the settlement. Later, Frank's office, along with the attorneys for Ortho Pharmaceutical, also formally notified the court that the case was settled.

That a case would be settled between the time that the justices voted an opinion out of Conference on a Thursday and the public issuing of the decision the following Monday was relatively rare. It was not a weekly occurrence, or even a monthly occurrence, but it happened often enough that there were standard procedures to be followed. Either the chief justice or the clerk of court would get all the forms in order and notify the other justices that a settlement had been reached, that the case was no longer before the court. On the following Monday morning, when the copies of the decisions due to be issued were stacked on the front desk in the clerk's office at the usual ten o'clock hour, standard procedure dictated that *Ortho Pharmaceutical v. Heath* would not be among them.

It was a spectacular Fourth of July weekend, with a special national celebration dubbed "Liberty Weekend", as the country celebrated the restoration of the Statue of Liberty on its one hundredth birthday. On Monday morning Jean took the early bus as usual. She transferred to the shuttle at Market Street station and disembarked at her stop near her office, carrying her heavy briefcase overflowing with work that she had taken home for the holiday weekend. She was at her desk when Joe Quinn appeared at her door. He stopped briefly, then slowly walked into her office, shutting the door behind him. There was something odd about the way he carried himself. Maybe it was the look on his face or the look away from her, not at her, before he began to speak. "To this day, I remember the chill that ran through my body," Jean said decades later.

"We are going to go ahead and issue the opinion in Frank's case today," Quinn said. Unbeknownst to Jean, Quinn and the other justices had met that Saturday. Even though a settlement between the parties had been reached, they decided to do something that they never, ever, did.

"I'm sorry," he said, without any further explanation. Quinn then turned and walked out of her office.

"Joe and I had that brief conversation but then he never mentioned it again," Jean said. "No one on the court ever talked to me about it after that."

Jean was no stranger to controversy. She had experienced more than her share of criticism over the years. She had had her legal opinions challenged; been chased out of one state for taking on powerful interests; had her appointment to the supreme court investigated; had the governor who appointed her publically question whether he would do it again if he had the choice; and she had tolerated consistently poor treatment by a colleague for years. In one way or another, those instances were all meant to raise questions about her experience or qualifications, her legal acumen and judgment, or her views, beliefs, and philosophy. But she had never been subject to any questions about her integrity. Ever.

But now, with the decision to release the opinion despite the settlement, Jean felt that was exactly what her colleagues were doing: questioning her honesty and integrity. She could conjure up no other explanation. They must have concluded that she had done something unethical, that she had broken the trust of the court, that she had leaked information about the case to her husband.

To have her colleagues call into question her integrity was devastating. Even worse, they were questioning Frank's integrity as well. "It was just the most awful feeling," Jean said. "And then the whole thing turned into such a nightmare."

According to Justice Mullarkey, "It simply should never have happened. When parties in pending cases reach an out-of-court settlement in the period between Thursday Conference and the following Monday's issuance of the opinions, the court had a clear protocol and that was to pull the cases. The opinions simply did not get released." But the court didn't follow its own procedures in this case.

Still, there was no immediate clap of thunder around the courthouse. No furious round of meetings or further discussion, heated or otherwise, among the justices or clerks or the staff. There was no public outcry or notice. To court insiders it was simply an odd diversion from normal procedures. Years later, few justices or clerks who worked at the court during that time had any recollection of the case, the settlement, or the action to issue the opinion against the court's own protocols. Years later, almost no one remembered any specific conversations or chatter in the office about the unusual issuing of an opinion that had been settled. While some were aware that the normal protocol was not followed, few knew about the convening of the justices for a special Saturday session over the July Fourth holiday weekend, but they all were surprised when told of it, for it was simply unheard of.

For the other justices and court staff, the Monday following the holiday was just another typical start to the week on the court, with copies of the opinions ready for release stacked neatly on the front counter. For Jean and Frank and their family, it was anything but. Along with the shiver that engulfed Jean as Quinn turned to leave her office came the dread about what would likely follow.

The court's decision to release the opinion despite the settlement, with its inherent implication that Jean was suspected by her colleagues of informing Frank of the deliberations and decision, was painful enough to live with. But soon the implications turned into direct accusations and legal actions. The attorneys for Ortho Pharmaceutical filed suit, requesting that the settlement be set aside, formally alleging that Frank Dubofsky was privy to confidential internal information about the pending supreme court opinion. Jean and Frank's private agony became a public disgrace.

In addition to Frank's efforts to salvage the settlement that Jo Ellen Heath had waited so long for, the Dubofskys were suddenly in a fight to salvage their reputations and their professional careers. "Supreme Court Justice spouse accused of inside information on lawsuit; Leak from Supreme Court alleged." [43] "Justice's spouse accused of gaining inside information." [44] "Justice Dubofsky denies she revealed evidence." [45] The headlines were a crushing blow to both Dubofskys. Each hired lawyers and agonized over the best strategy to fight the charges.

Supreme court justices do not ever comment about cases before the court. But this was different. Jean felt she had no choice but to make a public statement. "I felt like I had to tell people that what was being suggested was simply not true," she said.

And so she did, through a prepared statement that she wrote herself. "As is my practice in any case involving my husband's law firm…I did not participate in *Ortho Pharmaceutical Corporation vs. Heath*. I have not told my husband….or anyone connected with his firm anything about the case or its status during the time it was pending on appeal. My husband does not have access to any confidential information in my office or the court about any cases pending before the court, and I never discuss with him any confidential matters before the court."[46]

What Jean didn't say in her statement, but what she believed to be true, was that underlying the suggestion of impropriety were thin threads of persistent gender stereotyping, dating back to the time when women were not welcome in the law profession. The generally accepted and openly voiced assumption and rationale for excluding women from the profession went something like this: women were not well suited to become lawyers and judges because they could not be trusted to honor confidentiality. They could not be trusted because they would tell their husbands everything.

Jean's colleagues on the court appeared surprisingly oblivious to the repercussions that their decision unleashed. At the time, when Justice Quinn was asked by a journalist about the allegation that inside information might have been passed between spouses, he was taken aback. What charges? There were no such charges, Quinn insisted. "I have no scintilla of evidence…or indication there is any kind of a leak. It is incredible to me that anyone could make that accusation."[47]

Some twenty-seven years later, Quinn continued to be flummoxed that the release of the opinion led others to conclude that the court in any way had doubts about Jean's trustworthiness. His recollection of the specifics, of who said or did what and when, was hazy about the whole time period. He remembered that the phone call about the settlement came late in the day on Thursday, that Friday was the July Fourth holiday, and that the justices who were in town gathered that Saturday, which was something very, very unusual. But he didn't remember the decision to release the opinion as a very "big deal".

"As I recall the discussion that Saturday, it was along the lines that we were trying to make sure we were open, transparent, so that no one would accuse of us of trying to hide anything," he said. "By releasing it, I think some of us thought that meant we were being open."

Quinn had nothing but total admiration for Jean and it never occurred to him that the decision to release the opinion would lead others to think the justices were accusing Jean of anything. "Others might have been questioning whether there was a leak, but not the justices," Quinn said. "I am sure at the time that I didn't realize that it would create such a problem for Jean or that she would think we were questioning her integrity."

Whatever the intent, the questioning led the Colorado Bar Association and a legislative committee to launch separate investigations, while lawyers filed suits and counter suits and motions to determine whether or not the settlement offer was valid. When it became clear that the controversy was destined to drag on in the courts and in the media with no end in sight, both sides to settlement eventually agreed the best way to resolve things was to jointly hire an independent attorney to investigate and make a formal recommendation for how to resolve the matter. Each side stipulated that they would then adhere to the recommendation and withdraw their various legal claims.

It was a long six months for the Dubofsky family. Frank was livid, both at the accusations and about the hundreds of thousands of dollars in attorney fees they were accumulating. Jean, her heart broken, was worried about Frank and her own reputation, but also about the effect on the boys, concerned that Josh's crying and not wanting to go to school had something do with teasing by some of his friends about what was being said about his parents. Jean and Frank's friends didn't believe any of it, but that was little consolation.

In December, the investigating attorney completed his work. His conclusion was that the final settlement reached that Thursday afternoon in July was conducted and reached lawfully and in good faith and should be honored. There was never any improper conversation or information sharing between Jean and Frank, the investigator stated, fully exonerating both Dubofskys.

"It is undisputed that the settlement was valid and proper in all respects. The facts disclosed by the investigation demonstrate clearly and without doubt that nothing improper or unethical occurred, and the settlement was an arm's length, valid bargain," the statement read.[48]

It was a strong statement of exoneration, but other than relief that it was finally over, there was no celebration in the Dubofsky household. The *Denver Post*, which months earlier had run the story about possible leaks with this headline on its front page: "Colo. Supreme Ct Justice, Husband accused of inside information,"[49] did not place the news that nothing wrong had ever happened on the front page or on any of the thirty-eight pages of Section A. The tiny seven-paragraph news brief was placed at the bottom of the page, forty-one pages into the day's paper, just below an update regarding an escapee from the Arapahoe district court building. The headline said simply: "Legal dispute ends for justice, lawyer-husband," and the short article did not use any of the strong exoneration language contained in the statement. Not the "clearly and without a doubt" that they had done nothing wrong phrase. Not the "undisputed" agreement that the settlement was "valid and proper" phrase. Instead, after reiterating all the charges once again, it utilized only one direct quote from the investigator's statement: "the totality of the circumstances surrounding and leading up to the July 3rd settlement has been thoroughly investigated."[50]

The questioning and innuendos continued long after the December statement of exoneration and the settlement of the legal dispute, due in large part to Jean's long ago nemesis, Ralph Cole. Senator Cole, who engineered the months-long investigation into Jean's appointment to the supreme court six years earlier, resurfaced to investigate her again. Well into the 1987 legislative session, Cole continued to make potentially libelous statements and hold hearings about what he referred to as a recent case at the highest levels of the court system where secrets were leaked. And he continued to lobby for legislation to make such behavior a Class 4 felony.[51] There was never a doubt to whom he was referring.

Although it may not have been a conscious, firm decision on her part, it is likely that on that fateful Monday in July of 1986, before Joe Quinn had made it back across the hall to his office, Jean Dubofsky had already decided she had had enough. Through the court years she had resisted becoming angry at the treatment by Erickson, resisted becoming deeply disappointed in the laissez-faire attitude that the other judges held toward his behavior. But this was different. That her colleagues, some of them friends, could have doubts about her trustworthiness, that they could set in motion, either purposefully or inadvertently, a public discrediting of her or the questioning of her ethics and integrity, was almost too much to bear.

"I think I knew then that I couldn't stay," Jean said. But she also knew she couldn't leave in the middle of the controversy and investigations. That would leave the impression that she must have done something wrong. So she waited.

Every Monday morning Jean showed up for work and every week looked a lot like every other week of her tenure on the court. She concentrated on her cases and worked equally hard to hold her head up high, to not show evidence of the load of anger and hurt that she carried with her. Over the Christmas holidays, Jean reviewed the list of the more complex opinions that she had been assigned to write, and laid out an aggressive schedule to ensure she would be able to complete those cases in a timely manner. Unbeknownst to anyone on the court, to anyone except Frank, Jean made her decision. She would leave the court in the spring.

She felt at ease, finally, having made the decision. Unfortunately, as had happened in the past, a call from Topeka soon interrupted that sense of ease.

15

Topeka. Again.

Paul Eberhart celebrated his eightieth birthday in May of 1986 and Eleanor celebrated hers the following year. As the years went by, Jean's parents no longer traveled as often or as far as they used to and rarely made the drive to Denver. Jean still made occasional trips back to Topeka to check on her parents, and they appeared to be doing well. Her father had made it through a minor bout of cancer and her mother struggled with asthma, something that had developed when she was in her sixties. But overall they seemed healthy, well able to care for themselves and still very active in the community, regularly attending luncheons, lectures, and church suppers. "They were fine, chugging along, neither one of them seeming to have any big issues," Jean said.

Still, Eleanor had begun to think about the possibility of a move to a new retirement community that had opened in Topeka. Run by the United Methodists, it was one of the early versions of an eldercare facility at a time when the nursing home model had just begun the transformation into a continuum-of-care model. The campus had small cottages and apartments, some with garages for those who were still driving and active and wanted to live independently but were eager to have maintenance and home upkeep issues taken care of by others. A central health center was located on site to serve acute care needs, and nursing home beds were also available when increased medical care was required.

Eleanor thought it would be a perfect place for her and Paul. After Jean accompanied her mother on a visit to the facility, Jean thought it might be perfect as well. Eleanor didn't express particular concerns about her own health or issues with Paul, or suggest any urgency about making such a move. But she was a practical sort, and with her own asthma making her feel more vulnerable, and her ongoing worry about Paul and his moods and mental health issues, Eleanor wanted to be prepared. She didn't want to be a burden, should anything happen, and thought a move to this new community was the answer.

"We had even found a little duplex there and Dad could have kept his dog and it would have been just fine. But Dad wouldn't move. He just wouldn't hear of it," Jean said. "He would not have had his basement with his darkroom and his workbench and all his things. I understood why he didn't want to move, but Mom really wanted to do it."

Eleanor did what she had always done her whole life. She didn't push or insist. She would raise the idea from time to time, hoping to start a discussion, maybe get Paul to see things her way. But he would simply refuse to discuss it. And so they went along, as people do. Until one day in early 1987, the day when the phone rang with a call from Topeka. It was partly about her father but, even worse, this time it was also about her mother.

From time to time Eleanor would have a scary asthma attack and would have trouble breathing. Though often momentarily frightening, on those days she treated it with an inhaler, which she had at home and used regularly. The inhaler always got her through those episodes. Until the day of the call when the inhaler just wasn't enough.

"She had a very, very bad bout," Jean said. "This was the first time an ambulance had to be called. My dad called 911, but he didn't call soon enough." By the time the ambulance came, Eleanor had been too long without oxygen and she would never be the same again.

There was a piece of Eleanor that was just gone. She was able to communicate some, but not necessarily always rationally. "She couldn't walk anymore, so she was in a wheelchair, and she couldn't do anything for herself. She was just so impaired mentally."

Her mother's debilitating new health issues weren't Jean's only concern; she worried about her father as well. His type of mental illness, his type of depression, had long cycles. While someone might have an underlying depressive-like personality, a full-blown, deep clinical depression occurred rarely, often as far apart as twenty years. It was almost exactly twenty years since Paul's last bout of depression that left him hospitalized for almost a full year.

When Jean asked her father what exactly had happened that day of Eleanor's attack, why it had taken so long for the ambulance to get there, and why her mother had gone so long without oxygen, she never received anything but a vague explanation. She had no way of knowing, but she had her own guess as to what happened. "Dad likely was headed for a deep depression. It was time," Jean said. "So Dad was probably depressed and probably lying down and couldn't quite bring himself to get up and pay attention to Mom when she had her attack."

Just as Paul's deep depression was cyclical, Jean's life in 1987 would turn out to be very much like her life twenty years earlier, when she had to make regular trips back to Topeka and fight her way through constant worry about her parents, and the lingering questions about how this could have happened and what she could have done differently.

In the winter and spring of 1987, Jean traveled back and forth to Topeka to make arrangements for her father's care and to settle her mother in a nursing home. The nursing home was called Aldersgate. It was part of the same retirement complex that Eleanor had wanted to move to the year before.

If Jean had any second thoughts about her decision to leave the court, there was clearly "no turning back after Mom had her asthma attack," Jean said. She already had good reason to leave the court. Now she had another. "I wouldn't have forgiven myself if I didn't pay attention to what was happening with my mom and dad."

Jean soon began to plan for her post-supreme court life. The first thing she did was research how long justices in other states waited before they took on appeals and appeared before former colleagues. She thought an appeals practice would be the most natural fit and her likely next career move, but she wanted to be careful. She needed to be careful. Now more than ever, she wanted to be sure that no one would suggest that she was doing anything inappropriate or unethical. She discovered that most former justices waited between six months and a year before taking on appeals cases. She learned of one justice who waited as long as two years and decided that should be her gauge, her yardstick. She would wait at least two years, just to be sure.

Jean pondered whether teaching might be an option in the interim. So much of her life at the court had been academic in nature—the research, writing, and analysis. Teaching law students would be much the same as mentoring and teaching clerks fresh out of law school, she thought. She also had extensive experience speaking before groups, being on panels, sitting for interviews, and making speeches. She was comfortable that this combination of experiences would prepare her for the classroom. If she were able to teach at the University of Colorado Law School, located just across town, for the first time in years she would be working in Boulder. Without the daily commute to Denver, Jean would have more time for family and friends.

Jean picked up the phone and called Betsy Levin, the dean of the law school. "I have a 'what if' question for you," she told Levin. "What if I were thinking of resigning from the supreme court and wanted to come to the law school to teach for a year? Would there be a place for me?" As dean, Levin often brought in "visitors" to teach for a semester or two. Sometimes they were professors from other law schools, sometimes exceptional legal scholars or other notable members of the legal profession. "Jean was a state supreme court Justice and I thought she would be a good addition," Levin said. "A few of the faculty complained because they thought she wasn't scholarly enough, that writing opinions wasn't the same as producing scholarly work. But I thought we should have her come." When the dean formalized the offer of a visiting adjunct position for the coming academic year, the pieces of a new beginning began to fall into place.

Before she could turn to teaching, Jean still had a number of particularly challenging opinions to write, and during her final months on the court she kept her focus on those cases. She delivered the opinion in *Fields v. People*, a right-to-a-fair-trial case often cited in subsequent years. The opinion held that excluding jurors simply because of their Spanish sounding surnames could be a basis for arguing that a defendant had been deprived of a fair trial.

In April, Jean wrote the opinion providing relief against unfair tax assessments when a rental apartment to condo conversion occurred. "I know it sounds strange," Jean said, "but I think that case more than many other cases probably helped a lot of people." At the time, there was a surge in the number of apartments being converted to condos, and the sudden high valuation led to prohibitive taxes being thrust upon those taking ownership, making it difficult for many to stay in their homes.

Her last important opinion as a justice on the Colorado Supreme Court refereed a battle between the governor and the legislature over control of federal block grant money. In *Colorado General Assembly v. Lamm*, she ordered that when it was necessary for the legislature to allocate matching funds from the state coffers, the legislature had the legal authority and control, and when there were no matching funds, it was the governor who had the control of the federal block grant money.

In the late spring, Jean gathered her secretary and her clerks and let them know she was resigning. "The boys need me at home and it's time for me to try something new," she told them. Then she shared the news with Joe Quinn. A few weeks later, Jean formally submitted her letter of resignation to Governor Lamm.

The language of her resignation letter was pro forma, very business-like, very Jean-like. In the letter, as in her conversations with staff and colleagues, Jean gave no hint of the toll the accusations and the investigations had taken on her personally, or of the acute disappointment she felt in her colleagues for their actions that had led to the questioning of her integrity and honesty. Nor did she hint at the depth of her pain and grief over her parents' dual health crises, or of the additional responsibilities and burdens that she was now shouldering because of her parents' needs. The letter to the governor was brief. One simple sentence captured a few simple cumulative truths about this stage in her life. "The time has come for me to do something else [and] I need the mental stimulation of new challenges and a change of scenery."[52]

Over the course of her final week in the office, Jean said private goodbyes to her staff and some of her friends on the court. Each day she packed up a few things and took one more photo or piece of artwork off the walls and had her clerk help carry them down to her car. There was no going-away party, no final send-off. She simply turned out the lights in the middle of the afternoon one day and made her last drive back to Boulder, stopping at the grocery store to pick up butter and a package of chocolate chips. That night she needed to bake the next batch of chocolate chip cookies that the boys had come to count on when they opened their school lunch boxes each day.

16

Professor Dubofsky

When Jean backed out of her driveway to begin her commute to work for the first day of her new teaching job, the trip lasted all of five minutes. It was a whole new world compared to two decades of commuting an hour each way to Denver. The law school was almost exactly two miles from her home.

Jean was ready. She was eager. She was looking forward, not back. The only thing she wasn't was rested and relaxed. After delivering her final opinions and cleaning out her office, she and Frank took the boys on a trip to Italy. By the time they returned, the worries and burdens of caring for her mother and father had escalated. "I was back and forth to Topeka a lot that year because, in addition to my mom, my father was not doing very well," Jean said. "After Mom went to the nursing home, Dad spiraled downhill. You just couldn't leave him for very long without checking in on him. I was really worried about both of them all that year."

Her classroom workload was waiting for her as well. After waking up before dawn most mornings while on the court and working the two hours on the bus back and forth to Denver, she had assumed the workload that came with teaching would be—had to be—more manageable. But Jean had never taught before. She'd never selected textbooks or cases or journal articles or developed a course syllabus. Before she knew what she had gotten herself into, she had agreed to teach three very different courses her first semester: criminal procedure, land use planning, and local government law. She was eager to teach all of the courses, but it became clear long before the first day of classes arrived that it would be all she could do to simply keep her head above water.

"When you have to put your notes together for the first time and teach three different topics, it was a lot of work," Jean said. "It felt as though I was just a year or two out of law school, just coming on to the faculty. It was another starting all over again kind of feeling." At first, every week felt like swimming up stream, trying to simply be prepared well enough for the next class session and appear as though she knew what she was doing.

The teaching load would have been more manageable if Jean had been more like other visiting adjuncts. Most adjuncts arrived from another university with all the materials, textbooks, and syllabi for courses they had already been teaching. It might have been more manageable, too, if she were a beginning full-time hire, because new faculty members were given a reduced load, often only one new course preparation at a time. And it would have been more manageable if her colleagues at the law school had been supportive and believed in sharing.

Most of the faculty were supportive, thrilled even, that Jean had been asked to teach. She knew many from the community but most of the newer, young faculty members were supportive as well. The women faculty members especially took great pride that CU had not just hired a former supreme court justice, but the first woman on the court and the youngest to get there. But not all professors were pleased about Jean's hire.

When she asked one long-time faculty member—who was teaching another section of the very same criminal law course—which textbook he was using, he refused to tell her. "I couldn't believe that he simply refused. It seemed logical and a good idea that we'd each use the same textbook, since we were teaching the same course the same semester." That was Jean's first hint that some on the faculty were displeased that she was now among them and were not hesitant about making their displeasure known. "The people who didn't want me at the law school, mostly the conservative old timers, were about as hostile as could be," Jean said. "So openly hostile that it just seemed pretty peculiar."

As a visiting adjunct she was not invited to faculty meetings, didn't serve on any faculty committees, and had neither the time to ponder what the hostility was all about, nor the interest in the dynamics of the law school politics. She had all she could do to prepare for each week's classes, meet with students, and grade the essays and exams. And like so often in the past, she knew people would be watching her and judging her, so it was important to do well. When some made it obvious they thought she did not belong, it motivated her to prove the dissenters wrong.

Jean was essentially on her own at CU and she did fine on her own, especially as the semester wore on. With much of the initial preparation behind her she found her work rhythm and settled in. She loved so much about the job. She loved the intellectual challenge. She loved the exchanges with the students.

Later in the fall as that first challenging and hectic semester was coming to an end, she was approached by two members of the faculty appointment committee—the group assigned to recruit and make recommendations about faculty hires. David Getches and Charles Wilkinson were two of the most respected members of the faculty, knew Jean from the neighborhood and civic activities, and had been very supportive of Jean's temporary hire as a visiting professor. They asked if she would consider applying for a permanent full-time position.

To the extent that Jean had any longer term career plans, becoming a college law professor wasn't something she had pondered. She had thought that teaching would be an interlude between her court years and a future appellate practice, a time to decompress and contemplate her future, to ponder whether her instincts that an appellate practice was where she wanted to head next, was, indeed, the right next thing.

Still, when she was asked to consider applying for a full-time teaching job, her immediate answer was "sure". It was less a well thought out or strategic career decision than a "why not?" reflex. She still hadn't fully recovered from all the tumult of the previous few years and had neither the desire nor the energy to invest heavily in another major professional change just yet. And it felt good to be asked to stay. To be wanted. Staying put at CU sounded like a fine idea. And who knows, she told herself, maybe teaching and not private practice will turn out to be the perfect "what's next" for me.

The hiring process at CU was not all that different from other law schools. Throughout the fall and winter, the appointment committee received applications and proactively reached out to recruit individuals they deemed worthy. The committee reviewed the candidates, invited a select few to visit campus to deliver a lecture, meet with faculty and students, and sit for a formal interview. For candidates like Jean, who were already on campus, the committee assigned a faculty member to observe a class or two and provide a written evaluation.

Howard Klemme, an experienced and well-regarded member of the law school faculty, sat in on two of Jean's local government law classes and provided the appointment committee with a two-and-a-half-page memo evaluating her teaching methods and her ability. It was glowing. "Her teaching style encourages participation from many students… and she guides the discussion quite ably with…a solid sense of direction," Klemme wrote. He cited Jean's ability to use various methods of discussion to provide "a clear understanding of the basic law involved" and create an atmosphere conducive to "a very sophisticated discussion, adroitly guided by Jean, in which many students participated, almost entirely on a 'volunteer basis.'"

Klemme noted that her preparation for class was thorough. "It was apparent she had thought through the materials in great depth and had identified some broad basic themes…to help interrelate the materials in a very meaningful way." Klemme had taught this same class for years and his greatest praise for Jean came when he discussed his own curiosity and admiration for how Jean, teaching for the first time, and teaching this particular course and material for the first time, "was covering a great deal more ground than I have been able to in recent years."

"Jean's secret lies, I believe, in her exceptionally careful preparation, her thoughtful identification of the important basic legal rules, and her ability to get a class to recognize and assess the core policy issues involved with those rules," he wrote. "It is truly remarkable to see so much coverage being undertaken with so much depth and…achieving so much understanding on the part of students."[53]

When the appointment committee completed its review, the candidate they settled on was Jean Dubofsky. The next step was to take their recommendation to the entire faculty for a formal vote, a necessary step before the dean of the law school could advance the name to the central administration. By this time, the current dean was an "acting" dean, a replacement for Betsy Levin, who had left the school rather suddenly and taken another position before the start of the fall semester.

With or without a new dean in place, the process moved forward. The tradition was that the appointment committee would present its recommendation at a faculty meeting and, usually after a brief presentation and discussion of the candidate, the faculty would vote to accept the recommendation of the appointment committee. Usually.

Jean with her mother, Eleanor Eberhart, in 1942.

Eleanor holding Jean's hand in
downtown Topeka.

Paul Eberhart, Jean's father,
as a young professor.

Note: All photos without a credit listed are courtesy of Jean Dubofsky.

Paul and Eleanor and their children, Jean and Allan, in 1953.

Jean—a high school senior—at the moment her name was announced at the All-American Table Dinner as the 1960 Betty Crocker Homemaker of Tomorrow, April 28, 1960.

Vice President and Mrs. Nixon visiting with the Betty Crocker Homemaker state winners.

The 1960 Betty Crocker winner posing for press photos at the Capitol with Senator Andrew Schoeppel.

Kansas political leaders, left to right, Congressman William Avery, Senator Andrew Schoeppel and Senator Frank Carlson, enjoying a moment with Jean at the All-American Table Dinner.

After writing a weekly column for the *Topeka Capitol Journal* during high school, Jean follows with a stint on the *Stanford Daily*. She was promoted to night editor freshmen year.

Jean in Europe in 1962 during Stanford semester abroad program.

The destruction on the Washburn campus after the June 9, 1966 tornado.

Senator Frank Carlson with Jean and a fellow intern in the winter of 1963.

Nattily attired, Jean poses in her parent's driveway on a visit home.

Jean wearing the customary robe for her role as keynote speaker at the 1968 Topeka High School graduation.

Frank and Jean on their wedding day, September 14, 1968.

In the fall of 1966, Jean mingled with the Washington political elite at the wedding of her close friend, Margy McNamara, daughter of defense secretary Robert McNamara. Attending were President and Mrs. Johnson, Vice President Hubert Humphrey, and Senator Robert Kennedy.

Jean and Frank with their menagerie and skiing near their Sugarloaf cabin in the early 1970s.

'I'M FROM THE AMERICAN CIVIL LIBERTIES UNION, AND WE'VE HAD A COMPLAINT . . .'

Pat Oliphant cartoon illustrating the controversy over whether Ann-Marie would be allowed to play baseball with the boys. The woman saddling her way up the rope depicts the attorney who brought the case, Jean Dubofsky. *Denver Post*

Ann-Marie Sandquist

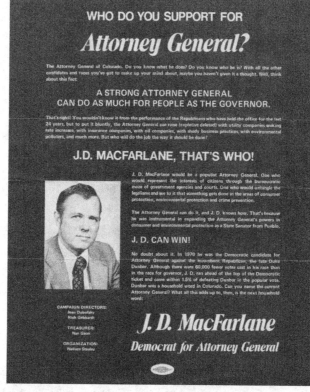

J.D. MacFarlane campaign flyer during his 1974 race for Colorado attorney general notes Jean as one of the campaign directors.

Jean Dubofsky, deputy attorney general, Judy Henning, chair of the Commission on the Status of Women and Robin Johnson, president of the Colorado Board of Education at a National Women's Agenda Day event. *Rocky Mountain News*

Governor Richard Lamm and the first woman justice of the
Colorado Supreme Court as she takes her oath of office on July 10, 1979.

Portrait of the seven Colorado Supreme Court justices during Jean's final court term.
Back row, left to right, Howard Kirshbaum, Jean Dubofsky, George Lohr, Anthony
Vollack. Front row, William Erickson, Joseph Quinn, Luis Rovira.

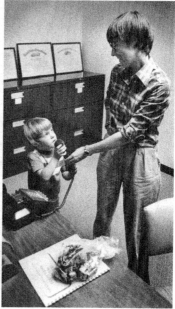

Frank and Jean with Josh on the left
and Matthew on the right.

Josh Dubofsky helps his mother
move into her office at the
Colorado Supreme Court.

Jean with her family the day she was sworn in as the first woman justice.
From left to right, Bob Taylor, Jean's uncle; Jean holding Matt
and Frank holding Josh; and her parents, Eleanor and Paul Eberhart.

Jean speaking about *Romer v. Evans* at CU in the fall of 1995. *Daily Camera*

A March 10, 1988 gathering of protesting law students at the CU Law School after Jean was denied a teaching position. *Daily Camera*

Governor Roy Romer and Mayor Wellington Webb lead No on 2 protest in the fall of 1992. *Rocky Mountain News*

Pat Steadman, a young organizer campaigning against Amendment 2 in 1992. Photo courtesy of Pat Steadman

In December of 1993, Colorado ACLU head James Joy and Dubofsky answer questions at a press conference following the Bayless ruling deeming Amendment 2 unconstitutional. *Rocky Mountain News*

Posing before Boulder County Courthouse in the fall of 1995. *Daily Camera*

Surrounded by the media, Jean answers questions on the Supreme Court plaza
after arguing before the nine justices on October 10, 1995.

Mary Celeste with Jean Dubofsky as they exit the doors of the Supreme Court.

On oral argument day, plaintiffs, lawyers, and the Colorado support team surround
Jean on the plaza of the U.S. Supreme Court.

Richard Evans and Jean Dubofsky embrace following the May 20, 1996 U.S. Supreme Court ruling striking down Amendment 2. *Rocky Mountain News*

Mayor Leslie Durgin and Jean embrace after hearing the news. *Daily Camera*

The joy of a few, as thousands celebrate the Supreme Court decision. *Daily Camera*

But there was nothing usual about this particular faculty meeting, this particular recommendation, this discussion, or this vote on that first Friday in March of 1988. Professor David Getches made an eloquent speech on Jean's behalf, as did others. But then a few spoke in opposition. Some spoke with great passion and for a long time about her lack of academic credentials and the lack of published articles in scholarly journals. The discussion went on and on. It soon became clear that the usual perfunctory acceptance of the appointment committee's recommendation was not going to occur this time.

"We were all so taken aback because it was the first time something like this had happened," said one faculty member supportive of Jean's appointment. "There was always a good bit of deference to the appointments committee. Part of what was shocking to me was I just don't remember this kind of contentious discussion, or such a lengthy discussion, going on about any other candidate before. And I don't remember anyone ever being voted down."

But that is what exactly what happened with the vote to approve offering a full-time position at the law school to Jean Dubofsky. "I was shocked that the opposition to Jean was enough to thwart her appointment. I was shocked at the hostility and how it happened. We just didn't see it coming. And I just don't remember thinking we should have seen it coming. I was devastated," this same faculty member said. "I couldn't believe it."

The secret vote, as is the custom in academia, apparently fell one vote short of the two-thirds majority needed to approve Jean's appointment. Consistent with the behind-closed-doors world of academic hiring decisions, there was no announcement nor any official acknowledgement of what had occurred. The acting dean, the members of the appointment committee, and other faculty members were all at a loss about what to do or how to handle the situation. Rumors began to leak out and the administration was forced to confirm that the rumors were true. Jean Dubofsky had been denied a full-time teaching position at the law school.

Questions, confusion, misinformation, and accusations followed. Within days, the news sparked an explosion of outrage and emotion at the law school, at the university, in the town of Boulder, and in the news media. Students, reporters, and community leaders demanded answers about what exactly had happened and why. The acting dean of the law school and the president of the university received phone calls and letters from a host of community leaders, including the mayor and other elected officials, demanding an explanation.

Among the letters sent to the dean was one from Senator Ralph Cole, the same Ralph Cole whose thirst for casting aspersions upon Jean's character earlier in her career seemed to know no bounds. But Cole came to Jean's defense this time. "While she and I have differed very much on a lot of matters, nonetheless I have found her to be a lady whom I believe possesses high intellectual qualities [and] I firmly believe that writing as many opinions as she did would be a fitting substitute for lack of publications in law reviews. In short, I think it is unfair to reject Mrs. Dubofsky."[54]

The most public display of outrage and indignation came from students. Some urged alumni to refuse further financial contributions to the law school; others organized protest actions or attempted to organize class boycotts. According to news reports, somewhere between two and three hundred law students—out of a total enrollment of 450—donned armbands, held signs, and protested in front of the law school administration building. "One student had printed out all of Jean's supreme court opinions on a roll of paper, and he was theatrically trying to wrap the building with them. It was pandemonium," according to Sandra Saltrese, a law student turned protest leader. "We were on the street with orange armbands and we were going to shut down the school. It was like the 60s and 70s."

Student leaders held meetings where the crowds spilled into the aisles and packed rooms to overflowing. The gatherings were opportunities to express their outrage, frustration, and anger at what had happened, but also gave the faculty and administration a chance to provide answers. "I thought, naively, that there was a meritocracy so of course Jean would be asked back. I thought that's how it worked," Saltrese said. "So I was very angry and was close to dropping out. I remember two women faculty members speaking at one big gathering and it really was something, very moving. They understood because they were upset too." Instead of dropping out, a small group of the protest leaders met with the dean. But no answer or explanations were forthcoming and no reversal of the decision seemed possible.

Leaders in the community spontaneously began to reach out to one another, outraged, angry, and ready to do something, if only they could figure out what that something might be. One of those well-known civic leaders was Josie Heath, a Boulder county commissioner by then and Jean's close friend. "I did not know the CU president well, but I called him up and said a group of us wanted to visit with him," Heath said. "We had already talked to the dean and we had talked to the chancellor but everyone we talked to said they were not the person to talk to. So we went over to talk to the president, but he was unwilling to do anything either. We were just being passed around from one person to another."

But the questions remained. Everyone had questions. The students, the press, CU supporters, and community leaders. And the list of questions was long because of the secrecy. Why was Jean turned down for the job? What was the rationale? What exactly happened at the faculty meeting? What happened leading up to the faculty meeting? Did the faulty members who voted against Jean genuinely view her as unqualified or were there other pressures or factors at work? How could Jean be denied a position due to the absence of a sufficient record of scholarly publications when the position was defined as "entry level", and entry level faculty appointees were most often fresh out of law school with no publishing record. How was it that the faculty recently approved the hiring of a male faculty member, another practitioner without a publication record, but also without as distinguished a career as Jean's?

All anyone had to go on were rumors and speculation. Journalists based their reporting on the rumors and speculation and used unsourced quotes to describe what might have occurred and the reasoning behind the vote to deny Jean a teaching post. With few answers forthcoming from the administration, reporters wandered the campus and spoke with whoever was willing to talk to them. They heard the purely academic explanation, the desire to recruit only widely published scholars with stellar reputations as legal theorists. They heard the ideological explanation, the desire of conservative faculty to resist tipping the liberal/conservative balance on the faculty by hiring someone like Jean. They also heard a personal explanation, the concern that Jean's prominence and notoriety would overshadow the reputations that others had worked years to achieve. And they heard the academic politics theory, that it was all about Betsy Levin, the former dean. Levin had invited Jean to come as a visiting professor in the first place, and the group of faculty members who had opposed Levin as dean, had made her life difficult, and had finally driven her out, would not then be content to acquiesce to any pick made by Betsy Levin.

But the most commonly acknowledged explanation, at first only hinted at, soon became the most obvious, assumed, and voiced explanation. It was blatant sexism, pure and simply. Maybe even illegal and unconstitutional gender discrimination. Sexism wasn't the big elephant in the room that *no one* would talk about; it was the big elephant in the room that *everybody* was talking about. It became a central theme in almost every news article that was written during that period of unrest. For one week it was as if a dam had broken at the university and suddenly it was a fitting time to acknowledge a simmering, underlying reality of life at the law school, at CU, and maybe even of life in general.

The institution, the law school, the dean, and especially the small group of faculty members who had voted against Jean were suddenly blanketed with accusations and questions about the motivation, judgment and culture behind what many felt was a grave and inexplicable injustice. It was a public relations disaster and a crisis for the school. Part-time faculty threatened to quit. Law school alumni leaders announced plans to end their fundraising efforts. Recruitment for the next law school class was being threatened and the entire community was up in arms.

"I think it was a real stain on the school," former law student Sandra Saltrese said. "I think the community was ashamed." And, as names of the "no" votes on the faculty began to leak out, it was a stain on their reputations as well, when they were labeled with a broad brush of criticism for all manner of sins the community had judged them to have committed.

The one person who had been mostly absent from all of the private discussions and who said very little to the press, at least initially, was Jean Dubofsky. Those who hoped Jean would help clear up the mystery of what exactly had occurred soon discovered that Jean had less knowledge about the details of the process and decision than just about anyone. Jean had not known that her name was going to be discussed at that Friday faculty meeting. She was not on campus that Friday, was not in town most of that entire week. After teaching her class on Tuesday, Jean informed the dean, then left a note on the office door apologizing that she had to be away for a few days due to a family emergency. Jean was in Topeka one more time. Eleanor Eberhart, Jean's eighty-year-old mother, had died. "She just stopped breathing one night," Jean said. "Her heart gave out."

That trip was as bleak as she could have imagined. It was an exhausting and wearing time, filled with sadness and grief, the short-term practical logistics of a funeral service, and the longer-term challenge of making a plan for her father. It was all a bit of a blur to Jean, as these things often are, going through the motions, keeping busy, doing the next thing that needed doing.

Frank returned to Boulder after Eleanor's funeral and Jean stayed on in Topeka for another few days to meet with her father's doctors, attempting to stave off what was likely to be her father's even deeper descent into depression and the inevitable hospitalization that would follow. Jean was still in Topeka when two law school faculty members came by the Dubofskys' house to share the news of what had occurred that day at the faculty meeting. When Frank called her later that night, she was stunned by the news. Not just that they had denied her a position, but that they had chosen that day of all the days.

"I just couldn't believe that they met and held the vote while I was in Topeka for my mother's funeral," Jean said. "My colleagues knew that she had died. I had put a little sign on my office door, right across from the main office. They knew. I'll never understand what they could have been thinking." In truth, while Jean may have not known that her name would be coming up for a vote that day, or even that a faculty meeting would be held that day, the date for the faculty meeting had been set long before news of Jean's mother's death was posted on her office door. But to Jean, it was one more indication of a hostile culture and working atmosphere.

She returned to Boulder to a week of protests and picketing, with headlines and photos spread across the front pages of the daily newspapers, culminating on the weekend with a meeting between the dean and faculty and fifty prominent citizens to discuss what the school could do to restore calm, salvage its reputation, and move on.

Jean's friends and supporters, along with student leaders, gathered separately to ponder what their next move might be. They insisted that she was clearly a victim of illegal discrimination and they wanted her to sue the university and make them pay, whoever "them" would turn out to be. They wanted her to fight on her own behalf, but also on behalf of all the women who had experienced much of the same treatment as Jean had. For if the faculty vote against Jean sparked the uproar, smoldering resentments lurking just below the surface fueled the fires. Jean was not the first woman at the university to be "run out of town".

Inevitably, when the conversation turned to what happened to Jean Dubofsky someone would nod knowingly and say: "No surprise, really. You know the same thing happened to (...........) don't you?" And the blank was filled in with the name of a chancellor or a president, a department head or a dean, a former professor or prominent scholar, one capable woman after another who had come to CU and then, just as quickly, had gone from CU. All were "run out of town," the short-hand phrase often used. Added to those tales were examples of the women who had stayed, and then faced uphill battles for tenure, for top assignments, for recognition and respect.

"I know what they did to Jean was personal to her," one female CU faculty member said. "But it was personal to a lot of us because it happened to us too. It was very consistent with so many other things that had gone on. So if you are asking me if it was surprising or not, I would say no. It was not surprising at all."

Betsy Levin, the dean who had invited Jean to teach, was the last casualty before Jean. "She had been brought in from the outside and she was very capable," Jean said. "But that same little group, Nagel and his crowd, made Betsy's life miserable. They ran her out just before I got there." Jean was referring to Professor Robert Nagel, the faculty member viewed as the leader of the opposition to Jean's appointment.

Nagel, perhaps the most highly regarded member of the law school faculty, was one of its more conservative professors with weight and influence in academic and legal circles. After Levin arrived as the new dean, Nagel seemed to embrace every opportunity to show his displeasure with her. Academic deans come with flaws, make their share of mistakes, and are deserving of a fair share of criticism. Levin was no exception. She was not beloved or held in the highest of esteem by the faculty as a whole. But few deans were treated as poorly as Betsy Levin, particularly by Nagel and a few other faculty members who belittled almost every decision she made.

"It was tough. I was miserable most of those years," Levin said, looking back at what happened at CU. "I was a woman, yes, but I was also not a lawyer. I was an outsider, I was Jewish, and I was a Democrat. So there were plenty of ways I didn't fit what that group wanted."

"It was just consistent with what most women face," said one faculty member. "You have to be almost perfect. Once a vulnerability appears, certain people will just go after you. I thought Betsy was treated terribly. When she got the chance, she left."

Jean came to understand the history of how poorly so many women had been treated and understood why the issue was not just about her; it was about a culture resistant to change, and it was about the students, especially the women students, and other women faculty members, too. But Jean was not interested in fighting or suing. She just wanted the whole thing to simply go away.

The school leadership came up with such a plan—a plan that would make it all go away. Jean's appointment failed by only one vote. When one of those "no" votes told the dean he was willing to change his vote, a resolution appeared in sight. A faculty meeting was scheduled for the following week. There would be another vote and the decision would be reversed. The faculty would approve the addition of Jean Dubofsky to the law school faculty. And the whole brouhaha would be put to rest.

The only snag was Jean. When Jean heard about the plan for a second vote, she told friends and colleagues that she would refuse to accept the appointment if offered. She asked that no second vote be taken. Her supporters were disappointed and many attempted to talk her out of it. They had fought for her for all the right reasons and they had won, they told her. With a new vote, she could stay. The school needed her.

A piece of her felt as if she owed them more than simply withdrawing. But she couldn't do it. It was a very personal decision. She decided that she simply could no longer work in a place where disdain, prejudice, and the smallness of others would be daily companions.

"I was disappointed when she decided not to stay," Saltrese said. "But I saw her and talked to her and I understood. Why would you want to be here, in this environment, after everything they did?"

"It's hard to sort out exactly what all the pieces were to my decision," Jean tried to explain years later. "Part of it was that I didn't need this kind of thing in my life anymore. But I suppose the reason I probably said 'enough', that I couldn't do it anymore, was because my mom had just died." She was just too depleted, too tired.

Overwhelmed by her own personal grief and emotionally at sea, she could not summon up even one ounce of outrage on her own behalf. Mostly what she felt was relief. "I felt stunned when I first heard that I had been turned down for the position, but almost immediately I felt relieved too. If there had been that one vote difference, I might have found myself with some very long, lonely, unhappy years ahead."

Jean typed out a brief statement announcing that she had withdrawn her application and no longer wished to be considered for a teaching position, and she formally requested that the process for a re-vote not move forward. While expressing her appreciation for those who had given her support, Jean wrote that she could not remain at the law school. "The opposition to my appointment would make it difficult for me to become an effective teacher and a productive scholar at this institution."

She hoped to put an end to the furor, and her plan was to go away quietly. Until a note appeared in Jean's faculty mailbox, a note from Bob Nagel, who led the effort to oust her. Attached to his note was a copy of an opinion piece he penned that would soon appear in the *Daily Camera*. In the piece Nagel not only defended the vote, he added insult to injury.

The purpose of his op-ed, he wrote, was to explode misguided myths that had been circulating, criticizing the vote against Jean, and to defend the secrecy of faculty deliberations and decision-making. He argued that evaluations of candidates' work and credentials would be less candid if done publically; fewer people would apply if they knew that "their alleged professional deficiencies would be exposed for all to see." Instead of jumping to conclusions that some of the faculty had improper motives, he wrote, critics should have assumed that the "faculty knew of facts or considerations [or] the existence of explanatory information" that had not been made public.[55] The insinuation was clear: if people knew the facts that the faculty knew, if they knew of all of her "deficiencies", they would realize just how unqualified Jean was.

Nagel then went on to describe why underlying personality traits or character flaws would make individuals "with very fine reputations... and impressive titles" poor candidates as law professors. And, without naming any particular faculty members, he managed to disparage the credentials of all women professors at the law school by suggesting that current women faculty members were hired, not because of their qualifications, contributions, and stature, but because they were given special consideration to fill affirmative action requirements.

"I was outraged with Bob Nagel's letter to the editor," according to one of those professors. She had been hired away from another law school where she had earned tenure in three years and was on a fast track, considered to be a rising star, with a serious publishing record at a very young age. "I was one of very few women law professors at the time, and when CU made me an offer, they were eager to have me. Little did I know that I would end up being called an affirmative action hire."

"Even though he didn't name us," another female professor said, "his comments were such an insidious way of belittling and demeaning women and minorities, by calling them simply affirmative action hires. And then saying we don't need another one of those belittled Jean as well, saying we would only be interested in her because she was a woman and not because of her accomplishments."

If there was a last straw for Jean, it was when Nagel cited the hiring of a woman to be the law school dean as evidence of how supportive he was of hiring women at the law school. He was referring to Betsy Levin, who had left CU months before, driven out after what others have described, and Levin confirmed, were many, many years of terrible treatment by Bob Nagel and others.

Jean had sat back, had tried not to get drawn into the whirlwind, tried not to do or say anything that would fan the flames. But when she read what Nagel wrote, when she saw how craftily he attempted to further sully her reputation, credentials, and qualifications, and those of other women faculty, it was all too much. Jean felt the outrage that so many others had been feeling and expressing and for a day, just one day, she did what she almost never did. She fought back. And publically. The *Rocky Mountain News* characterized it this way: "Former state supreme court justice Jean Dubofsky has finally doffed the kid gloves."[56]

She told reporters about Nagel's working behind the scenes to round up votes to prevent her from becoming a faculty member. "What he is not telling you is that he was the leader of the opposition against me," Jean said, "apparently starting from when my appointment as a visiting professor was announced." And, she said, how dare he use the hiring of Betsy Levin as dean as an example of how welcoming the school is to women when "he was the leader of the opposition that Betsy Levin experienced when she was dean here."

By the time the *Sunday Camera* was preparing its Week In Review section, Jean had finally expressed a good number of thoughts that, in addition to the topic of her experience at the law school, summed up her struggles as a woman throughout her career. Under the section entitled WORTH REPEATING, was Jean's quote, as it appeared, caps and all:

I HAVE HAD ENOUGH OF PROVING AND REPROVING MYSELF. I DON'T HAVE THE NEED TO WORK TWICE AS HARD AS ANYONE ELSE TO BE THOUGHT AS GOOD. I DON'T THINK I NEED TO BE POINT PERSON ON ANY MORE BATTLES.[57]

Jean's recollections of that terrible week remain vivid many years later. But in the midst of all that was awful, were moments that made her smile. The Thursday after Jean had asked that her name no longer be considered for a faculty position, as she was concluding her criminal procedure class, one of the students came forward to present her with a bouquet of flowers. The entire class stood and applauded. They clapped. And clapped. And clapped. Jean was deeply moved. "I thank you all very much for all the support you've given me," she told them. As she slipped out the door, the applause began again, one more time.[58]

Jean also received a greeting card in the mail that week, signed by some of her faculty supporters. The front cover was a Gary Larson cartoon with two illustrations. The first showed a group of six people, clueless expressions evident on their faces, standing together in a sailboat. The other showed three people in a car, half hanging out the windows, not bothering to look where they were going. The captions read: "Ship of Fools" and "Car of Idiots". When she opened the card, another caption was handwritten in large letters: "Faculty of Morons".[59]

PART FOUR

Equality or Hate?

A Stunning Election Defeat

The Battle for Gay Rights

17

Equality or Hate?

Looking back at the law school chapter of her career, Jean viewed the outcome, if not the process, as a fortunate turn of events. "I'm so grateful that in the end it didn't work out at CU," Jean said. "If I had stayed teaching, I never would have had the freedom to work on such wonderful cases." That freedom came when she created for herself the optimal work environment—a law firm of her own, as an appellate attorney.

She had her own office, her own secretary, and an occasional intern or clerk or young associate, depending on the workload. She took the cases she wanted and worked at her own pace, which was often intense and concentrated. She charged what she thought was fair, which sometimes was not to charge anything at all. She was known for saying yes to help out a friend, or a cause, or fill a need. Best of all, the need to spend even an ounce of energy proving her worth or justifying herself to colleagues was gone. The fog of sexism, subtle or blatant, no longer clouded her workdays.

Working by and for herself suited her on so many levels. Her office was in Boulder, just a few minutes away from home and the boys' schools, and close to the friends and community she had become such a part of. She was able to create more time for family, including yearly travel adventures, and became more active in the women's bar association, often mentoring young women lawyers. She returned to teach on occasion, not at the law school, but in the women's studies department. She did what she wanted to do.

Jean's life was balanced. And her legal career flourished again. Little more than two years after she left the bench, she began appearing before her former colleagues. She lost an occasional case, but mostly she won. Case after case. Year after year. And, as always, at the heart of most of her cases was an injustice. She soon became involved with attempts to remedy one particular injustice: the unfair treatment of workers who had been injured on the job.

In the early 1990s, after an increasingly conservative Republican legislature enacted a new employer-friendly workers' compensation law, Jean began partnering with Pepe Mendez, a well-known and well-respected workers' compensation attorney. Because of the new law, employers found ways to skirt their obligation to employees after they became unable to continue working due to injury on the job. Various categories of injured workers were often left out in the cold, without work options and without compensation, and increasingly they turned to attorneys like Mendez for help.

Because of the intricacies of the new law, Mendez began to have less success in pressuring companies to provide adequate compensation. When forced to go to trial, he often found judges who felt the new law tied their hands as well. The only place to find relief for his clients became the difficult appeals process. Which is why he picked up the phone and turned to Jean for advice.

Mendez sent over a draft of one of his first appeals and asked Jean to review it. Jean immediately saw problems in the way he approached his arguments. "After she read my brief on one of the first cases, she said, 'Pepe, you are making too legalistic an argument....You've got to write it so the judges understand what you are saying.'"[60] Mendez decided that the solution was not for him to take her advice but, instead, to hire her to take the case. And then he just stood back in admiration, he said, of her special knack for knowing how to translate the legal case into a personal story, and then transform that personal story back again into a strong legal case. At the appeals level, Jean successfully argued why and how one or another provision of the legislation was contrary to case law or was a violation of equal rights or equal protection under the Constitution. Whenever Mendez lost a case at trial, he would hand the case over to Jean and, almost invariably, she would win on appeal.

If Jean were recast into her legal services role lobbying at the legislature, she would likely have led the charge for repeal of this unfair law. But with the changing make-up of the legislature, despite her considerable skills, rolling back that law would have been a long, difficult, and perhaps impossible journey. "Being an appeals attorney was different than working for legal services," Jean said. "But it was another way to make new law, through court cases."

According to Pepe Mendez, "Jean handled some big, important, long lasting cases,"[61] that led to greater justice for many more than the individual clients involved. Over the course of a decade and a dozen cases, she and Mendez helped chip away at and dismantle the most onerous impacts of a bad law, opening the door to fairer treatment for thousands of workers injured on the job. Frank insists that this series of winning appeals on behalf of injured workers was the most impactful work of Jean's career, work that began because of a simple phone call from Pepe Mendez seeking Jean's help.

But most would argue that it was another phone call that led Jean to do her most important work. It was a call that brought her into the middle of the latest and biggest battle over injustice and discrimination—the battle over gay rights. Like other battles over injustice, it was a battle that had been brewing for decades.

The animus towards and marginalization of homosexuals in America has a long, complicated, and shameful history, which is why for a very long time few dared to admit their homosexuality openly, sometimes even to themselves. But increasingly during the 1970s, mostly in large cities, groups of gays and lesbians began to come together, began to open their doors, to peek out, trying to gauge whether or not it was now safe to "come out". Gradually, over a period of years, tens of thousands did come out and began quietly telling family and friends of their sexual orientation. Many transplanted themselves to San Francisco and other cities that seemed more welcoming and safe. With that increasing sense of community and a feeling of safety in numbers came a growing empowerment that transformed itself into civil rights activism. That activism, especially at the local level, often led to increased legal protections as hundreds of cities and towns, counties and school districts, began to enact laws prohibiting discrimination based on sexual orientation.

The most attention-grabbing battle over including protections for homosexuals in a local anti-discrimination ordinance occurred in Florida in 1977. The national spotlight came, not when Dade County commissioners passed an addendum to the county's human rights ordinance prohibiting discrimination based on "affectional or sexual preference," but when Anita Bryant, a former Miss Oklahoma and Miss America runner-up, launched a widely publicized campaign to repeal the ordinance. More crusade than campaign, fueled by religious fervor, the repeal effort became one of the biggest stories of the year, exploding into the national psyche, leading daily news headlines and the nightly television newscasts for months.

Bryant was not a pre-eminent celebrity by Hollywood standards, but she gained some measure of fame as a pop singer with wholesome songs that occasionally made the national Hit Parade Top 100. Her breakout performance came not as a pop star but as a spokesperson for the Florida citrus industry. A deluge of TV commercials captured her All-American looks and sincere, sweet voice proclaiming that "A breakfast without oranges is like a day without sunshine." Anita Bryant and Florida orange juice became synonymous with a Mom and Apple Pie image of America, and those TV ads lofted her into celebrity stardom.

Bryant used her fame to launch a nationwide movement against gay rights. She founded *Save Our Children*, an organization she used as a platform to advocate for repeal of the Dade County ordinance. After this wholesome, all-American-beauty-turned-pop-star-turned-orange-juice-queen began her campaign to repeal Dade County's gay rights ordinance, she became more famous than ever.

"I believe there are evil forces round about us...and we do not want our children to see the sexual sickness," she argued, describing her motivation. "It's not a political issue, it is a moral issue. God is very plain concerning these kinds of sins." Her crusade espousing her conservative Christian beliefs about the sinfulness of homosexuality and her concern over the threats homosexuality posed to children was successful. The Dade County gay rights ordinance was repealed. Or, as Bryant described it, "God said NO!" [62]

While that victory represented a serious setback to legal efforts protecting gays and homosexuals from discrimination in Florida, the Anita Bryant-led campaign had a much broader effect nationally. It elevated the battle over gay rights into the national spotlight and galvanized the fledgling gay rights movement to action. It also emboldened another emerging powerful force, the religious right. The tentacles of the religious right had just begun to stretch their influence and reach far beyond the world of faith and ministry into public policy and politics. Soon the clash of these two powerful forces would also capture the national spotlight, in what some thought to be an unlikely place: Colorado.

In Colorado, it would be no surprise that Boulder was one of the first cities to respond to calls for increased protections against discrimination of gays and lesbians. Boulder, thirty miles northwest of Denver, had once been a more typical, relatively conservative

Colorado town, but its population grew in the 1970s from 37,000 to 70,000 and it gradually transformed itself into a much more progressive city, earning the liberal leftist moniker, The People's Republic of Boulder.

In 1974, Boulder's newer city council members, led by charismatic civil rights activist Penfield Tate II and a group of liberal, activist women very much in the mold of Jean Dubofsky, passed a human rights ordinance that included prohibitions against discrimination based on sexual orientation.[63] These council members likely had moved farther to the left more quickly than the city's voters, because almost immediately efforts to repeal the reference to sexual orientation began. The public uproar that followed the council's action forced the council to place the issue on the ballot and allow the voters their say. Much to the surprise and dismay of many, the voters rejected the actions of the city council and protections based on sexual orientation were removed from the city's human rights ordinance.

The city council in another Colorado town had better luck. By the 1970s, quirky, tiny, famous Aspen had emerged out of its silver mining past and transformed itself into a ski resort and cultural outpost for the rich and famous. When the city council there enacted its anti-discrimination ordinance in 1977, there was no outrage, no call for repeal. The ordinance stood unchallenged.

Over the next decade in Colorado, a wave of attempts to enact local anti-discrimination ordinances was met with mixed results. Some passed, some failed to pass, some faded away without ever coming up for a vote. It would be left to the state's two largest cities, Colorado Springs and Denver, to define what kind of future Colorado's gays and lesbians would have. And define it they did by marching in entirely different directions, setting the stage for a five-year battle that became the most watched gay rights legal drama in the country's history. Eventually that clash landed on Jean's doorstep, propelling her to the forefront of what would be the most important battle of her career.

Colorado Springs, home to the U. S. Air Force Academy and three other nearby major military installations, was always staunchly conservative. Military families liked what they saw while stationed there and retired nearby. Republicans outnumbered Democrats two to one. It was not surprising that this part of Colorado would also be a welcoming and comfortable place for evangelical Christians to settle and raise their families. Nor would it be surprising that, when talk of adding protections against discrimination based on sexual orientation to the Colorado Springs human rights ordinance began to seep out, pressure mounted on the city council to shelve the idea.

What was surprising, however, was the city's dramatic transformation over the course of a decade from a comfortable conservative community into an evangelical mecca. Like a magnet, first one, then ten, then forty faith-based churches, think tanks, and social and political quasi-religious organizations relocated their national headquarters to Colorado Springs. The landing there of this new and growing religio-industrial complex to this promised land did not happen by accident or divine intervention. It was largely due to a small but powerful group of self-appointed business leaders and Christian zealots, including the owners of the city's famous Broadmoor Hotel, who set out to make the city *the* destination for the big business of the religious right and create a Silicon Valley-like hub for Christian organizations. The group called itself the Colorado Springs Economic Development Corporation, and they used land donated by the owners of the Broadmoor to lure one organization after another from around the country to relocate to Colorado Springs.

Their efforts coincided with a national explosion of the power of the evangelical right as a cultural, political, and economic force. The movement burgeoned and led to the formation of new and influential organizations, spawning Mega churches, direct mail operations, and evangelicals with their own television programs, some owning their own television stations. Many came to make their home in Colorado Springs.

Denver, with twice the population, was only fifty miles north but, politically, worlds away from Colorado Springs. As the state capital and the dominant political force, Denver was the Democratic Party stronghold in a Republican state, electing first an Hispanic and then its first African-American mayor. It was also home to a growing and increasingly more open and activist gay population. Although old guard Democratic Party traditionalists and a predominantly blue-collar working class mindset made Denver a much less obviously liberal place than Boulder or Aspen, by 1990 a liberal leaning majority of the Denver City Council made passage of an anti-discrimination ordinance possible. Gay rights activists there saw an opportunity and ran with it.

After months of preliminary work, a two-word addition to the Denver Human Rights Ordinance prohibiting discrimination by reason of "sexual orientation"[64] successfully made its way through all of the appropriate council committees. Both support and opposition slowly gained steam over those months of committee hearings, and by the time the ordinance appeared on the city council agenda for a vote on October 10, 1990, emotions were running high. The council chamber was packed full that Monday night, crowds spilling out into the hallway and filling an adjacent room. Following three hours of emotional testimony and sometimes acrimonious debate, interrupted by the forcible removal by police of one man whose yelling disrupted the meeting, the language to add sexual orientation to the city's human rights ordinance passed by a vote of eight to four.

The victory was short lived. Almost immediately, a California-based anti-gay rights group whose national mission and organization were dedicated to keeping such laws at bay, joined forces with conservative groups in Colorado Springs. Together they organized a petition drive and successfully placed a measure on the Denver ballot to overturn the ordinance.

In the spring of 1991, while competing for voter's attention with a dramatic mayoral race, a contentious ten-week campaign raged over whether or not sexual orientation would remain in the city's human rights ordinance. The debates, forums, and coverage by local newspapers and TV stations opened a window on the all-but-hidden world of homosexuals for all to see. But if that window opened, it did so with just a crack. Despite the hope of many gay activists that the campaign would foster a broad public discussion about gays and lesbians and their place in the world, or advance understanding and change societal attitudes, that did not happen. This was a political campaign and those leading the campaign were solely focused on winning votes, not on educating the public about all things gay.

The liberal, progressive, and overwhelmingly Democratic voters of Denver were likely to support a measure to outlaw discrimination. But to expect voters to rally around a group of people barely out of the shadows, or overcome discomfort with, even fears about, the unfamiliar lifestyles of and the possibly threatening strangers in their midst, was judged too ambitious a goal for a political campaign. The campaign leadership urged supporters to avoid any debates about the thorny subject of homosexuality or the life choices and challenges of gays and lesbians. The fight was to be a fight against discrimination of any kind.

Opponents of gay rights took a different tack. They framed the issue as a question of whether or not homosexuals were deserving of "special rights", and then proceeded to describe homosexuals and their lifestyle as clearly unworthy and undeserving of such special rights. The "special rights" framing was the primary message in their public debates and with the media. Behind the scenes, however, in the privacy of churches, at neighborhood gatherings, and through phone banks and literature dropped on doorsteps, opponents promoted a more invidious message, freely characterizing homosexuals' lifestyle as deviant and morally repugnant. They equated homosexuality with bestiality and necrophilia, and they argued that enacting the anti-discrimination ordinance would lead to increased child molestation and sexually transmitted disease.

As reports of this kind of personal character assault on homosexuals grew, so too did the concerns of leaders of the gay community about the campaign strategy. Some insisted that the campaign had to embrace a stronger positive gay rights message; that it had to fight back against all of the scurrilous charges and defend the honor and character of gay citizens; that it had to set the record straight.

Judy Harrington, an experienced Democratic political operative who had the full support of the governor and other political leaders, directed the campaign. She insisted that in order to win, they had to keep the focus on civil rights and equal rights and not be diverted by the desire, however understandable, to educate voters about homosexuality.

"We never believed that 10% of the people (Gays and Lesbians) alone could come up with 51% of the vote; it was necessary to mainstream from the beginning," she stated.[65] The mainstream message was simple: repealing civil rights or legalizing discrimination against any group is wrong and must be rejected. The more Harrington was pressured by allies to make the campaign a vehicle for a wider message about homosexuals, the more she insisted that their opponents wanted the debate to move in that exact direction because they believed they would win that debate.

Harrington's strategy proved to be a winning one. On Election Day, May 21, 1991, 55% of Denver voters voted against repealing the ordinance. Prohibitions against discrimination based on sexual orientation would remain in the city's human rights ordinance. With that victory, Denver became the largest city in the U.S. to uphold a gay rights law.

The victory provided new legal protections and also gave some comfort to gays and lesbians. "I think it eases a lot of fears about the potential for such consequences as losing a job or being denied housing because of sexual orientation," Tony Ogden, a leading Denver gay rights activist, said at the time. "This is part of an evolution of awareness and action for both gays and straights. Many gays are afraid to come forward, fearing repercussions for revealing their sexual preference. Society's attitudes may change glacially, but at least with a guarantee of legal protection against abuse, gays can begin to disclose their troubles." [66]

Jean Dubofsky was not involved in the Denver battle but followed it closely, interested as always in issues related to social justice. But she paid particular attention to *this* fight because for Jean it was personal.

In addition to Jean's parents and her brother, another central figure loomed large in Jean's life—her Uncle Bob. Bob Taylor was her mother's younger brother and to him Jean wasn't just one of the nieces; she was the daughter he never had. From the time she arrived into the family, until his death decades later, Bob and Jean were essential ingredients in each other's lives.

Jean's uncle moved from Topeka to Nashville before Jean was born, and he made a life for himself working as a top buyer for Cain-Sloan, one of that city's largest department stores and the site of one of the first civil rights lunch counter sit-ins in the early 1960s. One of his roles in Jean's life was as the supplier of most of her clothes—from new school clothes and Easter Sunday outfits every year, to the many high school formal dresses and all of the outfits Jean wore during her

Betty Crocker celebration tour, to a trunkful of clothes that Jean found waiting for her when she arrived at Stanford.

But it wasn't just clothes. She and her Uncle Bob corresponded throughout her childhood and college years. He sent post cards from various travel spots and never missed sending Jean a card and a gift on her birthday. He penned short letters of encouragement or congratulations for various accomplishments and regularly sent suggestions about what sweaters might go best with which skirts. Jean's first airplane trip, when she was twelve years old, was flying to Nashville to spend time with her uncle. When Jean and Frank were married, a wedding for only the immediate family, he was the only one outside of Jean's parents and brother who was there. He was sophisticated and worldly, with artistic sensibilities and, in a way, Jean always felt she inherited many of those same sensibilities from him.

Throughout her life, Christmas was never Christmas until Uncle Bob arrived. And when he arrived, it was always with his friend, Gene, the man he made his life with in Nashville. Bob and Gene were together for sixty years. "From the time I was a baby, they came every year, a day or two before Christmas," Jean said. "They were family."

"When I was young, I don't think I ever really knew that Uncle Bob was gay. It certainly was never said out loud that Bob and Gene were homosexuals," Jean said. "But it was always Bob and Gene. I'm not sure when it was that it occurred to me that they were a gay couple because you not only didn't talk about things like that back then, you didn't think things like that."

Later, after Jean became a lawyer, and still without acknowledging the obvious, Taylor asked her to come to Nashville and meet with his personal lawyer to help with some legal documents, to sort out power of attorney and other will provisions related to him and Gene, their ownership of property together and their financial assets. "Bob wanted to be able to take care of Gene should Bob die first."

Jean and her Uncle Bob did not ever discuss his homosexuality. "I suppose I would have liked to have talked to him about that part of his life. But I never raised the topic," Jean said. "I thought about it, but it was his life and he was the one to define it the way he wanted. He had drawn whatever boundaries were comfortable to him, and it wasn't up to me to decide to cross them. Maybe being gay wasn't the light he wanted to be seen in. I don't know. I guess I'll never know."

Given her relationship with her Uncle Bob, Jean had a special interest in what was going on in Denver. Though discouraged about the tone and hateful portrayals of gays, she was relieved that the effort to overturn the ordinance had failed. But, just as the vote by the Denver City Council to pass the ordinance had not been the last word on the issue, the election also turned out not to be the last word on the issue. With its winning campaign, Denver's broad gay rights coalition showed that it knew how to flex its political muscle.[67] But that flexing likely served to further invigorate the opposition, already at work plotting their next steps in the backrooms from Colorado Springs to California and Washington D.C. The election night celebration at the Mammoth Events Center on East Colfax Avenue had barely ended when rumors began to circulate that anti-gay rights forces were getting ready to strike again.

The leaders and major financial donors behind the national organizations dedicated to holding back the growing homosexual rights movement may have failed to stem the tide in the more Democratic and liberal capital city of Denver, but they were not done with Colorado. It was a Republican state. A conservative state. A Christian state. They were not going to allow *their* state, the state that had increasingly become the national home of the evangelical movement, to become a state where the homosexual lifestyle was welcome.

By opening day of the 1992 Colorado legislative session, a group now calling itself Colorado for Family Values (CFV) was armed and ready. During the summer and fall they drafted ballot language, circulated petitions, and gathered signatures for another initiative. This time, however, the battle would not be fought one city or town at a time. It would be fought on the statewide level. This time the goal was not simply to overturn one city's ordinance; it was to roll back all current policies, statutes, and ordinances in every city, town, county, and government entity in Colorado that provided anti-discrimination protections based on sexual orientation.

In addition to undoing any current such protections, the proposed ballot initiative would also prohibit all governmental bodies in Colorado from enacting any in the future.

It was a stunningly ambitious goal, and it arrived in the form of a one-sentence, six-clause, 75-word amendment that, if passed, would become part of the Colorado Constitution. It would be called Amendment 2.

> *Neither the State of Colorado, through any of its branches or departments, nor any of its agencies, political subdivisions, municipalities or school districts, shall enact, adopt or enforce any statute, regulation, ordinance or policy whereby homosexual, lesbian or bisexual orientation, conduct, practices or relationships shall constitute or otherwise be the basis of or entitle any person or class of persons to have or claim any minority status, quota preferences, protected status or claim of discrimination.*

Immediately, many of the same activists and political leaders mobilized again, this time to begin preparation to mount a campaign to prevent this amendment from becoming part of the Colorado

Constitution. It was a very difficult time for many gays and lesbians who barely had recovered from the final ugly weeks leading up to the Denver election. They felt beaten up, stigmatized, and more isolated than ever. When the early meetings to discuss how best to fight Amendment 2 harkened back to the internal battles, power struggles, and strategic differences that arose during the Denver campaign, many felt beaten down again. This time, though, some fought back more strenuously.

"There was tremendous conflict,"[68] according to Judy Harrington, who had signed on to manage the new campaign against Amendment 2. The most acrimonious debate was over the control and philosophy of the campaign. This time, unlike during the Denver campaign, representatives of various factions and organizations in the gay community were vehement that they be a part of a campaign steering committee, overseeing the campaign and its strategy. But the state's political leadership—Roy Romer, the governor; the new mayor of Denver, Wellington Webb; the Democratic Party power brokers and consultants--was equally insistent that turning the campaign into a community building exercise or an educational effort about homosexuality or a conversation about the challenges of being gay was the surest road to political defeat. The political leaders made clear that the campaign would be run by political professionals, not a committee of gay activists.

That this campaign would also *not* be an advocacy effort on behalf of gays and lesbians caused a greater stirring of discontent within the gay and lesbian community. With more gay activists feeling newly empowered to speak, and new leaders within the community emerging, the discontent began to find a voice. From ACT UP, an in-your-face cohort that had its roots in the politics of national gay pride and AIDS awareness movements, to the quieter voices advocating for working within the system for incremental change, there were almost as many different opinions about what the statewide campaign should be about as there were gay activists. The campaign leadership fought to marshal all the forces behind a mainstream campaign with messaging and strategies that had proved successful in Denver and other campaigns. Critics balked, however, and challenged the leadership over whether this was the optimum strategy for either the short-term election win or the long-term benefit for gay people. Inevitably, then, in addition to battling anti-gay forces, battling within became ever-present as well.

As both fronts in the war raged on, a small group of mostly gay attorneys and activists, led by Denver attorney Mary Celeste, feeling alienated and unwelcomed in the campaign but very much still committed to the goal of preventing anti-homosexual forces from being successful, came together in the spring of 1992 to discuss how they might be of value. Their discussion quickly settled on the big *what if* question. The polls suggested, and many believed, that Amendment 2 was likely to fail. But *what if* it did pass? What then? The answer, they thought, was a lawsuit that would prevent the amendment from ever taking effect.

Pat Steadman, a fresh-out-of-law-school and a fresh-out-of-the-closet young gay activist who had been involved early on in the Denver initiative battle, had moved over to work for the statewide campaign. He was a campaign jack-of-all-trades, organizing, researching, and providing the campaign with legal support. And then he was given another assignment: that of a peacemaker.

"When some people decided to separate from the campaign and focus on a legal strategy, on preparing for a law suit after the election, it was not appreciated by the campaign," Steadman said. "The campaign was concerned that if it was known that there was a group working on a post-election litigation strategy, it could undermine the campaign's efforts to focus on preventing it from ever becoming law." His assignment was to be a bridge between the campaign and the legal group, where strong feelings of mutual distrust and animosity had blossomed. "I was supposed to help keep the litigation strategy under wraps and prevent this other group from working at cross purposes with the campaign," Steadman said. Soon he became deeply involved in their efforts, and he teamed up with Mary Celeste to become the group's leaders. Their mission and their focus was to prepare for a legal challenge—just in case.

These attorneys, who had little experience beyond general domestic law, met weekly, compiled research regarding how to structure and support a lawsuit, discussed potential legal theories, and began making a list of potential plaintiffs. None of them had ever attempted a legal challenge that came close to approximating the effort that lay ahead, and they quickly concluded that the best way to prepare was to recruit the most qualified attorney they could find to direct the effort.

They made two lists. One was a short list of the top attorneys in Denver who might have the stature, experience, and skill to take the lead and guide the effort. The other list was even shorter. It had only one name on it: the esteemed former Colorado Supreme Court justice, Jean Dubofsky. They wanted someone of stature and gravitas who would be taken seriously. Someone with appellate experience. Someone with intimate knowledge of the judicial system. Someone who had championed civil rights and expanded rights for those who were left out. Not everyone in the room knew all there was to know about Jean Dubofsky, but most knew enough to appreciate that she was exactly the right person to be lead counsel. If only she would agree.

Pat Steadman was designated to make the phone call, explain the mission, and get Jean to say "yes". Jean had never met Steadman, but he was well aware of her. He had been a student at the CU Law School when the uproar over the faculty vote to deny Jean a teaching position was at fever pitch just a few years earlier.

When Steadman called Jean to introduce himself, he explained the group's mission and told Jean they were looking for a pro bono attorney, but not just *any* pro bono attorney, because this was not going to be just any pro bono case. It was, he told her, possibly the case of a lifetime. *If* it ever became an actual case.

Jean was immediately inclined to say yes. She had been following the statewide campaign, just as she had followed the Denver campaign. Before she agreed, however, she wanted to learn more, wanted to speak with a few of her gay and lesbian friends. One of those conversations was with a neighbor and close friend, Jim Buchanan. Jim was an attorney and his son Wade worked for Governor Romer. Recently Wade had come out to his family as a gay man. Jim Buchanan described the involvement he and his wife Janet were undertaking with the family advocacy group Parents and Family of Lesbians and Gays (PFLAG), how much they had learned, and how important this issue was to so many. You have to do it, he told Jean.

She also spoke with her political friends, and when they reassured her that Amendment 2 was unlikely to pass in November, it made her decision even easier. She was happy to pitch in knowing it would be only for a few months, until Election Day. But it wasn't simply the likely short-term commitment or the advice of friends and political folks that persuaded her. She thought of her Uncle Bob and she knew that Jim Buchanan was right. She had to do it.

18

A Stunning Election Defeat

By early July of 1992, Jean was fully engaged leading the legal effort, reading and rewriting drafts of briefs already taking shape, directing additional research and case analysis, and communicating with attorneys for the national gay rights groups who were following the events in Colorado with great interest. With the advice of those groups and other constitutional experts, Jean drafted a forty-seven-page legal brief outlining the legal theories, circulated it for comment and improvement, and had it locked down and ready to go long before Election Day.

She provided the strategic guidance about the two kinds of plaintiffs that they would need to best challenge the amendment's constitutionality: individuals who had actively pursued policies or laws designed to provide protection from discrimination, harassment, or violence due to sexual orientation; and cities and towns with such policies and laws already in place. The lawyers and activists working with Jean were well connected in the gay community and aware of anti-discrimination efforts across the state. Soon they had a list of many individuals who would fit the bill.

As summer moved into fall, Jean began finalizing all the elements necessary to be prepared to file a lawsuit immediately after the election, if needed. They had gathered case law for a range of legal theories, had almost a dozen potential plaintiffs identified, and Jean circulated the legal brief one more time. Jean and the team were comfortable that they had done all they could do to be ready—just in case. All that remained was to wait. Late October polls continued to show that Amendment 2 would fail to pass, making a lawsuit unnecessary.

When Jean was asked if she would volunteer to guide and lead the effort, to become the attorney of record for a legal challenge should Amendment 2 pass, it was a case in theory only. Voting *for* Amendment 2 was essentially a vote to prohibit laws against discrimination and Jean, like many Coloradans, did not believe that the majority of voters would support an amendment that essentially legalized discrimination.

"I never thought Amendment 2 was going to pass. Never." Jean said. "No one thought it was going to pass." Preparing to mount a legal challenge should the unexpected occur, should Amendment 2 actually pass, was in many ways an academic exercise, a just-in-case case. If there were any worries about its possible passage, it was not due to the belief that the voters of Colorado were likely to deny gays protection from discrimination; it was due to concern over the possible impact that a series of bizarre political dynamics on the national level might have in shaping Colorado's election results.

In the year-long lead up to the 1992 November election, the number of electoral dramas being played out nationally, with twists and turns that left most heads spinning, added a layer of complexity to the political environment in Colorado. The presidential primary season took center stage for the first half of the year. On the Democratic side, the first act of campaign soap opera took place in New Hampshire, home of the first presidential primary. Revelations and tape recordings by a woman named Gennifer Flowers, who claimed that she had engaged in a long-term affair with presidential candidate Bill Clinton, then governor of Arkansas, temporarily took the air out of the Clinton campaign's sails. Two months later, revived by a Super Bowl Sunday *60-Minutes* interview that had Hillary Clinton standing by her man,

Bill Clinton finished in second place in the New Hampshire primary. He dubbed himself the "Comeback Kid" and gained the lift he needed to regain his footing and eventually fend off other primary challengers to earn the Democratic nomination for president.

On the Republican side, the New Hampshire primary provided drama as well, when conservative television commentator Pat Buchanan, in an almost unheard of act of party disloyalty, mounted a primary challenge of the sitting president, the first George Bush. Then, equally unheard of, Buchanan received 37% of the New Hampshire primary vote, dealing an almost crippling blow to the president and spurring other challengers to join the fray. When the primary calendar moved from snowy New Hampshire to the inviting warmth of the southern states, a former knight of the Ku Klux Klan, David Duke, began competing for votes in those Republican primaries.

At the very same time, a previously unknown and unusually quirky Texas businessman, Ross Perot, threw his hat into the ring and became an immediate darling. None of these challengers were able to wrest the Republican nomination from President Bush, but Perot then switched gears and relaunched his campaign as an independent third party candidate. Perot didn't win the presidency, but his wildcard candidacy did turn the whole election process on its head in many states across the country, including in Colorado.

Ross Perot's independent, maverick candidacy was a perfect match for Colorado's many free spirits, cowboys, and lost souls, drawn to its wide-open spaces, looking for the chance to find or reinvent themselves. Perot brought these and all sorts of other voters out of the woodwork: people skeptical of politicians or tired of the traditional party candidates, and people who rarely, if ever, voted. With those new voters added to the pool, anything could happen.

In Colorado, a hotly contested U.S. Senate race and thirteen statewide initiatives, eight of them constitutional amendments, added to the electoral drama on the right, left, and center. A lottery question to move funds from prisons to parks and open space, an education funding question, and a highly controversial tax limitation measure called TABOR, meant to ratchet down and limit government spending at all levels of government, were also on the ballot. There was even a bill-of-rights of sorts for black bears, one meant to protect the bears from overeager hunters. Patricia Calhoun, editor of the alternative weekly newspaper *Westword*,[69] later grouped the long list of things voters would have their say about into categories: the Good, the Bad, and the Ugly, with Amendment 2 rated the ugliest of all.

There was a chill in the air as Election Day approached. A surprise storm dropped heavy snow in Colorado, stranding hikers in Rocky Mountain National Park and closing roads, with near blizzard conditions hitting many parts of the state. Weather forecasters had missed the surprise snowstorm, and election prognosticators had failed to spot the political storm that was about to hit the state. Amendment 2, the amendment that was not supposed to pass, passed easily. When all the ballots were counted, and all the election results were made public, it slowly dawned on many Coloradans that black bears[70] had more legal protections than gay people.

The *Denver Post* called it a "stunning defeat for backers of gay rights,"[71] and the explosion of emotion that followed was as surprising as the loss at the ballot box. Election night began with jubilation for Democrats. Bill Clinton was elected the next president of the United States and Native American Ben Nighthorse Campbell's surprise win kept the U.S. Senate seat in Democratic Party hands.

But then came disappointment. Governor Romer's initiative to fund public education appeared headed down to defeat, while a conservative, anti-government tax limitation measure that would curtail government funding passed. The schizophrenic reaction of the people in the Denver ballroom that night turned to angry disbelief when the statewide returns on Amendment 2 made it appear that, as local television newsman Ed Sardella phrased it, the voters of Colorado had decided, to "legalize discrimination against homosexuals". [72]

Gay rights activists had planned an election night celebration at their campaign headquarters on Colfax Avenue, ten blocks from the Democratic Party's celebration at the Radisson Hotel. But that hoped for celebration quickly moved to apprehension, then to rage. Activists poured out of their campaign office and headed downtown, where the Democratic Party bigwigs were celebrating. They were looking for something or someone to blame. Hundreds gathered outside of the Radisson waving signs and shouting slogans. It was almost as if a mob had taken to the streets, but without a plan of what to do or where to go.

After making their way home from work in the midst of cold and blowing snow, Jean and Frank hunkered down for the evening to await the election results. The early evening news carried the story of five thousand people huddled together in the freezing cold for a dawn rally at Stapleton Airport, waiting for Bill and Hillary Clinton to swoop down for the final stop of their 1992 presidential campaign. With so many statewide initiatives on the ballot, a third party presidential candidate who once had a lead in the polls, and bad weather potentially keeping down voter turnout, few felt confident predicting results. Jean and Frank watched and waited, just like everybody else. They stayed up late enough to learn that Bill Clinton would be their next president but with the fate of Amendment 2 still unclear.

Governor Romer had left the Democrat's downtown victory party before midnight and returned home to the governor's mansion with mixed emotions. Democrats had won the White House, a huge victory, and Democrats had held on to the Senate seat. But two statewide initiatives that Romer had fought hard for had failed to pass. And the results of a few important initiatives, like Amendment 2, were still up in the air. He had just fallen asleep when the phone rang. "I got a call that there was a near riot downtown and they said I'd better get down there," Romer recalled.[73] Amendment 2 vote totals were in. The amendment that the polls said would never pass had done just that.

The angry crowd had disrupted the Democrats' victory celebration, and with more people spilling out into the streets, a leaderless and explosive powder keg of a mob had formed. When the governor arrived back downtown, he climbed up on the hood of a car in their midst with a megaphone in hand, hoping to calm and reassure the volatile crowd.

"It is not you who lost tonight," Romer shouted. "It is all of Colorado who lost tonight."[74] He then asked the crowd to walk with him. He led them on a slow walk up to the state capitol, a half-mile away. It was his way of showing solidarity with their pain, providing an avenue for them to express their outrage at the result through a protest march of sorts. It also served to disperse the growing crowd. By the time Romer reached the capitol steps, less than a hundred remained with him, and after further discussion with the governor, they agreed to go home. He reassured them that he and other political leaders would not abandon them or their cause.

Romer was genuinely moved by the pain the passage of this amendment had caused so many. He told them that night and would remind them often in the weeks ahead that he would continue to fight to provide protections from the discrimination that so many experienced. He reminded them that he had led the fight against the amendment and was a friend to the cause of gay rights. But he also told them something they did not want to hear: that he was also the governor and responsible for upholding the laws and respecting the verdict of the voters. Within days, Romer would go from chief advocate for gay rights to being the named defendant in a lawsuit.

In the days and nights that followed there was more rage and more grieving, more marches and more rallies. The morning after the election, at a hastily called gathering across the street from the state Capitol at the First Baptist Church, three hundred angry and upset activists met with a dozen elected officials. The atmosphere was electric with raw emotion, but the part-strategy session, part-wake, part-therapy session did little to salve the deep wounds of betrayal.

Denver Mayor Wellington Webb and Governor Roy Romer shared the same disappointment and shock at the result, but tried to tamp down the rage and reassure people. They pledged to work together to deal with whatever lay ahead, whether it be legal or legislative action, or increased law enforcement services to prevent the feared increase in hate crimes and intimidation. "I think the political leaders were trying to say 'We are shocked too, and we are on your side. We won't let them hurt you,' " said Wade Buchanan, a close aide to Romer. He had been by the governor's side all during the campaign and was there with him that morning at the First Baptist Church.

For Buchanan, this was an especially personal defeat. A Rhodes Scholar looking to make a life in the world of politics and government, he didn't head to Washington as many of his classmates did. "The natural thing, and what I had expected to do after Oxford, was to head off to Washington" to find a way to make a contribution in the public sector, he said. His family had deep roots in Colorado, however, and he returned to Denver with another goal in mind: to figure out how to live an honest life by telling his family and his friends that he was gay.

He was gay at a time when there was no road map to help him tell his family what he had only recently admitted to himself. No roadmap for how to handle the reaction of others. No way to gauge what the impact of coming out as a homosexual would have on his career, his relationships, and his opportunities.

"This was the late '80s. It was a very different world then," Buchanan said, looking back many, many years later. "I knew so many people who dealt with their sexuality, their being gay, and the discomfort of dealing with their family, by moving away and distancing themselves from their families. But my family was too important to me to do that. I had to figure out how to come back to Colorado and do it here."

Buchanan came home and stayed. Over a period of years he told his family, then close friends, including family friends Jean and Frank Dubofsky. And finally he told the people he worked with that he was gay. By the time of the Amendment 2 battle, most people in his orbit knew he was gay, but it wasn't until the campaign against Amendment 2 that his job as the governor's policy advisor began to encompass a new responsibility, that of point person on gay issues. He became an active gay rights spokesman, campaigning across the state, often debating leaders from the opposing side.

The election result was a humiliating surprise and a political setback for Buchanan's boss, the governor, and it was a demoralizing loss for the community and his fellow gay activists. But the final surprise, in a week of surprises, was how personally devastating the election results were for him and for so many others.

"I'd been through campaigns. I'd been through losses," Buchanan said. "But I was caught off guard at how personal it felt. I think it was four or five months before I stopped feeling like all I wanted to do was just hide." It was one thing to understand intellectually that you were not accepted by society in general, that you were an outsider, considered strange. But to Buchanan, the vote seemed to be a clear rejection and repudiation by hundreds of thousands of people. "It was a definitive statement, a black and white decision," he said. "The state had just voted against you and who you were."

Another activist in the gay rights battle, Sue Anderson, experienced similar anguish. Anderson had taken on the leadership of the struggling Gay and Lesbian Community Center in Denver, and was one of the most visible leaders in the community and the only full-time paid employee for an organization dedicated to serving the gay population. She had also been in the middle of the political fight, beginning with the battles over the Denver ordinance. By the time this Election Day came to a close, she was as tired as she had ever been in her life.

Anderson had been a bit of a skeptic, not as confident as others that Amendment 2 would be struck down. After the early returns came in showing good results in Denver, she breathed a sigh of relief, but she had little energy left for celebration. "I have very clear memories from that night. I was at campaign headquarters early on and it was good. So I went home and went to bed." She awoke early and looked at the newspaper, then quickly dressed and went into the office. "It was barely six-thirty in the morning and the phones were ringing off the hook. Calls were coming in from all across the country. The answering machine was filled up. I thought, 'Wow. Now what?'"

It was the personal nature of so many of the calls that struck her. "The onslaught of anguish and anger coming from our communities. We had people in pain, people crying, people just in rough shape. The community center was a social service center so my focus was on trying to prop up the community and trying to respond to as much of what was coming in as I could."

Quickly the personal turned political as various groups turned to action. One group mobilized to write emergency legislation designed to repeal Amendment 2. Another began aggressive fundraising efforts to support the establishment of new gay rights advocacy and education organizations. But the most focused and immediate attention related to legal efforts to prevent the amendment from becoming the law. Within days, the talk was of what Boulder Mayor Leslie Durgin characterized as "one humongous lawsuit."[75]

Overnight, Jean Dubofsky, Pat Steadman, Mary Celeste, and the small band of lawyers found themselves in the middle of a firestorm of activity. They had been quietly hard at work identifying plaintiffs, delving deep into court precedents, drafting language for a potential lawsuit, and writing each other memos about which legal arguments held the most promise for this theoretical case. Suddenly it was no longer theoretical. It was real. And it wasn't just in Colorado. In addition to directing the round-the-clock activity to prepare for their eventual first legal step, Jean and many of the others were drawn into the media vortex as well. It was a big national story, and it quickly became evident that everything from then on would play out on the national media stage.

It wasn't what anyone had planned for or wanted. With the rejection of legal protections from discrimination, Colorado voters had just given the gay movement its biggest electoral loss. But it also did something else that all of the efforts over the previous decades had failed to do. "We had begged and struggled" to tell our story, Sue Anderson said, but no one cared. Suddenly we had "ninety-four straight days of media coverage." Their story was now on the front pages of newspapers across the country, sometimes even leading the national news. It was not going to be a one-day story or a two-day story or a Colorado story. "We were in the media, and we were there to stay," Anderson said. And by "we" she meant millions of gay and lesbian Americans.

Phones rang off the hook as members of the media were all looking for someone to talk to, trying to understand. The campaign had packed up and gone away, so Pat Steadman and Sue Anderson and Wade Buchanan and a half-dozen others who had been a part of the fight from the beginning were left to answer those phones, to step up and become the face and the voice of the gay rights movement in Colorado.

And thirty-three miles to the north, Jean Dubofsky was steeling herself for a legal battle that she thought she would never have to fight. A battle that would challenge her like no other, with the lives of millions in the balance.

19

The Battle for Gay Rights

In those first few days after the 1992 November election, chaos ruled. Colorado was branded the "Hate State", and political and business leaders feared that a devastating economic earthquake was about to strike the state after a boycott, organized by national gay rights leaders and fueled by Hollywood celebrities, spread like wildfire. Dozens of groups cancelled plans to hold their national conventions in Colorado; big cities forbade employees from traveling to the state; and a record number of vacation travelers cancelled hotel and ski reservations. One of the state's most important economic engines, tourism, appeared ready to sputter to a stop.

Governor Romer, Denver Mayor Webb, and other top elected officials, who only days before had been in full support of their friends in the gay community, were now in the awkward position of being on the opposite side. A campaign against the state of Colorado, a campaign to punish the state, was counter-productive, the officials argued. They pleaded with their friends to call off the boycott, to give the state a chance to respond, a chance to find out a way out of the turmoil the election results had created.

Mayor Webb set out on a national tour in an attempt to persuade anyone who would listen that the Amendment 2 vote did not represent the true values of the state, and to reassure them that there was a plan to prevent the amendment from going into effect. He met with big city mayors and appeared on the Arsenio Hall television show. But the boycott had taken on a life of its own, and even Webb's close

Democratic friends, especially his Democratic friends, felt they had no choice but to take a stand against a state that would not protect one class of citizens. Talk and promises would not be enough. Unless and until state leaders found a way to prevent the amendment from becoming law, the boycott would not only continue, it would expand. Demoralized, Webb cut his tour short and came home.

All eyes turned to the litigation strategy aimed at overturning the amendment, and to Jean Dubofsky and the group of lawyers who had formalized their status as a legal defense organization, the Colorado Legal Initiatives Project (CLIP). Within hours of the news that Amendment 2 had passed, offers of legal help poured in from across the state and the country, more than Jean knew what to do with. Every national gay rights organization, dozens of Colorado attorneys and law firms, and legal scholars and law professors from the most prestigious colleges and universities were all eager to offer advice and support. But in those very first days, there was no time to return calls or discuss offers of help. No time to seek additional advice or bring more attorneys to the table. The only thing that Jean and the CLIP legal team were focused on was filing their lawsuit fast and filing first.

"We wanted to file suit quickly in order to beat anyone else to the punch," Jean said. "We were afraid someone would just go file some random suit" that would have no chance of preventing the amendment from becoming law.

It almost happened. David Bath, a state legislator being prosecuted for molesting a fourteen-year-old boy, argued for dismissal of his case because he would not be able to get a fair trial, given that the majority of the voters of Colorado had supported Amendment 2.

"The Bath case was exactly the kind of case that we didn't want to become the case to test Amendment 2. We didn't want that limited kind of challenge to move ahead of ours because it would muddle things," Jean said. David Bath's lawyers might or might not have been able to get their client off with an Amendment 2 defense, but their arguments would not have been the vehicle for testing the fundamental constitutionality of the amendment.

Jean had been prepared to move quickly. Calls went out the day after the election to confirm the participation of the individual plaintiffs that had already been identified. But there was one hold-up: the cities that were set to become plaintiffs could not legally join the suit until after Election Day. Even with expedited procedures, days ticked by as city councils, city attorneys, and mayors processed the legal paperwork necessary to approve their participation as plaintiffs. Members of the CLIP legal team monitored federal and county court-houses, watching and waiting anxiously each day, hoping that no other case would be filed first.

Finally, on Thursday, November 12, nine days after the election, Mary Celeste, Pat Steadman, Jean Dubofsky and James Joy, Director of the Colorado ACLU, walked up the steps of the Denver City and County Building, which served as the county courthouse, and officially launched the lawsuit, *Richard G. Evans et al versus Governor Roy Romer and the state of Colorado.*[76] The lawsuit challenged the amend-ment's constitutionality, citing violations of equal protection, freedom of speech, freedom of association, establishment of religion, and the right to petition the government, all guaranteed by either the First or the Fourteenth Amendments to the U.S. Constitution.

Constitutional challenges percolate up through both state and federal court systems. Historically, civil rights cases were filed in federal courts, primarily to take cases out of the hands of the locally appointed, often racist, local judges that ruled southern courts in the 1950s and 1960s. Colorado in the nineties was not the South of the fifties but, still, Jean surprised a lot of people when she made the somewhat unusual decision to file in state court rather than federal.

It should not have come as a surprise. The Colorado justice system was her home. She was familiar with the nooks and crannies of every part of the system and knew many of the judges personally. Most had been appointed by Democratic governors Lamm and Romer, and they were likely to be more sympathetic than federal judicial appointees, the majority of whom were nominated by Republican presidents Reagan and Bush.

Jean's decision to file in the state court was about more than her own comfort or trying to game the system, however. Amendment 2 was placed on the ballot through the petition process, requiring the signatures of thousands of Colorado citizens. The majority of the voters of the state supported the amendment. The right place for the court battle, Jean felt, was in the court closest to the people of the state. The Colorado court, not the federal court, was the right place for this battle to be fought.

The CLIP team had successfully negotiated their first and biggest hurdle, filing a lawsuit. That filing started the clock on a lengthy legal process that ultimately would determine the amendment's constitutionality. But, and this was a big "but", filing the lawsuit would do nothing to immediately prevent the amendment from becoming law while the legal case played itself out. Jean's next hurdle was to find a way to block the amendment from becoming part of the state constitution before January 15, the date mandated that it take effect. After tense conference calls and heated individual conversations, it became evident that reaching agreement on the best strategy to prevent the amendment from immediately taking effect would prove difficult.

In mid-December attorneys gathered in the conference room at the Denver city attorney's office. It was the first time all of the attorneys were together in the same room. The purpose was simple: to hammer out a plan to stop the amendment from taking effect. Coming to agreement on a plan, however, proved to be surprisingly painful.

"Tensions ran high....[and] although the roomful of lawyers were all on the same side of the case they were about to launch, the group, at the moment, seemed more divided than united...the coalition of attorneys appearing on the verge of collapse" a number of times.[77]

The original group of CLIP lawyers had expanded to include city attorneys from Aspen, Denver, and Boulder—the three plaintiff cities, and attorneys from the Denver ACLU office, the national ACLU's Lesbian and Gay Rights Project, and the Lambda Legal Defense and Education Fund, the national gay rights organization dedicated solely to advancing civil rights of gays and lesbians. With that expansion came new voices, fresh perspectives, and conflicting points of view.

The disagreement among the lawyers centered on whether or not to immediately seek a preliminary injunction—a temporary restraining order of sorts—to block the law from taking effect. Suzanne Goldberg and Matthew Coles, representing Lambda and the national ACLU, argued that once the amendment became law, the legal burden would dramatically shift, making an already formidable challenge even more difficult. Proving "actual" harm to the plaintiffs, rather than a theoretical harm, was a much tougher legal case to make.

John Worcester, the city attorney for the city of Aspen, agreed with the strategy of seeking an immediate injunction to prevent the amendment from becoming law but for an entirely different reason. One of his city's biggest and most lucrative ski events was yet to come, Gay Ski Week. If the amendment took effect as scheduled, the national boycott would explode and lead to full-scale hotel cancellations. The economic hit on Aspen would be devastating to that small city that relied on the ski and hospitality dollars garnered during the limited number of ski weeks each year.

Jean did not disagree that preventing the law from going into effect was critically important, but she was hesitant. Filing for a preliminary injunction would trigger an immediate court hearing, a trial, with each side compelled to call witnesses, present expert testimony and provide evidence. Their small team of Colorado lawyers had been well prepared to file a lawsuit. But they were not well prepared to go to trial.

"I wanted to avoid having to go to trial immediately if we could find another way," Jean said. Seeking a preliminary injunction meant they would be in court in weeks and, in her judgment, they would need many months of preparation to argue the case successfully. Without adequate preparation at this early stage, she worried they might lose, and the entire cause would be lost. Darlene Ebert, the attorney handling the case for the city of Denver, tried to reassure Jean that she need not be so concerned about the prospect of going up against state attorneys at a hearing sooner rather than later. Ebert had recently argued a different injunction case and the state lawyers had not been well-prepared. We are on a mission, Ebert told the group, they are just doing their job. We'll be fine.

Still, Jean argued that they hold off. She wanted to give the governor and his legal counsel time to sort through their legal options. She had been around the Capitol, knew many of the key legal and political players, and she understood how things worked behind the scenes. If the governor could find a legal or administrative vehicle through his executive powers to block the amendment from taking immediate effect, she explained, that would allow them time to prepare sufficiently for a full trial later in the year.

Most of the other attorneys were not persuaded by Jean's argument and continued to push for what they believed to be the obvious and necessary next step: the injunction. The heightened tension over this first internal dispute seemed headed for a showdown, but within a few weeks' time the disagreement became moot. Lawyers advising the governor made it clear to Jean she was barking up the wrong tree. There would be no behind-the-scenes maneuvering, no way out. The governor was legally obligated to certify the election results on January 15 and that was exactly what he was going to do. To prevent the amendment from becoming law, she had no other option but to seek an injunction.

The attorneys moved past this first clash over strategy, but the already fraying relationships suggested the clash might have been a proxy for a more fundamental question: whether or not Jean Dubofsky was the right person to head the legal team.

It was not a new question. Long before Election Day, an attorney who was part of the original CLIP group forcefully argued that Jean should *not* be the counsel of record because she was not a lesbian. When national gay civil rights organizations joined the fight, their lawyers also began to question Jean's selection to lead the legal team. Not only was Jean not a lesbian, they argued, she lacked gay civil rights litigation experience, and her one-woman firm appeared ill-equipped to handle such a monumental case.

While the logistical concerns of staffing and resources were valid, Jean had a plan in place to manage those. And she thought the suggestion that she lacked civil rights litigation experience was absurd. She had no doubt that the depth of her knowledge and experience prepared her well for this case. But Jean thought the question about whether or not they ought to be hiring a gay or lesbian lawyer to lead the case had merit. When she was first approached about taking on the case, Jean had raised the very same question, especially after some in the group had voiced strong feelings that the case *should* be led by a homosexual. Jean asked Steadman and Celeste to reconsider whether they might be right.

"There was some grumbling by a few, but most of us never thought it should be someone who was gay. That just didn't seem like an important consideration," Pat Steadman said. In fact, having someone who was not gay or lesbian, someone with stature and gravitas in the legal community, might be the best strategy to ensure the case would be taken seriously as a mainstream civil rights issue and not just a gay issue. Steadman challenged those arguing that only gay lawyers be considered with this question: Do you really think that as we mount a battle against discrimination based on sexual orientation that one of our first decisions should be to discriminate against someone because of *her* sexual orientation?

Jean understood the discontent as partially a product of the natural tension between organizations dedicated to and motivated by a national gay rights agenda, and "locals" focused on specific issues of law in Colorado. Historically, in all major civil rights legal battles, the national organizations' focus on setting precedent and litigating big constitutional principles was often at odds with the concerns of attorneys responsible for one specific case. This tension and more was in evidence when Jean and lead plaintiff Richard Evans attended the Lambda national conference the week after the election.

"We had barely arrived at the airport, and I immediately got the brush-off from some of the key leaders of the two national groups who were supposed to be helping with the legal effort. They wouldn't even speak to me," Jean said. "I heard later that the Colorado attorney so opposed to my taking the case in the first place had been out there working the lesbian crowd. She was basically telling them that they shouldn't have anything to do with me."

Evans tried to soothe the strained relationships, but it was made abundantly clear during those days at the conference that most of the national gay rights leaders felt they knew what was best for advancing their cause. They viewed the Colorado group of lawyers, Jean included—maybe Jean in particular—as too inexperienced, too focused on Colorado, and too unsophisticated about the gay rights legal strategy to be taking the lead on an important case for their movement.

As time went on, it was the attorneys representing the interests of the national gay rights organizations who did most of the grumbling or questioning of Jean's leadership and not from the CLIP lawyers. "We couldn't believe it at first when Jean said she would do it. We knew she was the right person," Steadman said. "And as time went on, we were just so comfortable, so confident, knowing she was taking care of this for us."

———

Just before Christmas Jean returned to the courthouse to file a petition for a temporary injunction to prevent the amendment from immediately becoming law. As expected, the judge, Jeffrey Bayless, scheduled the hearing at his earliest open day after the New Year, Tuesday, January 11. Jean had confidence in her legal knowledge and experience, but she was not a trial attorney. To win in court, she would need trial lawyers, and she would need them fast.

The huge pile of pink phone slips that collected on Jean's desk in the days following the election included a message from Holland & Hart, one of the largest and most respected law firms in Denver. The firm's pro bono manager understood the significance of this case and wanted his firm to be a part of it. He offered the services of the firm's ligation team, including its chief litigator, Greg Eurich. Eurich remembered receiving a phone call letting him know that Jean had accepted the firm's offer of help, that a meeting had been scheduled, and that he should attend. He had no idea what role Jean had in mind for the firm but hoped that, as time went on, he would be able to give some small assignments to the many young associates who were particularly interested in being involved in this potential landmark case.

Eurich knew who Jean Dubofsky was. Every lawyer in Colorado knew of the former supreme court justice. "But I don't think I had ever met her before," he said. "I didn't really know what kind of help they would need, but I drove up to Boulder for the meeting."

When all the lawyers convened again, the group had grown to well over a dozen attorneys, all crowded around a conference table in Jean's Boulder office. Most seemed to know each other. "We were sitting around a table and just kind of brainstorming about who was going to do what," Eurich recalled. "Suddenly I realized that with the exception of one other attorney, there wasn't another trial lawyer in the room, nobody with any real court experience trying a complex case like this. And I thought, 'Oh my God, I'm not here to *help* their trial lawyer. I'm here because they think I am going to *be* their trial lawyer!'"

Jeanne Winer, another new lawyer in attendance, came to the same realization at about the same time. Winer had a history of activism within the gay and lesbian community and had been approached by CLIP months earlier to consider being one of the named plaintiffs. She agreed, happy to be a plaintiff or help any way she could. Jean Dubofsky knew of Winer, less from her gay rights activism than because of her reputation in legal circles. She was considered by some to be one of the toughest criminal trial lawyers in the state.

Dubofsky called Winer a few days before the same meeting to ask if she'd be willing to forego being one of the plaintiffs and instead help with the trial work. Like Eurich, Winer wasn't sure exactly what kind of help Jean was suggesting until she looked around the room that day. And like Eurich, she slowly came to the conclusion that she also wasn't there to help the trial lawyers; she was going to be one of the trial lawyers.

At the meeting, Jean also introduced Rick Hills to the growing legal team. Back in the fall of 1992, months before the November election, Hills, a young, would-be college law professor, arrived in Boulder. He was tagging along with his wife, a history professor who had accepted a teaching offer at the University of Colorado. Hills was a conservative Republican from a prominent accomplished family of lawyers with close ties to the Republican political establishment. He was not your stereotypical Boulder newcomer.

His budding legal career had already taken a few unusual turns. After a clerkship and practicing law briefly, he began work on a PhD in philosophy, with an eye toward academia. After one year, he abandoned his doctoral studies when he and his wife moved to Boulder. There he began teaching part-time at the CU Law School. The pittance he earned per course was not what he or his wife had in mind as a viable financial plan going forward.

"I went off to Boulder without any job or job prospects and a friend said, 'you have to talk to Jean Dubofsky, she needs an associate,'" Hills said. He had no idea who Jean was or what cases she was working on. An introductory phone call led to a long casual lunch that turned into a deep discussion about the legal framework for a pro bono gay rights case that Jean was involved with. Hills was hearing about the potential Amendment 2 case for the very first time, but he was not shy about opining on what theories might or might not be successful and why possible arguments being considered should be pursued or abandoned.

Maybe it was Hills' philosophy background or his academic bent, but whatever it was about him, Jean realized immediately that he was different; he did not think like most of the attorneys she knew. She was captivated by his intellect and his ability to quickly see connections, weaving one bit of case law to another to show how an argument could circle back on itself and collapse, or become a plausible option that could withstand scrutiny. "I remember thinking that he may have been the smartest attorney I had ever met," Jean said later.

In late October 1992, Hills accepted Jean's offer to come work for her. He would start after the first of the year. By then, they reasoned, the election would be over, the theoretical lawsuit would likely be moot, and there would be other complex appeals cases that Hills would assist with. Or so they thought. But by the time Hills arrived at Jean's office, the quiet appellate practice he thought he had signed up for had blossomed into a crisis hotline operation with phones ringing off the hook and the newly assembled team of attorneys preparing for a trial just days away.

Hills was about the same age as another attorney new to the group, Suzanne Goldberg, who arrived at Jean's office not long after he did. Twenty years later, she would be a distinguished professor, author, and scholar on gay issues, but when she arrived in Boulder she was as new to the field of law as Pat Steadman and Rick Hills. She was there to represent the views and the wisdom of her senior colleagues back at the Lambda offices in New York. Her assignment was essentially to help guide the case in a way that would be consistent with national litigation strategy designed to advance the cause of gay rights. Or, to put it another way, "I think she was sent to spy on us," said one of the local lawyers.

The national lawyers, including Goldberg, expected to be treated as the experts they were and assumed they would be shown proper deference. They often showed little patience for having to justify or explain rationales for their approach or legal analysis to the Colorado lawyers who, they felt, did not have the requisite level of expertise in civil rights law or in the specialty of gay rights law. And they often felt disrespected. At times, "the ACLU and Lambda lawyers sensed that Dubofsky did not fully consider their perspectives or value their collective experience in gay civil rights litigation. On disputed issues there was a sense, too, that Dubofsky didn't take fully into account the broader implications of the Amendment 2 challenge for lesbians and gay men nationally."

The uneasiness or questioning flowed in both directions. The way some of the national lawyers treated Jean, the way they spoke to her, their tone of voice, "was so disrespectful," according to Hills. "One lawyer was so aggressively rude and clearly furious that Jean had control of the case. Another was simply arrogant and preemptory, always with a tone implying, 'I know the right answer, you do not know the right answer, so you should just listen to me.' The attorney we worked closest with and talked to the most was always polite, but still often had a tone of suppressed impatience and tension in his voice, like he was trying to calmly explain things to people who just didn't understand. Worst of all, imagine Jean being lectured about the constitution by another young attorney, who like me, was barely out of law school."

Hills said he became a bit of a buffer, taking the phone calls, sitting through meetings, pushing back when necessary, being more confrontational, playing the bad cop to Jean's good cop. "Jean is such a sweetheart and she tried to be patient with everybody. She really did not want to be confrontational about it, but I just thought some of them were so rude and patronizing."

The complexity and the nuances of legal arguments, the changing nature of the trials, the diverging goals and purposes imbedded in various decisions all provided fuel for differences to arise and conflicts to fester. Jean would often say that the disconnects, the unease, and the differences in opinion between the national civil rights organizations and the local attorneys were predictable. Those who were focused on advancing a national gay rights agenda would inevitably have broader goals than those with the responsibility of ensuring that this one particular amendment not become a part of the Colorado Constitution. That those diverging goals would sometimes lead to fundamental differences in approach and theory was also inevitable.

In an ironic twist, part of the diverging legal approaches mirrored the threshold political strategy question that divided supporters in the Denver ordinance and the Amendment 2 campaigns: How much of the legal case was going to be about gays and lesbians and how much was going to be a basic civil rights challenge? The national lawyers, like the political campaign leadership, worried that if the case was all about gays and lesbians and bisexuals, they would lose. They thought that success would come through a straightforward theoretical civil rights challenge. Jean didn't share that view. She was just as sure from the start that the exact opposite was true. The case would certainly argue fundamental rights, but she felt confident that the only way they would be successful would be to make sure that the case was all about the real stories of ordinary people who happened to be gays and lesbians.

PART FIVE

20

Let the Trials Begin

It was January 11, 1993, opening day of the injunction trial, and the clock was ticking. Everyone in the courtroom was well aware that the next three days were make-or-break days. The plaintiffs would ask Judge Jeffrey Bayless to prevent Amendment 2 from becoming law. The state, the defendant, would ask that the will of the voters be honored and that the amendment be allowed to take its rightful legal place in the Colorado state constitution. The injunction trial would last only those three days and then it would be up to Judge Bayless to decide the outcome

It began that Monday afternoon with opening statements, a series of motions, arguments over motions, and rulings by the judge, all before the first two witnesses were called. Greg Eurich led an expert on legislative procedures through the background on the initiative and ballot process. A psychologist then provided definitions and context to set the stage for the coming discussion about sexual orientation and homosexuality.

The real drama and the heart of case began the next morning when the trial resumed. After the judge signaled it was time for the plaintiffs to call their next witness, it was Jeanne Winer's turn to take the reins.

When Winer and Eurich walked out of their first meeting with Jean and the other lawyers, they "were on a dead run in terms of getting prepared for that hearing," according to Eurich. They had no choice but to divide up the witnesses and dig in, each essentially working alone for weeks to prepare the witnesses they would be responsible for at trial. Winer took most of the plaintiffs. "I think we all thought I could relate to them better," Winer said. "They were my people and I felt very protective of them."

Winer felt the pressure any lawyer would in such a consequential case, but more so. She did not believe that Jean Dubofsky selected her to be one of the trial lawyers simply because she was a lesbian. "Jean wanted to win this case more than anybody and I had 100% confidence in her. If she wanted me on the case, I figure it was because she thought I was smart enough or skilled enough to do it," Winer said. "If I ever had any doubts, that Jean had faith in me was all I needed to reassure myself that I could do it."

But neither woman was naïve. It didn't hurt that Jeanne Winer was a lesbian. She was, however, neither a run-of-the-mill attorney nor a run-of-the-mill lesbian. Winer had variously been described as an ex-hippie Woodstock survivor, a member of the Boulder Socialist-Feministe community, an anarchist, and a former member of the Guerrilla Theatre Collective. She also had a second-degree black belt in karate.[78]

Winer described herself as a pit bull, a street fighter, someone on the legal team who wasn't going to play nice and wasn't going to be pushed around by the state. She suspected that was exactly what Jean was looking for, someone to complement the staid former supreme court justice and the impeccably proper 17th Street Denver lawyer, Greg Eurich. Winer was neither staid nor anything like the button-down attorneys in the big elite law firms. But she was good. Very good.

When she stood to call her first witness, she felt a special weight, unlike any she had experienced before. "I don't know if you were straight if you would feel that heavy a burden. It was personal to me and my friends and all of these people like me."

Her first witness was plaintiff John Miller. "Are you nervous?" Winer asked softly, after he was sworn in.[79] When Miller answered, "Yeah", Winer nodded knowingly. "So am I." To John Miller, Jeanne Winer did not seem anything like a pit bull or a street fighter.

Winer's first questions were all related to Miller's personal story. The state's attorney objected a number of times, questioning the relevance of putting the plaintiff's personal story into the record. Each time the state objected, Judge Bayless overruled the objection. These first rulings might have appeared inconsequential to observers, but they would set the framework for how much of the plaintiffs' personal stories would be allowed in evidence; they would determine whether or not Jean was going to be able to make the case be about gays and lesbians.

After the fourth or fifth quick objection from the state, Bayless stopped to elucidate on the reasons for overruling each objection. "Let me explain it like this," he said. "I think all counsel, and certainly the court as well, has struggled to get a handle on the issue that is here." When he referred to "the court" struggling to get a handle on the case, he was referring to himself. "Case law hasn't helped very much because very few cases have addressed this," Bayless said. So he was going to allow this line of questioning, not because he was sure of the relevance, but because he wasn't any more sure than anyone else what the case ultimately would be all about. The plaintiffs were going to have the opportunity to tell their stories.[79]

Soon the judge, the state's attorneys, the other plaintiffs' attorneys, and people all over the state and the country, who had just discovered this new sensation called *Court TV*, sat back and listened as Winer led witness after witness through the personal journey that led them to be part of a lawsuit against their own government. Their stories were mesmerizing. It was as if time stood still in the courtroom.

John Miller said he remembers realizing he was somehow different ever since he was eight years old, although it took him a lifetime to admit to himself and others what that difference was. He married twice, and after divorcing, spent many years raising his two children as a single father.

By the late '80s and early '90s, Miller was a Spanish professor at the University of Colorado campus in Colorado Springs and active in community efforts to support gay rights, including an attempt to pass a human rights ordinance. The Colorado Springs Human Rights Commission recommended to the city council that protections based on sexual orientation be included, but when it was introduced at the city council it raised a ruckus. The commission's staff director was removed from her position and the city council refused to go along with the commission's recommendation, voting it down by an 8-1 vote.

Miller was known on campus as someone gay students could talk to and he spearheaded various efforts on behalf of gays and lesbians at the school. As chair of the Faculty Council, representing the entire University of Colorado system, he fought to have protections from discrimination based on sexual orientation made a part of the university's policy. But it was a lonely fight. There likely were three to four hundred gay and lesbian faculty members in the four-campus university system, but Miller knew of only one other who was publically out as a gay person. Neither his university, his place of work, nor his city was prepared to make discrimination against people like him against the law.

Richard Evans was next on the witness stand. He came from a military family, fully expecting to follow his father and uncles into the Air Force, he said. But that never happened. Homosexuals were not allowed to serve in the military.

He testified that he no idea what being gay really meant when he was a boy but, looking back, he knew by the time he was seven years old that he was gay. That knowledge made his growing up years very painful and lonely. He did not tell his family about his sexual orientation until he was twenty-nine years old.

"Why did you wait so long?" Winer asked.

"Fear."

"Of?"

"Fear my parents would reject me," he said. "Fear that they would no longer have contact with me. That type of thing."

Winer slowly walked Evans through various parts of his life with question after question. Simple questions. Evan's answers were simple as well. Painfully simple.

"What was it like as a kid, in school? As a teenager, how did being different and knowing that you were gay and not acceptable to the majority of society affect you socially and emotionally?" she asked.

"I tended to be someone who isolated themselves from other people. I was known as a loner…was a bad student. I refused to go to classes…was not participating fully as a teenager. [I was afraid] that somebody would discover my sexual orientation and make an issue out of it. I became depressed and contemplated suicide."

"What does it mean to live a closeted life?" Winer asked.

"I did not have a lot of close personal contacts. I was not considered a friendly person or somebody who was reachable."

"Is this how you lived a good part of your life?" she asked.

"Yes, it was."

Richard Evans had been a state employee. He told the story of the process of his coming out at work and of a meeting he attended with Governor Roy Romer shortly after Romer was first elected governor. Evans did not know it at the time, but Roy Romer had his own coming out story, and part of that story had to do with meeting Richard Evans.

Romer, a Democrat, did not come early or easily to the cause of gay rights.[80] "I came from a rural Methodist culture and had a very strong aversion toward homosexuality," Romer said. "And I had it for a long time." But as a public leader he said he felt responsible to examine his "own truths". After he became governor, as part of his continuing process of examining and gaining understanding of homosexuals and gay issues, he held a meeting with a small group of gay and lesbian state employees to hear their concerns. When the meeting was breaking up, Romer thanked one of the men for coming.

"What's your name again?" Romer asked.

The other man looked away. "Look, I'd really rather not tell you. I get along better if people don't know who I really am."

"That really punched me in the stomach," Romer said. "That people couldn't be honest about who they were…could not be public about who they were."

Richard Evans was the state employee who told Romer that he was uncomfortable giving the governor his name. That exchange with Evans impacted the governor strongly. Strongly enough that he moved forward with an executive order forbidding employment discrimination based on sexual orientation. Strongly enough that years later Romer still remembers that meeting, that employee and that conversation.

Evans told that story of the meeting with Romer on the witness stand. He said he feared retribution, that he might be singled out, ostracized, or even lose his job if people knew he was a homosexual. He described how he slowly began to "come out" at work and then later began actively working to promote gay rights when he changed jobs and went to work for the newly elected Denver mayor, Wellington Webb. As part of his responsibilities with the city, Evans began to act as a liaison to the gay and lesbian community. It was not an easy or natural transition to go from being in the closet, being afraid, to being very public about his orientation. Nor was it easy when he had reason to be afraid again after he helped organize a gay and lesbian association among city employees and his name and contact information appeared in the employee newsletter, the *Spotlight*.

The editor from one of the big statewide papers called Evans, concerned that the paper had received a hundred phone calls from city employees who expressed outrage that such a group was being formed and that the *Spotlight* would run an article about the new group, giving it legitimacy. Some calls were threatening, she said, and mentioned Evans by name. "She was extremely concerned about my personal safety and asked that I be careful in moving about the city and just take better care of looking out for myself." After that, Evans asked his apartment manager to remove his name from the building directory. He changed his phone to an unlisted number. He looked over his shoulder more often.

The next plaintiff to take the stand was Angela Romero, a Denver police officer in her thirties. Romero described two aspirations that she had as a young girl. She wanted to grow up, get married, and have children; and she wanted to be a police officer, a school resource police officer, just like the one assigned to her elementary school.

Romero graduated from the Denver police academy and eventually gained the promotion and the job that she coveted. She was assigned to be the school resource officer for ten schools in one of Denver's most impoverished neighborhoods, much like the neighborhood she grew up in. "I loved that job with all my heart and soul," she said on the witness stand. She thought she had a special gift for working with kids who shared her background. One of her school principals saw that special gift too and wrote a letter saying he was grateful for all that Angela meant to the school.

Romero's other dream, to be married and have children, almost came true as well. She dated a young man and he proposed. The arrangements had all been made, the invitations had been sent out, and her parents had already paid for the church rental and the reception.

But a month before her wedding day, deep anxiety and a sense of dread overwhelmed her. "I became real depressed," she said.

When her maid of honor asked Angela what was wrong, Romero told her why she couldn't get married. Romero had known she was different since she was six years old but she tried to ignore it, tried to fit in. While a marriage might have allowed her to have the children she wanted, and might have camouflaged her sexual orientation, it would have all been a lie.

Angela Romero called off the wedding. Despite trying to remain in the closet, mostly out of fear that she would lose her job, her sexual orientation eventually became known to others in the department. Within days of her supervisor learning she was a lesbian, Romero was removed from her school resource position, demoted, and reassigned to a patrol car.

"And do you think it was because of poor performance?" Winer asked Romero on the stand.

"No," Romero said, "it was because I was a lesbian, and they knew it".

Her patrol job back on the street had its share of inherent danger, the kind that all police officers face. But her days and nights became more dangerous because when she would call for backup when handling a particularly high-risk call, no one would come. She described handling a domestic violence call and a street incident when, as per department policy, she was required to call for backup. She'd call and then would wait, but no backup car would come.

One night an officer arrived to provide backup even though he was not assigned to do so. He told her he was upset with what others were doing to her. He had heard the radio traffic and he knew that the officers who were supposed to respond, who were assigned to back her up, were not coming. They were not coming because they had learned that she was a lesbian, he told her.

Like John Miller and Richard Evans, Romero reached a point where she decided she had kept silent long enough. She had to try to make things better. She began by writing letters to her superiors, describing policies and procedures that needed to change. She suggested simple things, like not allowing the word "fag" to be used on police radios. And critical things, like requiring that cars provide backup when called, even if an officer was known to be a homosexual.

The plaintiffs would take all day Tuesday and most of Wednesday to present additional witnesses—a prison chief, a mayor, a teen suicide expert, and others testifying about the public policy consequences if the amendment were to go into effect. After the plaintiffs' rested their case, the state began its case with a psychologist who treated homosexuals with the goal of curing them, and followed that witness with a political scientist. As the afternoon session was coming to a close, the attorney for the state told the judge that they would have only two more witnesses. One would not be available until mid-afternoon the following day and the other would take little time on the stand. Bayless suggested that it made sense for them to wait until after lunch the next day to reconvene.

The judge gaveled them back to order at one-thirty on Thursday afternoon. It was the state's turn to make their case once again. In their written briefs, in their opening argument, and with their first expert witnesses, the state focused on suggesting areas of legitimate state concern that the amendment addressed. One interest was to protect the sanctity of individuals' personal, religious, and moral views. Local ordinances amounted to a government stamp of approval on conduct that violates the tenets of many religious beliefs, they argued, and was, in essence, allowing local government a role in promoting homosexuality, crossing the bounds of the separation of church and state. They also elicited testimony to support their contention that the proper place for any such laws was at the state, not local, level and that states have a clear interest in having uniform state laws.

On the final day, the state called only two witnesses: a pollster dissecting research to ascertain the true motive of the voters; and a civil rights champion concerned that adding gay rights to the civil rights agenda might dilute the focus on true civil rights, might water down the state's capacity to enforce civil rights protections to those truly in need of protection.

By late afternoon on the final day, the two sides prepared to make their closing arguments and, once again, the plaintiffs would go first. Jean Dubofsky rose and made her way to the microphone. Instead of beginning her closing argument, however, Jean informed the judge that she first needed to make a motion and then proceeded to do so.

"I make a motion today for a temporary restraining order," she began. "Last night I received a call from the governor's counsel saying that Mr. Tymkovich's representation to the court, and to us, that Amendment 2 would become effective at midnight on Friday was not correct." Instead, the governor's office informed her that the amendment would take effective at midnight on Thursday night. That night. Just hours away.

Jean's motion asked for a temporary order pushing back that deadline for twenty-four or forty-eight hours to allow time for the trial to be concluded and provide the judge adequate time for his decision. Judge Bayless, already showing the strain of having to decide the case under an extremely short timeline, could contain his frustration no longer. His explosion headed straight in Jean's direction.

"For six weeks the court waited for a motion for a preliminary injunction, and it was not filed," Bayless said. "And then once it was filed, the court pushed very hard to get this hearing moving so that this last-minute pressure wouldn't be here...And then within eight hours, now you want this all of a sudden?" There was no missing who he meant when he used the term "you." He held Jean responsible for the predicament.

"It was pretty ugly. Judge Bayless was essentially yelling at Jean for putting him in this time crunch," Eurich said.

Jean responded quietly but firmly. "Your Honor, we waited to file…because we spent a number of weeks discussing with counsel for the state whether they would agree to a temporary stay." She then reminded the judge that he was well aware of her various efforts to move expeditiously to a trial on the merits because he had been the judge to deny a stay of the amendment a month earlier.

Bayless was not placated by her explanation. She should just go ahead with her closing arguments, he instructed, because he wasn't prepared to rule on the new motion she had just sprung on him. If she wanted to include any additional arguments for why he should grant a temporary restraining order, she would have to do that with her closing arguments.

In a conversational tone, Jean commenced with her closing argument. It was, however, more a story than a legal argument. She began by answering one of the threshold questions Bayless would be weighing: Is it likely that if Amendment 2 goes into effect it would cause irreparable harm?

Jean wove together the stories of Richard Evans and Angela Romero and John Miller and all the discrimination they had experienced, all the work they had done, all the policies and ordinances and executive orders they had helped create to make such discrimination illegal. The harm was clear, she argued. All of those protections would disappear if Amendment 2 went into effect.

She then turned to a second two-part threshold question: Did the plaintiffs have a sound legal theory and have sufficient evidence to suggest the likelihood that a constitutional violation occurred? To satisfy Bayless of both, she began with the story of what had happened in California thirty years earlier when voters adopted a constitutional amendment that allowed individuals the freedom to decide who they would and would not rent, lease, or sell a property to. That amendment essentially enshrined in the California State Constitution the right to discriminate against African Americans, preventing them from living where they wanted to live.

The California amendment was passed in response to gains made by the civil rights movement to make it illegal to discriminate based on the color of your skin. "You might say there's been a gay, lesbian, and bisexual civil rights movement" here in Colorado, Jean said. "[And] Colorado Family Values, like the realtors in California, is attempting to roll back the civil rights protections for gays, lesbians, and bisexuals that have been obtained in this state." The only difference is that in Colorado discrimination on a much broader scale would be allowed, not simply in housing, but in employment, in public accommodations, with insurance, and even in schools. The California amendment was found to be a clear constitutional violation; Amendment 2 would be as well, she argued.

To further show the likelihood that the courts would find Amendment 2 unconstitutional, Jean pivoted to one more case, a case she always referred to as the hippie food stamp case.[81] When the sixties sub-culture of wandering free spirits—"hippies"—was denied the benefits that everyone else was entitled to, the Supreme Court ruled that it did so not out of any legitimate government interest but simply because of bias and prejudice. That was what was going on here, Jean argued. And laws motivated solely by antipathy, bias, or animas towards a certain group are, on their face, unconstitutional. The only motivation behind this amendment to restrict gays and lesbians from obtaining protections was bias and prejudice.

Jean then began a critique of the state's case. During the previous three days of the trial, Jean pointed out, the state made no attempt to defend the arguments made by the supporters justifying the need for the amendment. The state didn't argue that homosexuals are child molesters because there is no evidence that is true, Jean said. It didn't argue that gays and lesbians would cause their children to become homosexuals because the evidence and expert testimony showed that homosexuality is likely fixed as early as age four and that parents do not determine a child's sexual orientation. And it didn't argue that homosexuals should be denied protections because they interfered with a family's religious values because it can't. "There is simply no crisis in family values in Colorado," Jean said.

Jean reminded the court that the state provided no argument for any legitimate government interest in barring homosexuals from needed protections against discrimination because there were no legitimate government interests; there was only hate. And the evidence of that hate was provided by the supporters of Amendment 2: a hate-filled anti-gay video; a similarly offensive multi-page brochure that had been mailed or left on the doorsteps of hundreds of thousands of households, filled with claims equating homosexuality with pedophilia; multiple examples of letters and speeches and expert testimony calling homosexuals immoral and repellent.

Finally, as Jean neared the end of her remarks, she returned to the question of the harm that the amendment would cause if allowed to go into law. All that is legally necessary to prove irreparable harm, she argued, is to show that the plaintiffs would be denied their basic constitutional rights. That is harm enough, and we have clearly done that, she told the court. But there are further examples of the harm that could be done if the court does not rule to prevent this amendment from becoming law.

"Beginning at 12:01 tomorrow...between 175,000 and 455,000 people in this state will assume a second class status when Amendment 2 becomes effective." They will lose the governor's executive order that provides employment protections; they will lose the current insurance statutes that require equal treatment; they will be subject to discrimination in housing and employment, she argued; and they will become even more isolated, even more fearful for their safety if they become identified as gay or lesbian. She listed cities and towns that would lose their human rights ordinances, would lose their policies that protected police officers, or would lose programs to encourage HIV sufferers to come forward and be treated.

John Dailey, Colorado's deputy attorney general, closed for the defense and reiterated many of the arguments made in his opening statement. The plaintiffs' were simply wrong about their claims or misunderstood or were flawed in their theories and arguments. There was no equal rights claim, no First Amendment claim, no freedom of expression violation, and no likelihood they would be successful arguing any of those claims, he said. He minimized the impact of the amendment and countered the plaintiffs' suggestion that it would deprive gays and lesbians of their basic civil rights. And he reiterated his arguments that there are state's interest being served by the amendment. It provides uniformity in laws statewide; it prevents a dilution of the state's capacity to enforce current civil rights laws; and it serves to protect citizens' rights to be left alone to raise their children in accordance with their own moral values and religious beliefs, he asserted.

By the time Dailey concluded, it was well after the usual five o'clock adjournment time. And it was Judge Bayless' turn to speak once again. Clearly feeling burdened with the decisions before him, he ruminated on his conundrum. He described how hard he had worked to review all the briefs prior to trial and to read all the depositions and other material placed into evidence each day. It was only now, after closing arguments were made, he said, that he finally had all the facts in front of him. He worried out loud, talking to himself as much as he was talking to the filled courtroom, about how little time there was for him to properly weigh all of the information now in his possession: if he did not rule before midnight, Amendment 2 would become law.

He also had Jean's motion for a restraining order before him and he had to rule on that motion as well. A key legal test for issuing such an order, Bayless explained, is whether or not the status quo would be changed if one were not granted. He was convinced that the status quo would undoubtedly be changed if Amendment 2 became law at midnight, he said. Which left him with a choice between ruling on the case before midnight or granting Jean's motion and issuing a restraining order to give him time to prepare to make his ruling.

"The question is," he said, "Can I render a decision on an issue that I consider to be very significant, very important, not only to the legal community but also to the voting public, given the time frame?" He reflected on the California case that Jean had cited and recalled that "a part of that reported decision included that the court chose to take a little time. I think that court was wise in making that decision."

Finally, Bayless was ready to rule. He did as Jean had suggested, ordering a twenty-four hour stay that would block the implementation of the amendment until he had a chance to rule on the injunction, which he would at five o'clock the following day.

When the judge gaveled the court back into session at the following day, he said that after he took the case home with him, he spent hours trying to make sense of the three days of testimony, and it had taken him until two-thirty in the morning before he made up his mind whether or not to grant an injunction. After that, Bayless said he tried to sleep but couldn't. So he began to outline the opinion and was writing and editing right up until the last minute when the opinion had to be printed and copied, just before he stepped back into the courtroom to deliver his ruling.[82]

His ruling was simple: Amendment 2 would not take effect until a full trial on the merits of the case and any subsequent appeals settled the question of the amendment's constitutionality. Bayless reasoned that harm would be done if it were allowed to take effect. And he judged it likely that the plaintiffs would prevail in making their case on the merits, partly because the state had failed to make a persuasive case that there was a legitimate state interest in limiting the rights of cities and towns to enact policies and laws protecting gays and lesbians. The amendment appeared motivated solely by bias, he said, and that provided a likely avenue for the plaintiffs to argue successfully that it violated the equal protection guaranteed by the Fourteenth Amendment of the U.S. Constitution. That was all the plaintiffs needed to do: convince the judge that they had a *likely* avenue to pursue that could lead to a determination by the court that the amendment was unconstitutional.

The Bayless ruling for the plaintiffs in the injunction trial was a huge victory. It meant that the amendment would not become law, at least not until a final determination was made at a later trial that would rule definitively as to the constitutionality of Amendment 2. News of the decision captured bold headlines in all of the Colorado dailies, but it was not simply Colorado that took note of this potentially far-reaching decision. It landed on the front page of the *New York Times*, along with a quote from Lambda attorney Suzanne Goldberg: "The gay and lesbian community can breathe a collective sigh of relief."[83]

The Bayless decision was monumental for gay rights supporters. But his ruling also presented some legal challenges when he, inexplicably, combined the two central and separate legal arguments into one. The plaintiffs argued that Amendment 2 denied fundamental equal protections guaranteed by the Constitution, and that it did so based on biases and animus, rather than any legitimate state interest. Bayless wrote, mistakenly conflating two different arguments, that the Constitution guaranteed "a fundamental right not to have the state endorse and give effect to private biases." The Constitution guaranteed no such thing, however, and the plaintiffs never made any such arguments. The plaintiffs received the result they wanted, but the partially scrambled legal ruling raised new questions and left the case more muddled and confused.

21

A Risky Legal Gambit

Early in the injunction trial, Judge Bayless described his own struggle to "get a handle on the case" and suggested that no one in the courtroom knew what the case would ultimately be about either. With little direct language in law, in court opinions, or in the Constitution to provide definitive guidance, there was no clear or obvious path to determine the constitutionality of the amendment.

From the earliest days of preparation for a possible legal challenge, a panoply of constitutional claims, including religious freedom, rights of association and privacy, due process, and individual rights versus governmental interest were all considered, and many of these arguments made their way into memos, briefs, and the courtrooms. Yet, a clear conviction about which claims, theories, and arguments might or might not be most effective was elusive. Ultimately the plaintiffs' lawyers agreed that a Fourteenth Amendment equal protection claim held the most promise, and that became their central focus.

Settling on this claim narrowed the constitutional focus to this simple but profound clause of the Fourteenth Amendment: "No State… shall deny to any person within its jurisdiction the equal protection of the laws." But narrowing the constitutional focus did little to settle a number of complicated and controversial strategic choices over which theories and arguments would best support this claim. One of the thorniest arguments that Jean choose to pursue, despite pushback by many of the national gay rights lawyers, involved the legal concept of suspect class.

When it is evident that a group of individuals is singled out for unequal treatment and is subject to a range of discrimination simply because of the color of their skin or their racial and ethnic identification, the courts give this group suspect class status. They do so because of the suspicion that such infringements might be based on race or ethnicity. Infringements based on race or ethnicity are not permissible under the Constitution. If granted suspect status, stricter scrutiny and a higher bar of proof applies and any actions that potentially limit or infringe upon the constitutional rights of this suspect class group require a much higher, stricter standard of review by the courts. As part of the higher standard, the reasons for limiting such rights would have to be compelling, not simply rational.

The concept of identifying a group as a suspect class became particularly salient during the civil rights years when blacks were subject to a set of Jim Crow laws that deprived them of many basic rights guaranteed to whites. Jean wanted to persuade the court that gays and lesbians had suffered much the same kind of discrimination and wanted the court to consider the plaintiffs as a similar suspect class, or something close to it. If she succeeded, it would make it more difficult for the state to prove its case; its attorneys would be forced to show that the state had a compelling reason to intervene in local government efforts to protect homosexuals. Also, it would force the state to show that Amendment 2 was an appropriate, narrowly tailored approach to accomplish their stated goals, and that no other less restrictive solution was available.

One of the specific arguments the state would offer was that it had a legitimate interest in having a uniform set of anti-discrimination laws at the state level, rather than city-by-city and town-by-town variations. While it seemed like a reasonable, perhaps laudable goal, Jean wanted the courts to hold the state to a higher standard, to require the state to prove that having uniform laws at the state level was essential, not just preferable. And she wanted the state to have to show that the solution, amending the state constitution, was the only, best, and least restrictive way to advance the state's interest in promoting a uniform set of laws across the state. If she could get the court to see gays and lesbians as a suspect class, it would up the ante, trigger the stricter scrutiny, and impose these higher hurdles.

It was a risky legal gambit. The federal courts had never shown any willingness to consider homosexuals in that same way as racial groups. Nor had they ever hinted that they were open to moving in that direction. On the contrary, the courts had generally sent clues at every opportunity that race and ethnicity were one thing, but identifying other groups as a suspect class was not going to happen. To many on the legal team, it seemed like a losing proposition from the start.

Jean did not necessarily disagree with their assessment. "In an honest legal world, sexual orientation should be a suspect class; it met all of those standards," Jean said. "But I knew that the court for its own reasons was never going to go there. But just because you are not going to get the court to go where it should go, that doesn't mean you don't use it to accomplish something else." The something else was the concept of quasi-suspect, sometimes called suspect-lite, an intermediate standard of scrutiny.

Even if the court would never get all the way to treating homosexuals as a suspect class, arguing persuasively for it might move the court to fall into the quasi-suspect no-man's land that moves the court to a standard of proof that lies somewhere short of the higher hurdles of compelling state interests and strict scrutiny, but well beyond the low hurdle of a simple rational basis test. And that quasi-suspect territory might give the state just enough additional trouble making the case that it had a legitimate interest in setting restrictions on local anti-discrimination laws.

Another "something else" that Jean was after was being able to prove the harm and the devastation of the discrimination, which was essential to winning at the injunction trial. In her judgment, the only way to accomplish that was through the personal testimony of the plaintiffs. And the only way to insure that the personal testimony would be allowed, would be admissible in court, was to make a claim that justified such testimony. The suspect class claim would open the door to court rulings allowing the personal testimony of the plaintiffs into evidence.

Attempting to prove suspect class was not just a risky gambit on the legal level, it was also risky and problematic on a philosophical and personal level for many gays and lesbians. One underlying precept to qualify for suspect class involves immutability. Your race or ethnicity is determined at birth, for instance. It is genetic. Whatever your race at birth, it is immutable. You can't change it.

The plaintiffs would have to convince the court that homosexuality was not a choice, but pre-determined and immutable, much like race or ethnicity. The arguments would point to genetics and DNA and the theories suggesting that the personality and the personal characteristics that make one a homosexual are essentially hard-wired and unchangeable, established at birth, something you have no control over, not something that is acquired later on in life. But such arguments were anathema to many homosexuals who felt that choosing to be who you were was part of what they were fighting for. Worse, such genetically based arguments fed directly into the medical model that suggested homosexuality was a defect or malady in need of a cure. Some worried this argument could easily end up crossing over the line to an illness model, the antithesis of the argument that homosexuals are just like everyone else.

In the January injunction trial, the plaintiffs' testimony provided the first layer of evidence about how obvious their homosexuality was at such an early age. But the October trial would be the place for building the second layer of proof, with scientific and expert evidence to show that sexual orientation was set early and was immutable. Lawyers on Jean's own team were a bit uneasy about what they were being asked to do.

Jeanne Winer, like many lesbians, understood homosexuality with all its complexities, understood that there were as many explanations for their sexual feelings, sexual preferences, sexual orientation as there were individuals. She understood that many thought the fight for gay rights was a fight for the freedom to be who they were, about the freedom to choose who they loved. To have so much of the case riding on trying to prove immutability, something she did not believe was universally true, especially for lesbians, was uncomfortable for Winer, and for many gays and lesbians. "I wished we hadn't tried to do suspect class," Winer said. "It got so muddy, some things were crazy and stupid and we went too far."

But Winer had faith in Jean Dubofsky and, once Jean laid out the legal theory and the goal, Winer's job was to provide witnesses and elicit testimony to support those legal arguments. She dug in and produced convincing scientific testimony about the genetic roots and the immutability of homosexuality. But she didn't always feel good about it.

The attorneys from Lambda and the ACLU made clear that, had they been lead counsel, they would have done things very differently. They did not want the case to be about homosexuals but about the Constitution. They did not want the case to be fact-based but based on theory and precedent. At the outset they would have gone for a summary judgment or facial challenge, arguing that on its face, the Constitution prohibits Colorado from barring any group of its citizens from seeking antidiscrimination protections. The case would never have been about gays and lesbians. It would never have been about Angela Romero or Richard Evans.

And attempting to prove that homosexuality was immutable would not have been at the heart of the October trial. That difference in approach was just one more example of Jean going her own way, over the objections of many around her. "I heard about it all the time, how uncomfortable it made people to be trying to prove immutability," Jean said. But in her judgment it was necessary to win the case. Although she listened to concerns and understood the unease, she thought her professional responsibility required her to make the best judgment she could about legal strategy, even when it offended the very people she was trying to help. "I suppose I felt that one of my responsibilities was to ensure that those kinds of personal and emotional reactions weren't getting in the way of making the sound legal decisions. Maybe there was a benefit to having someone who wasn't a lesbian making those kinds of calls."

22

Appealing for Justice

Nine months after the injunction trial, all the players in this drama were back together at the courthouse for the October trial to decide the constitutionality of Amendment 2. The plaintiffs' legal team still experienced many of the same tensions and disagreements over legal strategy, and in many ways, the trial on the merits of the case closely resembled the January trial. But along with the similarities came differences between the two. The most obvious difference, on the very first day of the second trial, was the venue.

Instead of Judge Bayless' first floor courtroom, this time they were summoned to gather in Courtroom 3 on the second floor of the Denver City and County Building. Legal essayist Jeffrey Rosen described the room as a "neoclassical jewel, with its mustard walls and gray Vermont marble and polished oak backboard. It is a platonic ideal of a courtroom, which is perhaps why Viacom commandeered it in the mid-1980s to film several episodes of the new 'Perry Mason.'" [84]

Bayless opened the trial with an explanation: the move from his courtroom was needed because, with all the attention the case had garnered, they needed a larger space. The roomier Perry Mason courtroom, however, presented challenges. The show's producers were allowed to replace the original lighting fixtures with a pair of very ornate, but barely functioning, Beaux-Arts chandeliers. The chandeliers, still hanging overhead, made it difficult for judges, lawyers, and witnesses to see one another. "So we will be in the dark a bit," Bayless quipped.

"For some strange reason, we also have spots where the microphones can't pick-up voices," he continued, instructing everyone to use the main stationary microphones. "No roaming around."

The length of the October trial, ten days instead of three, and the depth and substance of the evidence provided by both sides were the most significant differences from the earlier injunction trial. This time both sides relied extensively on experts—philosophers, biologists, sociologists, and political scientists—who testified for hours on end and in mind-boggling detail. Each side presented dueling facts and studies to buttress their claims or refute the claims of the opponent. Both sides also deposed dozens of additional expert witnesses during the eight months of preparation, and placed in evidence hundreds of additional pages of the deposed testimony to support their case.

The legal approach of the plaintiffs had not changed dramatically over the nine months. In January the plaintiffs persuaded Judge Bayless of the *likelihood* that they could prove that irreparable harm would be done if Amendment 2 went into effect; that an equal rights violation occurred; and that the amendment served no legitimate government purpose. At the October trial they would have to prove their claims. The testimony and evidence presented was all meant to support their argument that Amendment 2 failed important constitutional tests: it denied one selected group of Americans, homosexuals, equal protection of the laws; it denied them the fundamental right to participate in the political process, the equal right to petition their government and gain redress when subject to discrimination; and it was motivated not by any legitimate or compelling government concern, but simply by animus, bias, bigotry, and ignorance.

In addition to proving the claims, additional goals motivated Jean's selection of witnesses and the testimony sought. One goal was to create the most complete record possible. "If we end up at the U.S.

Supreme Court, we wanted to be sure that we had everything in the record we might possibly need because it was impossible to know for sure what we would be arguing as the case went on," Jean said. Depending on rulings by the district court and any future appeals courts, different legal theories and arguments might be necessary. To anticipate possible future court rulings, some of the plaintiffs' witnesses were called to provide testimony as a prebuttal to possible arguments the state might make in the future.

A second goal was to provide everyone, from the presiding judge to the world at large, an education. The trial became an introductory course: Gays and Lesbians 101. And the world was watching. Literally. *Court TV* was again in the courtroom and televised the trial live, gavel-to-gavel. For Jean, the trial was more than a legal case. It was an argument with society about social justice, and the key to winning that argument was education.

The testimony over the first days of the October trial built upon the vivid and powerful personal stories told by plaintiffs at the injunction trial, then pressed the claim that homosexuals should be treated as a suspect class. Winer and Eurich elicited testimony from scientists, geneticists, psychiatrists, and sex researchers to support the argument that sexual orientation was not a choice but immutable, a part of who people were from the start. Later, they turned to political scientists, historians, and philosophers to provide testimony buttressing the claim that the amendment was motivated solely by animus and prejudice, not by any legitimate government purpose. The attorneys walked the expert witnesses through a history of perceptions and misperceptions, violence and arrests, investigations and witch hunts, from the early Greeks through the Stonewall riots in New York City in 1969, up to the present day, including the campaign waged by Colorado for Family Values. Once again the key piece of evidence was the CFV brochure that contained some of the most hateful language and descriptions imaginable, unmistakably confirming the depth of animus towards homosexuals that was at the root of the amendment.

The state used its time and witnesses primarily to bolster their claim that the amendment served legitimate state interests and to refute the plaintiffs' suspect class arguments. The state's witnesses testified that homosexuals were not a disadvantaged group, or a group without political power, nor was sexual orientation an immutable genetic characteristic. And they argued that the rational basis test, not the strict scrutiny test that would be triggered by suspect class, was the appropriate test of whether or not the government's interest was legitimate.

Witnesses for the state testified that Colorado was being taken over by gays and a gay agenda that threatened religious freedom and infringed on the right of families to believe in, and raise their children with, a different set of moral values. They also argued that children might be harmed if homosexuals were given special rights, that protecting gays from discrimination would cause a resource problem in protecting others from discrimination, and that having different ordinances city-by-city, or policies agency-by-agency, would create contradictory laws and harmful factionalism.

The state's witnesses that held the most interest to Coloradans were Tony Marco, Will Perkins, and Kevin Tebedo, the three men most responsible for and most closely identified with Colorado for Family Values, the initiative to put the amendment on the ballot, and with the campaign that followed. They shared their understanding of homosexuality and their reasons for pursuing the amendment. Their goal, they said, was to quell a rising gay agenda that they felt threatened the moral and religious fabric of the state, and to prevent homosexuals from being given special rights that might eventually lead to affirmative action and other worrisome requirements. They argued that since the majority of voters in the state agreed with them, it should become the law.

The plaintiffs' and the defendants' lawyers often butted heads and pressed each other with objection after objection, leading to some very trying and heated exchanges. Each side challenged the other over the validity of competing evidence and studies on sexuality, genetics, biology, morality, crime statistics against or by homosexuals, prevalence of homosexuality, and the history of homosexuality. As one day ran into another, the testimony ranged from tedious, to esoteric and philosophical, to humorous, and neither side revealed any smoking gun or appeared to score any major case-turning points. Still, each day garnered press attention in both local and national newspapers, often with colorful front page headlines: "Sexual orientation 'gene-linked;'"[85] "A judicial circus is in town."[86]

Eventually, after nine days, after all the witnesses, the objections, and the final motions, each side made their closing arguments. It was their last opportunity to give meaning to the evidence presented and provide the judge and the public with an understanding of what the trial had been all about and what was at stake.

Jean began with a recap and critique of the state's arguments that the amendment served legitimate state interest. She insisted that there was no compelling state interest, the standard she wanted the court to apply. She also addressed a range of other claims that the state included in their brief but did not argue at trial. She did so, she told the court, in order to create the fullest record possible, in anticipation that the case would be subject to appeals.

Jean concluded by returning to the evidence presented months earlier at the injunction trial. She reminded the court of the great harm that would be caused, of the testimony of the plaintiffs, and of the fundamental argument that she had made from the first day of the first trial: there was no real purpose, no legitimate purpose, no compelling purpose for the amendment; it was simply motivated by fear and hate and bigotry.

The first thing state solicitor Tim Tymkovich did when he rose to make his side's closing argument was place a large board on an easel. It contained a list of all the rights that would *not* be affected by the amendment. He referred back to this list again and again as he attempted to undermine the claims of the plaintiffs' lawyers that Amendment 2 would have a dramatic effect on the civil rights of gays and lesbians. He also tried to undermine the plaintiffs' claim that the motivation behind the amendment was bias, and addressed the issue of suspect class, refuting claims that homosexuality was immutable, or that homosexuals were powerless. He closed with a strong defense that the amendment served many legitimate and important state interests.

After gaveling the trial closed, Judge Bayless made plain that he would not be rushed as he was at the close of the injunction trial. Nor would he stay up all that night trying to decide how he might rule. In the end, Bayless took six weeks before rendering his judgment.

Using much the same language as he had in the first trial, Bayless deemed Amendment 2 in violation of the equal protection clause of the U.S. Constitution. "Colorado Ban on Gay Rights Laws Is Ruled Unconstitutional,"[87]

"Tossed out,"[88] "2 Unconsititutional"[89] were the headlines splashed across newspapers in Colorado and around the country. The entire front page of the *Rocky Mountain News* was devoted to the decision. "Amendment 2 struck down" was the headline and the half-page photo that accompanied the story captured the joy and relief felt by ACLU state director James Joy and Jean Dubofsky.[90] It had been a long journey to this trial and this decision. And the plaintiffs prevailed.

The battle over Amendment 2 was not over, however. Within days of this Bayless decision, the state launched an appeal before the Colorado Supreme Court, just as it had after his injunction decision in January.

When Jean stood before her supreme court peers and former colleagues during the two appeals to the state supreme court, it was both an odd and a familiar sensation. Joe Quinn had retired from the court by then, but her close friend, George Lohr, and her nemesis, Bill Erickson, were still on the bench, as were most of justices she served with. They were now joined by Mary Mullarkey, her colleague from the attorney general's office who had replaced Jean on the court. There was little she didn't know about the group arrayed before her.

In her old chambers, among friends, she was comfortable but not complacent or overconfident. Jean had been arguing before them for three years by then, but this case did not feel at all like any other appeal she had argued before. The justices must have felt the same way, that it was an extraordinary case, because the court allowed television cameras into chambers and, for the first time in the history of the Colorado Supreme Court, oral arguments were televised live.

The state's job was to persuade these justices that Bayless had been wrong in his reasoning and wrong in his ruling. Persuade them that there were legitimate and compelling state interests served by the amendment. Persuade them that the plaintiffs failed to prove that the amendment would cause direct or irreparable harm to anyone. Surprisingly, that job fell to Attorney General Gale Norton.

Appeals before the Colorado Supreme Court were generally the job of the solicitor general or a deputy attorney general not the elected attorney general. When Jean worked for J.D. MacFarlane, he would have been the last person in the office to make oral arguments at the supreme court. While Jean was sitting as a justice, she rarely saw an attorney general argue a case, even in big, important, controversial cases. Especially, in big, important, controversial cases.

But Norton, the attorney general, handled the oral argument herself during the injunction phase, a tactical error, because when matched against Jean, she never had a chance. Gale Norton was undoubtedly a good politician and maybe even a brilliant lawyer, but she stumbled that day. As one attorney who had been in the chambers said, "She may be very good at some things but it doesn't include arguing before an appellate court. She was not up to the task at the first appeal; she just was totally out of her element."

The justices ruled to affirm the Bayless injunction decision by a vote of six to one. The only dissenting vote, not surprisingly, was Justice William Erickson. In his dissent Erickson argued that the state *had* shown three areas of legitimate state interest: establishing uniform statewide laws, protecting religious freedom, and managing the resources well so that civil rights could be enforced.

After the October trial, when the state appealed again, the result was exactly the same, six to one. There were momentary cheers and great relief on the part of the plaintiffs' team when the Colorado Supreme Court affirmed the Bayless decision once again. They were heartened that the justices turned back most of the state's arguments about legitimate state interests and, although the opinion opened the door a bit to the state's concern over religious liberty, they closed it just as quickly, finding that a constitutional amendment was hardly the least restrictive or only means possible to address that concern.

In addition to finding the amendment unconstitutional, the Colorado Supreme Court decision the second time around gave the plaintiffs' team something else to cheer about. "They interpreted Amendment 2 as something that had 'meaning,'" Jean said. The justices concluded that the amendment, if allowed to become law, "would have a broad discriminating impact." This was a critically important interpretation. At various times throughout the long legal process, the state attempted to argue that Amendment 2 had no real meaning, that the plaintiffs' claim of broad impact restricting the rights and freedoms of homosexuals was unfounded. They occasionally compared Amendment 2 to the state's "English only" amendment, an amendment that never was enforced and never really had any impact on anything. "But the Colorado Supreme Court ruled that Amendment 2 was not something that was meaningless, that it had real meaning," Jean said. That was key because the U.S. Supreme Court would be bound by the interpretation of the state supreme court, if the case ever made it to the high court.

The ruling of the court, written by Justice Luis Rovira, caused some head scratching as well. Rick Hills, Jean's associate who came to play a decisive role in constructing the legal strategy, described it as something a lot worse than head scratching. "I was banging my head against the wall when I saw the opinion as it came off the fax machine." What concerned Hills was of concern to Jean as well. Rovira's opinion, and the concurring opinion written by Justice Gregory Scott, both relied heavily on the plaintiffs' argument that the amendment denied homosexuals their right to participate equally in the political process. While the political participation argument helped them through the trial and the appeals process in Colorado, getting the U.S. Supreme Court justices to buy that argument was an entirely different matter.

"I thought the political participation theory was a load of hog wash from the very beginning," Hills said. "Focusing on voting and claiming that state constitutions can't strip things away that people can vote on at the local level seemed like a goofy theory. We might have been able to persuade Justice Rovira of that, or get it past the Colorado justices, but I knew we would be dead on arrival at the Supreme Court."

The guts and the roots of the political participation argument came from the Fourteenth Amendment's equal protection guarantee. That guarantee, with the help of case law and legal precedents, morphed into an equal right to vote guarantee which, in the case of Amendment 2, morphed into an equal-right-to-participate-in-the-political-process, i.e. the right to seek relief through the local or state political process.

"We knew from the outset that the political participation theory had some potential weakness," Jean said. They hoped and expected their stronger argument, that there was no legitimate interest served by the amendment and that it was motivated solely by animus and bias, would carry the day; but the plaintiffs also presented other potential arguments, including the equal rights/political participation argument. Unfortunately, the argument that Rovira relied on most was the plaintiffs' weakest argument, the one that had the least chance of making it past the nine Supreme Court justices. And it appeared increasingly likely that the Supreme Court might be exactly where this case was headed. Although the state supreme court ruling is the end of the line for most cases that come up through the state court system, this case was not like most cases.

23

The Supreme Effort

Jean thought the decision of the Colorado Supreme Court should have been the end of it. It had been decided again and again, twice in district court and twice on appeal before the Colorado Supreme Court justices. Each trial, each appeal, each opinion and final ruling varied slightly, but the basic result was always the same: Amendment 2 violated fundamental guarantees of equal justice and was unconstitutional.

She was not surprised, however, when Gale Norton filed an appeal on behalf of the state of Colorado requesting that the United States Supreme Court accept the case for review. Months went by, as both sides watched and waited to see what the high court would do. On a cold raw Wednesday in February 1995, the Supreme Court announced its decision, granting certiorari in *Romer v. Evans.* There would be one more hearing and one more ruling. This time, the final ruling. The United States Supreme Court would have the last word.

The two sides couldn't have been farther apart in their arguments, but now that the case was headed to the Supreme Court, they shared the view that *Romer v. Evans* could be as pivotal for gays as the *Brown v. Board of Education* decision was for blacks, perhaps the most important civil rights case in a decade.[91] When the court announced it would take the case, Norton predicted it would become a "landmark decision." "The importance [of this case]…is reflected by the fact the court today turned down over 500 cases at the same time they took only one case, and that one case was Amendment 2," she said.[92]

After two trials and two appeals, there was a déjà vu quality about beginning for the fifth time the process of honing, adjusting, and repositioning their arguments. Even so, now that the case was before the nine Supreme Court justices, the familiar was dwarfed by the unfamiliar. The stakes were higher, of course, and that would be difference enough. But the players, the rules, the setting and the historic significance took the participants into uncharted territory.

Another change from earlier in the process was the quiet permeating Jean's law office. It was no longer a busy, bustling place; she was practicing alone again. Suzanne Goldberg had long abandoned her nest down the hall in the law library and returned to New York. The weekly gatherings around Jean's conference table and the daily hour-long conference calls were ancient history. Rick Hills, her legal soul mate, had moved to the University of Michigan where he and his wife both found fulltime professorships. Jean was happy for him and wished him well, especially since he agreed to continue to be available should the *Romer v. Evans* journey have more miles to travel. When the court announced they would take the case, the first person she called was Rick Hills. Together they made a plan, one final time.

The decision by the Colorado Supreme Court would be the decision before the U.S. Supreme Court, with oral arguments scheduled for October 1995, seven months away. It would be that opinion, written by Justice Luis Rovira, that Jean, Hills and the other lawyers would begin to take apart and put back together again. Their focus would be to persuade at least five Supreme Court justices of the soundness of Rovira's analysis and reasoning.

Jean and Rick Hills could talk in shorthand by now, familiar with what the other was thinking. They knew to trust each other's instincts, to take seriously each other's worry about the strength and weakness of various nuances of their arguments, and appreciate each other's readings of individual justices and what it would take to win each one over. They would have months together to prepare for oral arguments. Before they began that process of deconstructing and reconstructing the Rovira opinion, however, Jean had another matter to attend to. Something she needed to do alone.

The day the high court announced it was taking the case, Jean booked an airline ticket to Washington. A week later, Jean was sitting in the Supreme Court Chamber, in front of the nine justices, listening to that day's oral arguments. She was sitting in the observer's section, off to the side, not at the front row table near the podium where she would be in the fall when the oral arguments for *Romer v. Evans* were scheduled to be heard.

Her plan for this first trip to Washington was to get the lay of the land, to observe and absorb as much as she could about the process, the mechanics, the players, the peculiarities of each individual justice, and the traditions. She wanted to learn from others what she didn't know and what she should expect as the next six months would unfold.

She came armed with a list of more than a dozen names of key people to contact while she was there. Some were individuals who had reached out, offering help. Others were recommended as wise men, individuals she should talk to and learn from: senior attorneys in the Justice Department, former clerks of the current justices, experienced litigators who had argued frequently and successfully in front of the court. She was there to seek advice and to learn. But she was also there, maybe mostly there, to deal head-on with the question of whether or not she would be the one standing before the nine justices on the day of oral arguments. She was there because of the doubters who, once again, but now more forcefully and directly, suggested it was time for Jean to step aside.

There had been questions earlier in the case, of course, suggestions that Jean might not be the right attorney to lead the case. But it was different now. The question about whether or not, now that the Supreme Court had agreed to hear this historic case, it was time for the experts to take charge, was openly discussed in the offices of national gay rights organizations and around conference tables at prestigious law offices and law schools across the country. The sentiments expressed were familiar: The case was too important for a lawyer no one had ever heard of, a sole practitioner, an attorney who had never argued a case before the Supreme Court. Amateur hour was over and it was time for Jean to step aside, to turn the case over to the renowned constitutional law litigators with experience before the court. Or time for the New York or Washington or San Francisco-based civil rights and gay rights attorneys, who worked full-time on these issues, to take over.

Since only the plaintiffs could decide whether or not to replace Jean, one of the lawyers working on behalf of the national groups called Darlene Ebert, the attorney for the most prominent plaintiff, the city of Denver, and encouraged her to ask Jean to step aside. It was not a long conversation. "We had the utmost respect for Jean. She had proved every step of the way to be a superb attorney. Precise, poised, careful," Ebert said. "I told him there was no chance it was going to happen."

Jean not only knew of those conversations, she was occasionally even a part of some of them. During discussions of broader strategy issues among the legal team, the possibility of seeking a new lead counsel was hinted at. Matt Coles, a co-counsel on the case from the ACLU's Lesbian and Gay Rights Project didn't simply hint; he was very direct with Jean and he put it in writing. He urged her to pursue bringing in someone else to argue before the justices.

"It could go either way, and the outcome may well depend on oral argument," he wrote. "I know how much this cases means to you personally and I know how difficult it would be for you to watch someone else argue it a this point." But it was too important to let those feelings get in the way, he cautioned.[93]

Although there had been differences between Jean's team in Colorado and the staff of the ACLU, Lambda, and other national gay rights organizations, a healthy measure of respect grew among the lawyers participating in the case. They had come together, and all had contributed in different ways. Coles had been a central part of the legal team from the very beginning, had been on all the conferences calls, reviewed all of the brief drafts, and made cogent recommendations for improving various arguments. His suggestion that Jean turn over the case to someone else now that it reached the critical Supreme Court stage was not meant to show disrespect to Jean, or what she and the team had accomplished. He believed, as did many others, that it was not an unreasonable suggestion if, indeed, it was clear that the case would have a better chance of success with someone else taking charge.

The suggestion that Jean step down may have been partly about improving the chances of success, but it was likely also a revisiting of something that had been in the air since the very beginning: that Jean was not one of them, was not a lesbian. Throughout the case, when disagreements occurred, it often seemed that at the root of those disagreements were lingering suspicions that Jean's views and decisions might be lacking in some way because of her disconnectedness to the gay experience. Some of the gay rights lawyers believed that as competent as Jean was as a legal theorist, she might not have the same high level of skill and judgment as someone whose life work, passion, and very being were wrapped up in the cause.

"I understood," Jean said. "These were people and organizations whose whole lives were centered around fighting things like Amendment 2. I knew how personal it was to them." But if part of the rationale for why someone else should take over the case was because they thought this case was not personal enough to Jean, they were wrong. It was personal to her too.

She took the suggestions for a change seriously, however. It was no longer simply a Colorado case; it was an historic case of national consequence, the most important gay civil rights case in a decade, and she agreed that it was too important not to have the best advocate possible.

"I had to take a serious look about who should argue it because so many people were calling and offering and suggesting various people," she said. "I think every famous constitutional law professor in the country called me. And I was ready to let someone else argue the case if I thought that would give us the best chance. If it was obvious that someone could do it better, if I ever thought, 'oh yes, this is the right person', then I would have given it up."

Jean was not riddled with doubts about her own capabilities. In fact, she felt just the opposite. She had spent eight years as a supreme court justice in her home state, and by 1995 had another half-dozen years arguing before that judicial body. She lived and breathed the appeals process; she understood the crosscurrents and challenges. And she had no doubts about her own ability to handle oral argument in front of the U.S. Supreme Court. But she also wanted to be scrupulous about examining what was best for her clients, who by now reached far beyond Richard Evans and Angela Romero and all the other named plaintiffs, to the hundreds of thousands of homosexuals in Colorado who would be impacted directly by this decision, and the millions all across the country who would suffer if the Supreme Court did not rule in their favor.

"I wasn't afraid of making the arguments. I had done umpteen oral arguments by then. I wasn't intimidated about doing it. But I was intimidated by the fact that we could lose." After coming so far, she had to be sure that every next decision, every next step, brought them closer to what would be an historic win.

Jean laid out her own strategy and timetable for preparing for oral argument. Ascertaining whether or not to bring in someone else to argue the case before the Supreme Court was one of the first issues she needed to resolve.

"When I made that first trip to D.C. to begin the preparation, I went to talk with people in the Justice Department and solicitor general's office and lawyers around Washington," Jean said. "One of the things I asked about was whether I should continue to have the case or not; whether I should be the one to argue the case," she said. She had a list with her of the mostly highly recommended appellate attorneys and constitutional law luminaries that had been suggested as her replacement. "I didn't want to be blindsided if there was an obvious alternative to me."

As she discussed the case with the people she sought advice from, she slowly crossed one name after another off the list. During two separate trips to D.C. during February and March, and scores of meetings and conversations, she heard:

"He's brilliant but impossible to work with."

"They wouldn't put in the time."

"He's quirky and may not be respected by the court".

"He's eloquent but not doing it so much anymore".

"There's a question about how hard she might be willing to work."

"He tends toward being gimmicky."

"He has a great deal of credibility, but I don't think he'll be willing to do it."

"She's smart enough, but I'm not sure she's had enough direct experience with the court."

As Jean weighed the possibility of each person suggested or each person offering to take the case, she began to doubt whether any of them would come to know the case as she knew the case; would have the feel for the details or the knowledge of the history of the case, or of Colorado, that she had; would put in the work necessary or make the case their top focus.

She met with a handful of attorneys who had clerked for Justices Kennedy and O'Connor and other current justices, and consulted with appellate attorneys and Justice Department officials who often appeared before the court. Towards the end of her second trip, she visited with attorneys at the Hogan & Hartson law firm. The head of their appellate division was John Roberts, who would later be appointed Chief Justice of the United States. Roberts had clerked for the current chief justice, William Rehnquist, had argued often and successfully before the court, and had a reputation as one of the finest appeals attorneys in the city. He had a great deal of knowledge about the inner workings of the court and of the individual justices.

When Jean met with Roberts, they talked a good deal about the members of court, and discussed the legal theory and strategy options. Roberts advised Jean to focus on the first question she might be asked by the justices, which he thought would be "What does it mean? What, exactly, would the impact of Amendment 2 be?"[94] Then the conversation turned to whether or not Jean should seek someone else to replace her at oral argument. Roberts was well aware that Jean was under some pressure to do just that.

Although he understood the rationale for the advice she might be getting, he held a different view. He told Jean that it wasn't always necessarily an advantage to have one of the more well-known constitutional experts, or one of the same Washington lawyers who frequently came before the court do the oral argument. Justices often tire of the same old faces, he said. It was a view that Jean had heard before from a few others.

The most important thing, Roberts told her, was intimate knowledge of the record. Knowing the case inside and out would be key. You
know the case better than anyone. You've lived with it, you understand
the facts, the journey; you understand Colorado and the whole
history of how this case made it to this point, he said. Don't be in any
hurry to give up this case to someone else. You might just be the best
person to argue this case.

Maybe Jean heard what she wanted to hear. Or maybe she heard
what she needed to hear to be able to move on. She was impressed
with Roberts and could see how good he would be if he were arguing
the case. Jean mused later that he was the only one who, if he had
shown an interest, she likely would have invited to argue the case.

"If he wanted to do it, if he had told me that he thought he should
do it, I probably would have let him," she said. But he didn't say any
of those things. For a variety of reasons, Roberts couldn't do it or
thought it would be a conflict or that he just wasn't right for it.
When Roberts told Jean he thought she was the right one take this
case before the court, that settled it in her mind. She would argue the
case.

In truth, Jean wasn't looking to find someone else, wasn't determined
to find someone else. There was nothing she wanted more than to be
the one standing at the podium in front of those nine justices. Nothing she wanted to do more than finish what she had started so many
years before. Except for one thing. The only thing she wanted to
do more than argue the case was to win the case. If she had found
an alternative, someone better, she would have done the right thing.
But in the end there was no one else she felt more confident in than
she did in herself.

In addition to having confidence in herself to get it right, Jean
worried that someone else might simply get it wrong. Other members

of the legal team and some of the experts she met with in D.C. were still convinced the argument should center on the fencing out of an individually identifiable group from the ability to participate in the political process. Jean and Rick, however, remained convinced that the political participation argument was not a winning argument. One of the concerns Jean had about turning the case over to someone else was that another attorney might not fully appreciate the flaws of the participation argument, might not fully make the pivot away from equal *participation* to a stronger equal *protection* argument. Instead of giving them a better chance for success, Jean worried that bringing someone new in would do just the opposite.

The nuances of the participation vs. protection argument proved all absorbing. At one point she and Rick discussed whether to abandon the political participation argument altogether and not include it in their Supreme Court brief. But abandoning the original argument had its own pitfalls. It would have created such outrage with their legal partners that it could have upended the coalition. It might also have been viewed as a sign of panic, raising concerns that the plaintiffs were losing confidence in their own arguments. While discussed, it was just as quickly dismissed as a viable option.

In fact, keeping the political participation argument in the brief served another purpose. "Sometimes its good to give the court something they can reject," Hills said. "Give them some crazy theory or a Hail Mary pass they can reject, so after, when it rules against you on those things, it can rule for you on another theory and the court can look moderate, can appear Solomon-like."

Once Jean settled the question of who would argue the case, she moved forward with preparations and used additional trips to Washington to seek advice on strategy, on legal theory, on what to expect from various justices, on how to use amicus briefs, and what to include or not include in the briefs.

She occasionally wrote a summary memo after a series of meetings to highlight what she learned, what worried her, what she wanted to make sure she double-checked. Sometimes her notes were simply for her own use; other times she would send the summary memo on to Rick. He would do the same thing: mostly write short notes on conversations with others or summaries of memos he'd received, laying out what he had learned and what they needed to consider. Then they would deliberate over how to proceed, whom to enlist to help on what, what possible solutions or directions they should take to ameliorate some issue or redirect an argument. The clock was ticking again, with most of the concern and focus centered around how the case would be "briefed", how exactly to use the fifty pages allowed by the court, which theory or theories would serve best as the foundation of the central arguments, what evidence would be included or excluded, all based on calculations around which arguments might persuade or dissuade an individual jurist.

No discussion was needed about whether or not to include one piece of evidence; the CFV brochure that landed on hundreds of thousands of doorsteps just days before the election in November of 1992. More than any other evidence presented at the earlier trials, Jean wanted the justices to see for themselves what the battle over Amendment 2 had been all about. Not only to see, but to feel. The hate. The animus. The bias. The real reasons behind the amendment.

Another piece of the of the strategic puzzle related to amicus curiae briefs, the "friends of the court" legal briefs written by interested parties with strong views and advice to impart to the court. The number and content of amicus briefs are hard to control and, in fact, often have little impact, especially when an overabundance of individual briefs are submitted by numerous diverse interests. The justices rarely read or consider more than a few. But successful Supreme Court litigators often credit their success in part to the saliency and power of one or more key amicus briefs.

Jean received many offers of briefs, with various authors, organizations, and interest groups suggesting what they might focus on, so many that she worried the plethora of possible briefs had the potential to overwhelm the court. Her solution was to outline a plan for consolidation, with suggestions about who she wanted to write the key briefs, and which particular piece of the overall argument each one should concentrate on. Limiting the number and focus of the briefs, and having the most prestigious names attached to those few, increased the likelihood that clerks reviewing the briefs would note particular ones for the justices' attention.

Suzanne Goldberg, staff attorney for Lambda Legal Defense and Education Fund, volunteered to take on the job of riding herd on the many offers of help, consolidating and grouping them into a series of amicus briefs that met the strategic objectives. That assistance took a huge load of the shoulders off Rick and Jean who, in addition to working on the plaintiffs' brief, were focused on two amicus briefs in particular: one being prepared by the Clinton Justice Department and the brief being drafted by Harvard law professor and esteemed constitutional scholar, Laurence Tribe. Still worried about the flaws in the political participation theory, Jean and Rick worked closely with Tribe to find another way to advance their argument by framing it more directly as equal *protection*. If they were successful at this re-framing, and paired with the "no legitimate government interest argument," they felt they would have a strong two-part argument that would secure the five needed votes.

The court generally gave briefs from the administration serious consideration. Jean and others on the team had numerous conversations with lawyers in the Justice Department and were confident the administration brief would prove persuasive. National gay advocacy groups, civil rights groups, and members of Congress had lobbied the White House hard, and fully expected the Clinton administration to join the case on the side of the plaintiffs. But when the June deadline came to submit amicus briefs, the president had not yet signed off on the brief that the White House counsel's office had already fully vetted and recommended to the president.

Not ready to give up, one of the Justice Department attorneys called to ask if Jean would seek a one-week extension, hoping to give the administration time to resolve the impasse. Without telling him why, Jean asked the state's lead attorney, Tim Tymkovich, if he would agree to their request to extend the deadline for amicus briefs for another week. He agreed. In the end, however, the Clinton administration made a last minute decision not to file its brief.

"It was disappointing," Jean said. "And it was all politics," another indication of how far right the country was moving, and how fraught gay politics were at the time. Clinton had been elected with the help of gay Americans and with promises to end the ban on gays serving in the military but instead had settled on "Don't Ask, Don't Tell" as the nation's policy. With the president's refusal to weigh in with the court on behalf of the plaintiffs, he had once again disappointed and angered gay rights advocates who once had such high hopes for what could be accomplished during a Clinton administration.

With or without the backing of the White House, the Tribe brief, written on his behalf and on behalf of four other prominent constitutional scholars, remained the most crucial. It had been the focus of attention for months, the subject of phone calls, memos, discussions among Rick Hills, Jean, and Larry Tribe, and discussions that each of them had with other experts along the way.

Jean, Rick, and Tribe debated and obsessed over minute phrases that had potentially monumental impacts if they could get them just right. Their Rubik's Cube-like discussions calculated how far to move one piece of the argument, and in what direction, in order to satisfy or persuade one justice without such a turn undermining the support from another. Their main focus was on swaying justices Kennedy and O'Connor, taking care that any changed nuance not threaten what they considered three solid votes from justices Breyer, Ginsburg, and Souter.

In the end, the Tribe argument was a very direct one and, in hindsight, appears obvious: a law that on its face takes away from one group the protections that are available to everyone else is a clear infringement on the equal right to protection guaranteed under the Constitution. On that basis alone, Amendment 2 should be declared unconstitutional, he argued. On its face, Amendment 2 violated the Fourteenth Amendment's declaration that "no state shall make or enforce any law which shall…deny any person within its jurisdiction the equal protection of the laws."

Instead of adding carefully nuanced layers to the argument or further delineating through case law or legislative intent rationale to buttress the equal protection declaration, Tribe argued that the power of the argument lay in its directness, simplicity, and elegance. There need not be any further case law or precedent or interpretation to find Colorado's Amendment 2 unconstitutional. The Fourteenth Amendment is clear and unequivocal. The final Tribe brief language was incorporated into the plaintiffs' brief and became the glue that held all of their arguments together.

The final tinkering with the language of the briefs on both sides continued until the moment they had to be sent off to the printers in June. Once the briefs were submitted, preparation for oral argument began. Jean's preparation consisted of drafting responses to dozens of potential questions, then testing out phrases that might be more or less effective, more or less likely to steer her away from trouble, or catch the fancy of a particular justice. She also organized a number of question and answer sessions with various groups of experts to get the feel for questions coming her way at a rapid pace.

One practice session with a group of experienced appellate and gay rights attorneys proved particularly helpful. It was held in New York and organized by the ACLU and Lambda. "We just sat around for hours talking about one question or another," Jean said. "We discussed which questions to move off of quickly, which ones to use to make a quick turn to another point you want to get in, how to respond if a certain question came from one justice or another, that sort of thing."

It was also common practice at all appellate levels to hold formal mock arguments, full-dress rehearsals, with colleagues playing the role of justices. They were often held in rooms built to replicate a supreme court chamber. Jean, however, had never found them helpful. She felt the sessions tended to create a false set of pre-packaged rote answers that might not be responsive to the justices' particular concerns. She sometimes felt they often did more harm then good and she generally refrained from including a mock argument in her appellate preparation routine. It was, however, unthinkable to her colleagues that she would breach the de riguer practice session for her Supreme Court appearance, and so she agreed to hold one. Just one. "It was fine," Jean admitted. Both Jean and Rick remember being impressed with John Roberts, who played the role of one of the justices.

As the days crept closer to the scheduled argument, Jean and other members of the plaintiffs' team of lawyers began arriving in D.C. They settled into their hotel and worked out of donated office space, going over and over things for days on end.

Jean's close friends in Boulder knew she was in the middle of the demanding preparation for her argument before the court and had not seen a lot of her in recent weeks. So late on the Friday afternoon prior to oral arguments, the last person Josie Heath expected to hear from when she answered the phone was her friend, Jean. "The phone rang and I picked up the phone and it was Jean," Josie recollected. " 'Do you want to ride over to the football game with us?' Jean said. I said 'What? Where are you?' 'I'm at the airport. I just flew in.'" It was Matt's senior year, Jean explained. It was a big, big game and Matt was going to start. So, of course, Jean had flown home to be there.

Jean went to the game that night, spent time with Frank and Matt, then went for her regular visit with her father Saturday afternoon. Jean had moved him to Boulder a few years earlier and, while he did not live with the Dubofskys, he remained in need of regular care and attention from his daughter.

On Sunday morning, she drove to Vic's for coffee, a morning ritual when she was in town. Going to Vic's was usually just about coffee. But it also was part of another ritual for Jean whenever she was preparing for oral argument. It was Jean's place to figure out if she was ready, to test herself one more time, to be sure she was truly prepared to stand before a set of judges.

A coffee shop not far from their house, Vic's was nothing fancy. Sitting at the far end of a corner strip mall, it was almost hidden from view by the acre of parking spaces that separated the shops from the intersecting streets. Jean would get her coffee and sit at one of the tables in the far back, with only a blank legal pad and a pencil. There she would think a while and then begin writing what would be her opening or closing statement. Not in full sentences or paragraphs but in bullet form, key points, sometimes numbered or starred or under-lined, sometimes with arrows to move it later or earlier.

That Sunday morning, Jean pondered some of the basic questions as usual. Which justice might ask the first question? What kinds of questions might come soonest? And what would be her response?

Could she cite the exact perfect language of the exact opinion that would bolster her point? Using only what she had in her head—no notes, no folders—Jean used her time at Vic's to test whether or not she could nail the case when she was standing all alone in front of the justices.

Usually by the time she left she would have a list of items to review when she returned to the office, some notes about a precedent or an opinion or a law. On this Sunday, she did not leave with a list. Instead, on her legal pad was one big question mark: How will I begin? What, *exactly*, will be my next dozen words after I say "Mr. Chief Justice, and may it please the court,"

24

Nine Justices

Each new term of the U.S. Supreme Court begins on the first Monday in October. In the lead up to the 1995 term, the national legal press began to focus not on the first Monday in October but on the second Tuesday. *Romer v. Evans* "has become the most watched case of the term;"[95] an "historic battle" and the decision will be "hailed as one of the decade's most important civil rights rulings;"[96] will be a "watershed case," and not just for Colorado. The ruling portended "enormous consequences" for the gay rights movement nationally and for all the legal battles down the road.[97]

Jean Dubofsky, the relatively unknown appellate attorney from Boulder, Colorado, soon would be standing before nine Supreme Court justices to argue the plaintiffs' case. She felt ready. The immense weight, the responsibility, they were there too. But mostly, she felt ready. After three years of preparation, she had done all she could do. It was going to go however it was meant to go, she thought to herself

Jeanne Winer and Jean Dubofsky drove over together that morning from their hotel near Dupont Circle. When their cab pulled up in front of the U.S. Supreme Court on that clear, crisp Indian summer day in October of 1995, they saw bedlam in every direction. On the sidewalk, in the court plaza, and on the streets. Two long ragged lines snaked around the block, one for those with tickets and reserved seats and another for those without tickets, waiting, hoping they would be allowed inside the Supreme Court chambers to witness the proceedings for themselves.

The front of one line was more a disorganized campsite than a line. Chairs, sleeping bags, and backpacks, along with remnants of a large supply of half-eaten meals, lay along the sidewalk. The most determined of the crowd had spent the night, to improve their chances of obtaining one of the few open spots inside the courtroom.

Pat Steadman was one of those near the very front. The young attorney from Colorado had traveled to Washington for what would prove to be one of the most emotional days of his life. Fifteen years later he would rise to become a well-known and distinguished member of the Colorado State Senate. But it was his three years campaigning for gay rights and organizing lawyers in his home state to prepare for this legal fight that landed him on the doorstep of the high court this October morning.

In spite of the day's significance, Steadman appeared rumpled and disoriented, blurry-eyed and unshaven. He had camped out on the sidewalk all night to be one of the first in line in order to ensure that he would obtain one of the few remaining seats inside the court Chamber. Each side had been provided a limited number of reserved tickets, but there had not been enough for everyone involved in the case. Steadman had given his reserved ticket to another who had worked so hard.

Jean's son Josh was in the other line, the line for reserved ticket holders waiting for the doors to open. A Stanford University junior, he had flown across the country to be with his mother on this very special day. He had not slept on the sidewalk and he also did not yet have a ticket, but if things went as planned, his mother would find him and deliver a much-coveted ticket to the day's proceedings.

In addition to lines, groups were milling about, some small, some large, some with signs and banners, others marching in circles, shouting messages, all of them there to state their case or show support or simply to be present for that important day.

Satellite trucks lined up along the street, their telescoped dishes extended skyward. On the plaza, television crews were setting up and settling in for the day. It was a bit of a circus, but a relatively dignified one, as if the location and issue before the court demanded that. Etched overhead in the polished white marble atop the court building were the words "Equal Justice Under The Law." Far below, at the base of the eight columns atop the hill of steps that fronted the court, were puddles of waxy drippings formed from the remnants of the candle-light vigil that had begun at dusk the evening before and lasted through the night.

No one seemed to notice the two neatly attired women who made the long climb together up the steps, all fifty-two of them, leading to the entrance of the Supreme Court. They passed through the second row of majestic columns and disappeared.

Maybe Jean Dubofsky should have been awed by this beautiful marble temple of justice, but she wasn't. She'd lived among the archi-tectural symbols of democracy during her years working on Capitol Hill when she'd walked along this sidewalk fronting the Supreme Court almost daily. It had been a long time since Jean had lived in Washington, but she had always felt comfortable there. And she still felt comfortable this day, even with the special treatment she was accorded, the ability to simply ascend the steps and walk through the doors as if she truly belonged.

A security guard directed them down the hallway where the attorneys of the day were gathered. But Jean excused herself for a minute, turned and walked in the opposite direction, down another hallway to a side room near the clerk's office.

Frank, who had not made the trip with her but remained home with Matt, had called a law school friend who now worked at the court and was able to locate a ticket for their older son, Josh. Josh would be her family that day, there to support her.

And so, before taking her historic spot as the lead attorney arguing before the nine justices of the United States Supreme Court, Jean had one last thing to take care of. She went back outside, down the steps, and walked along one of the lines until she spotted Josh.

"Did you get some breakfast?" she asked, ever the mother. Then she semi-surreptitiously slipped the ticket into his hand. "Now don't lose this."

Jean walked up those steps one more time, through the towering columns at the top, and through the 17-foot high cathedral-sized bronze doors. She wondered to herself if every individual who entered there was made to feel so Lilliputian. This time she moved down the Great Hall that led to the oak doors of the Chamber, the all-white marbled hallway lined with busts of former chief justices—John Marshal, Taney, Taft, Charles Evans Hughes, and Earl Warren. Jean was flooded with images of the sacredness of the place and of the history that had been made there.

At exactly ten minutes before the hour, Jean Dubofsky, Rick Hills, and Jeanne Winer entered the Chamber together, and made their way to the front and through the rail to their designated place. The room was packed.

In the first row were Denver city attorney Darlene Ebert, their trial lawyer partner Greg Eurich, and Mary Celeste, one of the leaders of the original group of lawyers who had the foresight to begin preparation for this just-in-case case that made it all the way to the United States Supreme Court. There had been another line at a side door exclusively for attorneys who had been admitted to the D.C. Bar. Each of them had not only taken the time to apply to become a member of that bar far in advance, that morning they had left their hotel at three-thirty to be first in line to be sure they would not only get in the door but find their way to the most coveted seats, directly behind their legal colleagues.

The Supreme Court Chamber had a stately feel but, except for a thirty-foot ceiling, it was a surprisingly small and intimate space. Jean took her place at the long attorney's table that sat three feet below the slightly arched majestic mahogany bench where the justices would reside. The floor-length ruby-red drapes, fronted by four more soaring white marble columns, hung like a theatre curtain behind the bench. At exactly ten o'clock the justices slipped through three slits hidden in the curtains and, without ceremony, took their seats.

Every nook and cranny, every one of the churchlike pews in the Chamber was filled, jammed with people, elbow to elbow. It had been the hottest ticket in town for weeks. Jean couldn't see or didn't have time to see who else was there or where they were sitting. She was facing forward, her focus totally on the nine justices sitting in front of her. She didn't know that Betsy Levin, the CU Law School dean who had extended her hand to Jean years before, had waited in line, too, and had gotten the last of the eighty seats reserved for members of the D.C. bar. Nor did she know that Boulder Mayor Leslie Durgin, who was battling breast cancer, had skipped a scheduled treatment in order to attend.[98] Jean knew that Richard Evans was somewhere a few rows behind her, but not that he had already begun to cry.

Jean was gratified to see Ruth Bader Ginsburg sitting as one of the nine. Josie Heath always liked to say that if she had stayed on the Colorado Supreme Court, Jean, too, might have someday found a seat among those justices. Jean was sure that would never have been the case, yet she and Ginsburg could look in the mirror and see a resemblance to the other in the roads they had traveled. They shared Harvard Law and Ladies' Day and a lifetime of work seeking justice for others. They both had married attorneys who championed their careers in the law and were partners in raising their kids. Both had been excluded and demeaned and had found barriers along the way but simply walked around them to find their own path. Each figured out how never to reach too far, too fast, to instead just do the piece of work in front of them and do it well.

Once the justices were comfortably seated, Chief Justice William H. Rehnquist began simply. Without ceremony or greeting, he gave barely a nod towards the state's counsel. "We'll hear argument now in Number 94 1039, *Roy Romer v. Richard G. Evans*," he said.[99]

Tim Tymkovich, the solicitor general for the state of Colorado, was already standing at the podium, as he had been instructed, ready to begin as soon as the Chief Justice recognized him. The attorneys for both sides had received guidance about what to do, where to sit and stand, what to say, and how to refer correctly to the justices—Rehnquist would be "Mr. Chief Justice"; the others simply "Justice".

"Mr. Chief Justice, and may it please the court," he began, sounding calm and confident. This case, he said, was about the authority of the state over how to allocate lawmaking powers among state and local jurisdictions when it came to special protections for homosexuals, and the sole question was whether or not the state can reserve those lawmaking powers for itself. He cited *James v. Valtierra*, an earlier case decided by the court, referring to it as the definitive case that "authoritatively" resolved this question. That was as far as Tymkovich got before Justice Anthony Kennedy interrupted him at the one-minute mark. It was pretty much all downhill for the state from there.

Kennedy said he was not interested in the issue of allocation of power to make certain laws, essentially pushing aside the focus of Tymkovich's argument, and dismissing for the moment the relevancy of *James v. Valtierra*. The justice said he wanted to focus on something else first, the fundamental question of equal protection, what Kennedy referred to as the unique and troubling way Amendment 2 appeared to threaten those protections.

"Usually when we have an equal protection question, we measure the objective of the legislature against the class that is adopted, against the statutory classification. Here, the classification seems to be adopted for its own sake," Kennedy began. He then raised his voice and in a tone of incredulousness added: "I've never seen a case like this. Is there any precedent that you can cite to the court where we've upheld a law such as this?"

For a tick of the clock, life stopped in that courtroom.

Pat Steadman thought there might have been an audible gasp from the audience. But he wasn't sure because, like Richard Evans, by then he was crying too.

Steadman's night camped out on the sidewalk in order to be sitting in the audience had taken its toll.

"It was October so it wasn't exactly warm out," Steadman remembered. "And you don't really sleep. There are people everywhere, protesters chanting, full blown chaos all the way around. It was the most surreal experience and by the time the sun came out, people were fighting, cutting in line, crying, screaming, praying for you. The most bizarre experience. Such an ordeal. Two minutes into the oral argument I realized I was sobbing. It was partially because I was an exhausted emotional mess and partially because of what Anthony Kennedy said." Steadman was relatively new to politics, but by then he had learned how to count votes. "I knew then that Kennedy would be our fifth vote."

Tymkovich tried to explain that the case of *James* was relevant but Kennedy would have none of it. No, the justice said. That was a very different case. "The whole point of *James* was that we knew that it was low income housing and we could measure the need, the importance, the objectives of the legislature to control low cost housing against the classification that was adopted," Kennedy said. "Here the classification is adopted for its own sake...adopted to fence out, in the Colorado Supreme Court's words, the class for all purposes and I've never seen a statute like that."

Soon Justice Sandra Day O'Connor spoke up, the tone of her questioning suggesting even less patience with Tymkovich. "How do we know what it means?" she asked a number of different times. "The literal language would seem to indicate, for example, a public library could refuse to allow books to be borrowed by homosexuals and there would be no relief from that, apparently." He tried to explain that might not be the case, but O'Connor challenged his answer, interrupting and repeating her concern that the meaning just wasn't very clear.

"But how do we know that?" she asked more than once. "I don't read anything in the opinion that tells me what the thing means." The solicitor general's responses, to the extent that he actually was allowed to give an answer before being interrupted again, left things more confused, not less.

It was then Justice Ginsburg's turn to reinforce concerns over the potential breadth of the amendment. With this amendment, it appears that it means "everything," Ginsburg said. "Thou shalt not have access to the ordinary legislative process for anything that would improve the condition of this particular group....and I would like to know whether in all of U.S. history there has been any legislation like this."

Jean felt her whole body begin to relax when Kennedy first interrupted Tymkovich. "He was our fifth vote and if he was asking as his first question 'Has there ever been a law like this?' I thought, well, we might just have won our case." By the time Justices O'Connor and Ginsburg were through with their initial questions, it began to look like a rout. But only for a moment.

Justice Antonin Scalia then stepped in and tried to take the questioning in an entirely different direction, suggesting confusion over whether or not the subject of the amendment was sexual orientation or sexual conduct. If it was all about conduct, then it would be perfectly constitutional, he said, since many state laws criminalize a range of such behaviors. Tymkovich and Scalia bantered back and forth and together managed to either confuse or obfuscate whether the amendment spoke to more than conduct. This discussion clearly annoyed other justices who were trying to break into the conversation. And it annoyed Jean. "The amendment was clear. It had both words, orientation and conduct, in the language."

Justice Ginsburg and Justice Souter managed to elbow their way back into this debate. An aggravated Souter suggested that Tymkovich was possibly misleading the court or, at the very least, inaccurately characterizing the amendment. He went on at some length, eating up the state's precious allotted time.

Ginsburg pointed out other concerns, also at some length. She described how local governments had been the places in the past where people could go to get relief before it became possible to do so on a statewide basis. She used the suffragists as an example and asked Tymkovich if he thought a state amendment forbidding women from seeking the right to vote at the local level would have been constitutional back then. When he tried to answer in a manner that suggested he didn't quite get her point, Ginsburg challenged him to try to "cast your mind back to the days before the Nineteenth Amendment." The remark earned more than a few chuckles from the audience, a rare occurrence in this most serious of court chambers.

And so it went. Tymkovich's oral argument had been hijacked by the justices, one quickly taking the floor after the other, sometimes talking over the other, asking long questions that were as much making arguments as asking questions, often with one justice answering the question of another. "There was a point at which it seemed like Tim had literally taken a step back from the podium," Jean said. "The justices were just arguing among themselves and not really looking to him for anything."

Jean took no pleasure in seeing the justices batter the solicitor general. As she had experienced occasionally to her benefit in the past, rough treatment sometimes was meant to give judges cover so that later they would appear more even-handed when they voted for the side they had previously criticized so harshly. If not that, it surely meant that they were in a feisty mood, and her turn for battering would come soon enough.

Jean did take pleasure and comfort in the substance of the questions, however, when the debate among the justices turned to justification for the amendment. Jean's most effective argument was that the amendment lacked any rational government purpose, and she was content to have the justices sparring over that issue. As Tymkovich's time was coming to an end, it was clear that he had exasperated many of the justices. Justice Kennedy and Justice Breyer, in particular, were almost badgering him for his lack of clarity about what the amendment actually would or would not do. Answering that question was exactly how Jean had planned to open her argument.

When Tymkovich was finally able to wedge a request to save the remainder of his time for rebuttal into the back-and-forth between justices, all of ninety seconds remained. The Chief Justice thanked him, then directly turned to Jean. "Ms. Dubofsky, we'll hear from you."

Jean opened with the standard salutation, "Mr. Chief Justice, and may it please the court." Unlike Tymkovich, however, her voice was quite small and quiet, without gusto or strength, not a voice exuding confidence or command. Part of it may have been nerves, but it was also just her way. She had learned very early on that a quieter voice often invites more attention. As people have to strain to hear, they have to concentrate more.

She began as a teacher might, laying out the day's lesson, in the same manner that had served her well in other courtrooms. "Let me begin with how Amendment 2 should be construed and then discuss how our legal theories relate to its unique combination of breadth and selectivity."

"Amendment 2 is vertically broad," she continued, "in that it prohibits all levels of government in the State of Colorado from ever providing any opportunity for one to seek protection from discrimination on the basis of gay orientation."

If some expected a shift in the justices' behavior from the leaning forward, jockeying attempts to elbow themselves into the debate, cutting their colleagues off as they waited for their chance to jump in, it was not to be. Barely twenty seconds had elapsed when Chief Justice Rehnquist interrupted, stopping Jean before she had the chance to explain the second half of her description, the "selectivity" part.

Rehnquist's question was followed immediately by one from Justice Anthony Kennedy. Then another justice and another. The justices were not in the mood to sit back and allow Jean to make her arguments, and they gave her no more time to answer than they had given Tim Tymkovich. They bombarded her with question after question.

When she was allowed to answer, she consistently provided a brief "yes" or "no" statement, often quickly following up with a "but". But it doesn't matter because even without that, it is unconstitutional. But whether that were found to be true or not is immaterial to the constitutional questions. But that particular interpretation of the amendment is not necessary for this Court to find that Amendment 2 is unconstitutional.

With that series of "yes or no, but" responses, Jean managed to accomplish something the solicitor general was unable to do: provide clear and succinct descriptions of what the amendment meant and didn't mean. With each answer she took particular care to go to the heart of the unhappiness that Justice Breyer and others exhibited over the lack of clarity about what policies or laws the amendment did or did not allow. At one point, when Jean stated that the amendment's prohibitions clearly did include a certain type of policy, Breyer stopped her. "Well, what do we do when the counsel from the other side [is] saying it doesn't?"

Jean could have taken the bait and allowed it to become "he-said", "she-said"; or she could have directly accused Tymkovich of either dissembling or simply being wrong. But she did neither. Her description of what the amendment prohibited, she said, was not her *interpretation*, but the exact language of the Colorado Supreme Court in their written opinion.

"And where, exactly, did the Colorado Supreme Court say that," Scalia, the "doubting Thomas" of the group, asked, clearly not persuaded that Jean's answer was factually correct.

Jean did not miss a beat. With barely a downward glance, she answered: "It says that on page B dash 3, D 24, and D 25." It was her practice to handwrite page numbers from the briefs and appendices in the margin next to each key argument listed on her one-page typed outline. She almost never was asked, but it was always one of the last things she did the night before an oral argument. Just in case.

On these pages, Jean told the justices, the Colorado Supreme Court provides examples of protections that states and cities and government agencies would be precluded from enacting under the amendment.

Like dutiful students in a classroom, all of the justices simultaneously began to flip through their notebooks, trying to find the right page, whispering to one another or asking Jean to repeat those page numbers.

"Where?" "No, not that page." "E 25. Or is it D 25?" "In the white appendix?"

"D as in 'Does'?" asked the Chief Justice. "D as in 'David', or yes, D as in 'Does'," Jean answered. For a moment, the queries were all regarding which page and which paragraph. The sights and sounds of nine justices searching through their notebooks was a bit comical. Eventually they would all find the right pages.

Justice Scalia flipped through his pages like everybody else. "B 3? Where does it say that on B 3?" Scalia read a few sentences and, almost gleefully, announced that he didn't find what Jean said he'd find.

Jean pointed out politely that he needed to go to the first sentence above what he just read. Scalia bypassed acknowledging her correction and continued grilling Jean on other points of contention, as well as offering his own opinion, at great length, about special rights and special protections. Jean occasionally attempted to respond but realized she could not satisfy any of his concerns, finally only offering the observation that perhaps "we are having trouble with semantics."

Justice Souter interrupted Scalia's inquisition with a question of his own, which then led to more questions from other justices. But a subtle shift was unmistakable. The turning to the pages in the appendix became a figurative turning of the page in the tone and the rhythm and the content of the questions being asked. It was as if the spell of skepticism tinged with belligerence had been broken. The justices not only began to give Jean time to answer their questions, they gradually began to listen to her responses and ask related follow-up questions.

Most of the questions continued to address how narrow or broad a net the amendment cast, the same questions posed to the other side, as the justices sought clarity about the meaning and potential reach of Amendment 2. While Tymkovich's explanations were unsatisfactory and appeared to raise more issues than they resolved, Jean's answers seemed to reassure the justices, help simplify their decision, reduce confusion and anxiety over the possible wider repercussions of their decision. Her intent was to persuade them that, while the impact of the amendment to cause harm was wide and broad, resolving how wide and how broad had no bearing on the constitutionality of the amendment. Even a minimum, narrow finding was sufficient to constitute a violation of equal protection, she argued.

That was the message that Jean began to deliver, over and over again, using only slightly different words each time. It's true, she said, that in its broadest interpretation the amendment could mean lots of things. But the Court doesn't have to concern itself with or resolve how broadly the amendment might be interpreted in order to find Amendment 2 unconstitutional. She repeatedly used the phrase "at a minimum" to encapsulate how they could frame their analysis. At a minimum the amendment means this... or at a minimum the Colorado Supreme Court found that... Jean's message to the court was clear. Even if the court understands the impact of the amendment to be a small, narrow, de minimis discriminatory impact, she emphasized, that is sufficient to find it unconstitutional.

At one point, Chief Justice Rehnquist attempted to restate Jean's argument in the form of a question. Are you saying that we "can sustain the Colorado Supreme Court's decision overthrowing the statute by taking just what the Colorado Supreme Court said was the minimum meaning?" "Yes, that's correct," she responded. Soon, other justices were also using the phrase "at a minimum."

As her time was about to come to a close, Jean was asked the final critical question that had yet to be addressed. What about *Bowers v. Hardwick*, the 1986 Supreme Court ruling that sustained the Georgia law making sodomy a crime? The court did not want to touch that case; did not want their decision in *Romer* to be tied to that case in any way; did not want to open the Pandora's box that attempting to reverse *Bowers* would entail. And Jean let them off the hook.

You don't have to undo *Bowers*, she told the justices, to find Amendment 2 unconstitutional. Once again, Jean reassured the court that they need not break any previous barrier or plow new ground to rule for the plaintiffs.

With that, Chief Justice Rehnquist thanked her, the signal that her time was up. And, after thanking Tymkovich, announced that "the case is submitted." And that was that.

As is the tradition with important Supreme Court cases, at the close of oral arguments, representatives of the two sides made their way back down the marble hall and through bronze doors, and then down the dozens of steps to the plaza below where microphones had been set up. Matt Coles and Suzanne Goldberg walked down the steps with Jean, then stood before the waiting media to make brief statements and answer questions. A large group of applauding supporters was there as well; CLIP had raised money to buy plane tickets and book hotel rooms for the lawyers, plaintiffs, key supporters, and activists that had been part of the long legal journey.

For the rest of the day the Colorado group enjoyed being hosted and toasted at a series of events. First, a luncheon for invited participants, supporters and members of the media, although a few individuals who were not on the invitation list apparently crashed the event. "At the lunch, I remember being followed around by a man who kept putting his hands over my head and wanted to pray over me for all my sins," Pat Steadman remembered. "I couldn't seem to shake him."

Later there were additional conversations with the press, other social hours, parties, and celebrations that lasted well into the night. Steadman and others who had camped out on the sidewalk the night before, barely made it through the lunch before stumbling back to their hotel rooms and into bed, exhausted.

The Colorado contingent would fly back to Denver together the following morning. All except for Jean. She didn't attend many of the social events on the day of oral arguments and wouldn't be flying home with the group the following day. After the luncheon she returned to her hotel room, packed her bags and took a cab to the airport. "I had a bought ticket to fly home that same day. I think I was so afraid it might go badly and, if that happened, the last thing I wanted to do was stay around and have to face everybody."

But things hadn't gone badly, at least not for Jean's side. The *Washington Blade* ran an editorial cartoon with caricatures of Jean and Tymkovich standing on the steps outside after oral arguments, the pillars of the Supreme Court in the background. The cartoon shows a dignified Jean stating that she thought "the justices asked good questions." Tymkovich was drawn with tape over his mouth and unable to speak, wrapped in bandages, and scuffed up, as if he had emerged from a terrible beating.[100]

The *Denver Post* described both Tymkovich and the attorney general, Gale Norton, as appearing "shell-shocked" after the session ended.[101] Other reports stated that Tymkovich had served as a bit of a punching bag throughout the "tough, skeptical questioning"[102] while Jean's questioning was deemed "anti-climactic".[103]

Others may have viewed Tymkovich as battered and bruised, but he was not totally discouraged with what had transpired. He thought he saw evidence in the give and take with the justices that the political participation argument was not going to fly; and evidence that the court would be less likely to use strict scrutiny but instead would stick to a rational basis review, where he felt more comfortable that the state's arguments would meet the test.

Most of the reporting, however, had little to do with the two lawyers or the arguments they were able to make before the justices. Jean Dubofsky and Tim Tymkovich were but bit players in the whole drama. It was the justices who took center stage, both during the oral arguments and in the media coverage. On its front page the following day, the *New York Times* wrote that the justices debated "one another at least as vigorously as they questioned the lawyers before them."[104] The assessment could just as accurately have been that the justices debated each other even *more vigorously* than they did the attorneys.

In the end, the *Rocky Mountain News* and the *Denver Post* did the best job of capturing the pivotal moment of the day with their headlines quoting Justice Kennedy's opening salvo: "I've never seen a case like this."[105] At that moment, and soon after when Justice O'Connor made clear she, too, had grave doubts about the amendment, most court watchers believed the case was essentially over. Nothing Tymkovich or Dubofsky did after that likely mattered in the end.

That afternoon the nine Supreme Court justices withdrew to the Conference Room, the hallowed place where no clerks, no staff, no visitors were allowed. No one but the justices. They closed the imposing mahogany door and took their seats around the large polished oval table that commanded the room.

As was the custom, each justice would then speak in turn, the most senior to the most junior. Almost always it would gradually become clear as the discussion proceeded from one to another around the table where the case was headed. In this case, the discussion would lead to a decision to sustain or overturn the ruling of the Colorado Supreme Court. Once the outcome became apparent, the Chief Justice would assign a justice on the majority side to write the opinion. And then the waiting would begin again.

25

Waiting For History

The Supreme Court would hear many more cases during that fall and on through the winter and spring. Each justice would work on his or her individual opinions, circulating drafts, rewriting and circulating some more, until they deemed the opinion ready to take back to Conference once again for a final vote and agreement to issue the opinion as written.

Often it would take three or four months before the justices would rule, with no rhyme or reason to how long each case would take for a decision or which decisions might be expected to be released on any given Monday. Court opinions always came down on a Monday, except during the final weeks of a term when extra "opinion" days would be added for decisions still lingering. There would be no clues ahead of time. The only notice that the Court was ready to release a decision would come at eight in the morning via a phone call from the clerk's office on the Monday morning when the opinion was to be issued.

Jean initially thought it possible that the *Romer v. Evans* ruling could come quickly, perhaps even by the end of the year. But it became obvious soon enough that she was mistaken. January rolled into February and then into March. Jean made sure that on Monday mornings she was in her office early, long before eight o'clock, just in case that would be the Monday that the phone would ring. As Monday after Monday came and went without a decision, Jean's hopefulness and optimism ebbed and was slowly displaced by apprehension.

It didn't matter that on that day of oral arguments when Kennedy began his questioning by asking if there had ever been anything like this kind of law before, that Rick Hills had passed Jean a note saying "We've got him!"

It didn't matter that Jean felt sure Hills was right, that Kennedy's question signaled that they had won his vote, making it the coveted fifth vote needed to affirm the decision.

It didn't matter that after oral arguments Lyle Denniston, considered the most astute reporter covering the Supreme Court, smiled at Jean as they passed in the hallway outside Chambers and offered his congratulations. "You got it. 6-3," he said.

And it didn't matter that a friend of a friend had reported back from the secret world inside the Supreme Court that Anthony Kennedy had been assigned to write the opinion. Had Kennedy joined conservatives with a vote to overturn the Colorado court's decision, he would have been the last justice asked to write that opinion. If he was writing, he had to be writing for their side, had to be the fifth, or even the sixth vote, depending on where Justice O'Connor landed, that would affirm the decision and put an end to Amendment 2 once and for all.

None of that mattered. As March became April and April became May, Jean's concerns and anxiety grew. She'd learned over her years as a justice and as an attorney appearing before the court that whatever you think you know, you don't ever know. And so she worried.

"Of course, I worried. I worried about it all the time, right from the beginning. I worried about the reaction of people in the gay rights community to what I was doing. I worried about the merits of the case and getting the work done. It took an enormous amount of time just managing the whole thing. Dealing with the press and all the volunteers. Dealing with all the people who had theories. There must have been thirty-five professors who had theories that I had to listen to. I was worried about everything. But mostly I was worried that we would lose." Eventually she worried herself right into the hospital.

After the oral argument in October, Jean immediately returned to a backlogged caseload, which meant long hours and a good bit of travel. "I'd been to Canada for a deposition to be taken on one case, and I'd been an expert witness on some other case, so I'd been doing an awful lot of flying in the space of just a few weeks. I started getting an ache in my leg. It just felt as though my leg was full. It went on for a couple of weeks but I thought it was just all the flying."

One morning while stopping for her usual coffee at Vic's, she ran into an acquaintance that was heading across the street to the hospital to visit her husband. He had a blood clot in his arm. "She told me it was the oddest thing. He kept saying that his arm felt like it was full and heavy and felt achy. And it turned out to be a blood clot. I said to myself, 'Hmm, maybe I should call my Kaiser doc.' I went in to see him, being quite apologetic, 'I'm not really sure why I am here.'"

Her doctor checked Jean over and then used a measuring tape to see if there was any difference in the circumference of her two legs. That gave him the information he was apparently looking for.

"I was to go over to X-ray, he said. 'Go directly there, nowhere else.' So I went over and they did the X-ray. One radiologist called over another radiologist and said, 'Take a look at this!' I had a blood clot running from my ankle to my hip. They said they'd never seen anything like this before. So I got sent to a room in the hospital that was a kind of hyperbolic chamber, pressurized. I must have looked anxious, because the nurse tried to reassure me. 'Don't worry,' she said. 'I've never lost anyone.'"

Later, when one of the doctors asked Jean if she had been under any particular stress, Jean had all she could do to keep from laughing. Stress was thought to be one possible cause and Jean had to own up that, perhaps, they might be right about the cause. "I was in the hospital for a week on blood thinners. I survived."

On the third Monday in May, just as she had every Monday morning for months, she left the house early, stopped for coffee, and was alone in her office by seven thirty. Just in case. Alone, but not really alone.

Dozens of the attorneys and activists involved in the case, plus the hundreds who had gathered in the First Baptist church in Denver the morning after the election years before, and thousands of gay Americans all across the country had grown increasingly anxious about what the court would decide. They too had waited every Monday morning for their phones to ring. For someone to call them. Some even gathered in front of the Supreme Court each Monday morning. For more than seven months they had been holding their collective breaths and the waiting had become increasingly exhausting.

At exactly 8:01a.m. on Monday morning the twentieth day of May 1996, Jean's phone rang. "The person on the phone said only that this is the clerk's office at the Supreme Court and the decision is affirmed," Jean remembered. "They don't say anything more than that."

In acting to affirm the Colorado Supreme Court's decision, Amendment 2 was deemed unconstitutional and could not become part of the Colorado constitution. They had won. Jean ran across the hall to tell Frank, who was sharing the office with her at the time. Then she ran to stand by the fax machine, while trying to make phone calls at the same time. The written opinion was simultaneously faxed to all of the attorneys of record and so she stood patiently over her fax machine as the court's decision slowly began to spew forth, page after page.

"I called Rick Hills, and then I tried to call all the plaintiffs and Pat and Mary before they could hear from someone else." But she was too late. The word was out. She began receiving phone calls from those whose speedier fax machines had produced the decision minutes before.

As she was reading the section of the court's opinion where Justice Kennedy began citing the 1973 *Department of Agriculture v. Moreno* decision, the decision that prevented the federal government from denying food stamps to hippies, no one could see her as her left hand reached for the 3 x 5 card with four words she had written to herself three years earlier. It was still propped up on her desk: Hippie Food Stamp Case.

"It was the first thing I thought of when I took the case. It was the only case like that and I thought that might be how the court would see Amendment 2. I wrote myself that note and propped it up on my desk because I had learned by that point in my life that very often the first time you see a case, your first instincts are often good. And you need to remember that first instinct."

Kennedy referred to the Hippie Food Stamp case when he wrote that animus or hatred towards any group or the desire to harm a politically unpopular group is not a sufficient reason to treat any group, including homosexuals, as second-class citizens; that such animus is not a legitimate government interest and bears no rational relationship to any government purpose.

———————

Jean's son Matt was in his first period class at Boulder high school that May morning. By his own reckoning Matt had not been as aware of or as appreciative of the substance and weight of cases in his mother's professional life as his brother Josh. Josh had figured out that their mother arguing a case before the U.S. Supreme Court was a big enough deal that he flew to Washington to be there in person to watch seven months earlier. "I was eighteen years old and a senior and into sports," Matt said. "I honestly don't think I had much appreciation at all about the social and political implications of my mom's work." Until that day in May.

"I remember that day very well, mostly because one of the counselors came and pulled me out of class to tell me that she had won." Matt had not been one of the people who had been holding his breath, waiting for the court to rule. He knew there had been an important case that his mom and Rick Hills had worked on over the past few years, but beyond that he had no real awareness of the scope or importance or long wait for a landmark decision was swirling around the orbit of his life. There was no anticipation that this Monday would be different than any other Monday of his last month of his senior year.

"There certainly was never any expectation that I would be pulled out of class or anything like that. But what I remember most was that this counselor was so very emotional. There were tears in his eyes and it was obvious that it meant so much to him. I think the reason I remember it so well is because of how important what happened seemed to him. This was my mother, but it clearly meant more to him than it did to me, which was kind of a clue that this must have been big. That my mom had accomplished something huge."

That day may have been the beginning of a change in his perception of his mother as someone other than just "mom". "It took me a while," he said many years later, "but I think I eventually did figure out that she did some pretty special things." As a young father now, his appreciation for her remains fundamentally about the kind of mother she was, and all that she did to always make that role be her most important role in life. "But I realize now that she was also something else at the very same time."

His brother, Josh, described his sense of his mother in a very similar way. "For her family, she was just like what her mother was. She was there to raise the kids and do the cooking and totally be a mom. But then she was also like women of today, fully welcomed in and fully able to participate in public and professional life and to accomplish so much. She was like a bridge between these two worlds. She was not one or the other; she was both at the same time. And when I think about that, I think that is a pretty incredible thing."

———

Jean Dubofsky lived an ordinary and an extraordinary life. She experienced more than her share of incredible and memorable days and that Monday, May 20, 1996 was one of those days. Maybe the best of those days.

By noon word of the decision had spread and more than three hundred people had gathered in front of Boulder's city hall. It was part carnival, part celebration of how much the world had suddenly changed. The owner of a downtown restaurant gave voice to what so many felt for the first time. "Today I can stand here and not be a second-class citizen." [106]

Throughout the afternoon and into the evening, the streets filled with the sounds of beeping horns calling out from one car to another, part of an outpouring of unexpected powerful emotion that seemed to grip the entire city.

By evening more than 1,500 people rallied at the state Capitol in Denver. Some waved flags colored by rainbow stars and stripes,[107] while others used chalk to write "We Are Free!" on sidewalks and raised homemade signs with "Amendment 2 is Dead" and "6 to 3 for Sanity."[108] There were speeches and cheering, long embraces filled with tears and laughter, all in the midst of a dancing-in-the-streets kind of atmosphere. "I will never, ever, forget what it felt like that night," gay rights activist Tina Scardina said twenty years later.

Jean would never forget that day or that journey either but *Romer v. Evans* inevitably did begin to recede into her past with only occasional reminders. Little things. An unordered drink arriving from a flight attendant, sent back to her from a passenger who spotted Jean as she passed down the aisle. The only message a "Thank you." Or a bottle of champagne appearing on their table when Jean and Frank would be out to dinner. They would turn to look at who had sent it, and it would be a stranger with a glass held high, offering a knowing nod of gratitude.

————

When the Supreme Court handed down its ruling in 1996, it was in many ways the end of long journey. But in more important ways, more consequential ways, the court decision was a beginning, not an ending.

Twenty years later, the ripples from *Romer v. Evans* continue to impact millions of people. Before the court ruled in *Romer v. Evans*, gays and lesbians were often fired from jobs when their sexual orientation was discovered. Zoning laws prevented homosexuals from owning homes in certain neighborhoods and refusing to rent or sell to someone even suspected of being of being a homosexual was legal. Harassment and violence was common, with the police and the justice system often turning the other way. And sex between same sex couples, in the privacy of their own home, was a crime.

After *Romer v. Evans*, legislatures and courts around the country began to pivot away from laws and policies that fenced off gays and lesbians from the protections and rights that all Americans share. Slowly, and then not so slowly, through thousands of local and state ordinances and legal decisions upheld by one high court after another, gays and lesbians have become free to live and work where they want, and free to enjoy the same protections and benefits as all citizens.

Inevitably, new decisions by the U.S. Supreme Court and the opinions of Justice Anthony Kennedy, the court's swing vote, would be at the center of this sea change. And, whether coincidence or by design, those landmark decisions would always come on the very same day in late June, six years, sixteen years, and eighteen years later.

On June 26, 2003, in *Lawrence v. Texas*, Kennedy wrote—on behalf of the same 6-3 majority in *Romer v. Evans*—that the Texas law making it a crime for two people of the same sex to engage in sexual conduct was unconstitutional. The court would no longer be forced to use *Bowers v. Hardwick* as its guide.

On June 26, 2013, in the *United States v. Windsor*, in a 5-4 decision, Kennedy wrote that the Defense Against Marriage Act was a violation of the Fifth Amendment's equal protection guarantee. The federal government could no longer treat married same-sex couples differently when it came to benefits available to other married couples.

And on June 26, 2015 in *Obergefell v. Hodges* Kennedy wrote that the right to marry was a fundamental right under the Constitution. Same sex couples could no longer be denied the basic freedom to marry in any state or city.

With each new decision, Jean's her phone would ring with calls from friends who understood the history. Her history. Understood that without *Romer v. Evans*, there likely would not have been *Lawrence*. That without *Lawrence*, there might not have been *Windsor*. But with the three, there would be no turning back, making it all but inevitable that same-sex marriage would become the law of the land.

Her conversations with friends on the day of the *Obergefell* same-sex marriage decision were doubly joyful for Jean because just two days earlier the Supreme Court had ruled in another important civil rights case. Its decision fended off a challenge to the 1968 Fair Housing Act. No one had any reason to know of or remember Jean's involvement in the passage of that historic civil rights bill forty-seven years earlier. That was fine with her. But she knew, of course. And she remembered.

That week was another good week for justice. Which made it another good week for Jean Dubofsky.

Sources

This untold story relies on a rich lode of primary source material, including more than fifty hours interviewing Jean Dubofsky over the course of two years and a running two-day-long conversation with her when she accompanied me on a research trip back to her hometown of Topeka, Kansas. Interviews with Jean's brother, Allan, her husband, Frank, and their children, Josh and Matthew, provided an additional and important layer of perspective, insight, and clarity about various aspects of her life and history.

I also interviewed more than sixty individuals with unique connections to the times, the legal case, and/or Jean personally—lawyers, judges, clerks and staff; gay rights advocates and colleagues; childhood and college friends; political leaders, legal aid lawyers and statehouse colleagues; and reporters covering the time and events. Those first-person interviews and personal recollections provided the most extraordinary and revealing accounts of the details and perspectives of all facets of the life and times of Jean Dubofsky and serve as the foundation for the book's narrative arc.

When Jean generously granted me full access to boxes and boxes filled with a lifetime of private and personal files, a stunning documentation of her life through the decades, I was able to tap another rich collection of primary source material. Half of the worn and dusty cardboard boxes were retrieved from the basement of the family home in Topeka, Kansas. They were filled with photos, high school newspapers, press clippings, and family memorabilia. Most importantly, they were also filled with letters—more than 300—to and from Jean, her family, and friends, dating back to the late 1940s.

Other boxes came from Jean's basement and contained envelopes and folders overflowing with memos, professional correspondence, telephone messages, personal notes, photographs, news clips, report cards, travel records, pay stubs, and much more, chronicling Jean's adult life, from college to the present day.

To corroborate and clarify various accounts, I utilized a half-dozen archival collections (legislative diaries, reporters' notebooks, papers of prominent officials) located in the Western History Collection of the Denver Public Library and the Stephen H. Hart Library at the History Colorado Center. The largest archive, a comprehensive twelve-box *Romer v. Evans* collection, contained more than a thousand pages of memos, correspondence, handwritten notes of conversations and meetings, drafts of memos and briefs, news clippings and a trove of legal documents, including legal briefs, trial transcripts, and audio recordings of original proceedings.

Secondary sources were important as well and helped to enrich the broader context of the time and place and helped confirm specific facts and chronology. A handful of written profiles and television interviews helped sketch the outlines of Jean's life and hundreds of articles from the *Topeka Capital Journal, Denver Post,* the *Rocky Mountain News,* the *Daily Camera* and other local and national newspapers and magazines provided detailed coverage of Jean's involvement in cases or issues of the day, from her appointment to and leaving of the high court, to the controversies she was embroiled in during her years of prominence. Hundreds of additional articles in daily newspapers and weekly periodicals and legal journals provided rich contemporaneous accounts of the four-year *Romer v. Evans* saga, from local gay rights initiatives to the Amendment 2 campaign and its aftermath, to the Colorado trials and appeals, and the Supreme Court process.

I also immersed myself in the history of the times, watching newsreel coverage and documentaries and reading my way through memoirs, biographies, PhD theses, and seminal works of the civil rights struggle, the anti-war and women's movements, the founding of legal services agencies, the legislative history of various laws and the legal history of landmark Supreme Court cases. I spent time on the Harvard and CU campuses, at the U.S. Supreme Court, and even drove the dusty and winding roads of Belle Glade, Florida and Sugarloaf Mountain, Colorado, all to gain an appreciation for the times and places that influenced and shaped the subject of this story.

Citation Notes

Citations appear for all direct quotes taken from documents, news accounts, interviews conducted by others, and/or are available to the public, and for all materials available through any public source. In lieu of hundreds of additional superscript numbers cluttering every page to note an "author interview" citation, I use the following convention: all quotes *without* a citation come directly from author interviews. The source of the quote is identified in the narrative whenever possible. I honored the requests of many interviewees who did not want to speak for attribution by using "one justice said..." "a top aide to the governor remembered..." "a close friend described..." to identify the source as closely as I was able.

All interviews with the author were conducted during the period of July 2013 through March 2016. They were most often conducted in person and were recorded. Interviews conducted by phone were also most often recorded. When recording was not possible or when the interviewee asked that no recording be made, detailed and as close to verbatim notes as possible were taken, especially on the most relevant portions of the conversation. Brief summary notes about the broader context of each interview were often added as well immediately after each conversation. Specific quotes used in the book reflect actual words and phrases as recorded or noted, edited only for tense and syntax or when combining quotes from multiple conversations on the same subject matter to best render an accurate comment.

Most of the primary source material is unavailable to the public and remain a part of Jean Dubofsky's personal papers or in the author's possession. As much as possible, I have identified these sources in the narrative (E.G. "In a letter home to her parents." "In a memo from…" "In a handwritten noted dated…"). Additional citations are provided in the end notes when such narrative references may be inadequate or additional clarity is warranted.

List of People Interviewed

Sue Anderson
Adam Babich
Liz Birnbaum
Michael Booth
Jan Buchanan
Wade Buchanan
Emily Calhoun
Mac Danford
Lyle Denniston
Frank Dubofsky
Jean Dubofsky
Matthew Dubofsky
Josh Dubofsky
Allan Eberhart
Darlene Ebert
Greg Eurich
Livy Filipek
Dick Freese
Cary Hart
Gary Hart
Josie Heath

Richard Hennessey
Sally Francis Henson
Rick Hills
Tom Holland
Cindy Kahn
Terry Kelly
Howard Kirshbaum
Dick Lamm
Dottie Lamm
Betsy Levin
George Lohr
Kathy Maag
Jim Maag
Walter Mondale
J.D. MacFarlane
John Miller
Mary Mullarkey
Robert Nagel
William Neighbors
Margy McNamara Pastor
Bruce Pech

Joann Pfuetze
Lori Potter
Susan Westerberg Prager
Bill Prakken
Joseph Quinn
Magdaleno Rose-Avila
Sandra Saltrese
Tina Scardina
Morgan Smith
Pat Steadman
Wally Stealey
Tim Tymkovich
Curt Vazquez
Jeanne Winer
Mimi Wesson
Michael Zwiebel

Endnotes

[1] General Mills publications and correspondence, Spring 1960, Dubofsky personal papers. Questions retrieved fromhttp://thehairpin.com/ 2013/06/interview-with-a-one-time-betty-crocker-homemaker-of-tomorrow/ http://www.dailykos.com/story/2009/07/09/751822/-Are-you-a-Betty-Crocker-Homemaker-of-the-Future-or-Tomorrow-POLL#.

[2] All-American Table Dinner program, April 28, 1960, Dubofsky personal papers.

[3] "How Nice To Be a Pretty Girl And Work in Washington; Glamor, Excitement and Romance and the Chance to Serve the Country," *Life Magazine*, Vol. 52, No. 12, March 23, 1962, 28-35.

[4] Donnie Radcliffe, "The Water Street Group; 'New Frontier' Nostalgia At a Waterfront Reunion 20 Years Later," *Washington Post*, June 29, 1981, C1-3.

[5] Judith Richards Hope, *Pinstripes and Pearls* (New York: Scribners, 2003), 82.

[6] Ibid., 105.

[7] Retrieved from www.baseball-almanac.com/quotes/quodean.shtml.

[8] Oral history project, retrieved from ktwu.washburn.edu/productions/tornado/stories.htm.

[9] Honigsberg, Peter Jan, *Crossing Border Street: A Civil Rights Memoir*, (Oakland: University of California Press, 2000), 63-64.

[10] Mitchell Landsberg, "1968 Watershed A Quarter Of A Century Ago Seemed To Lurch From One Shock To Another As It Ended One Era, Began The Next." *Rocky Mountain News*, January 10, 1993, 122.

[11] Mondale, Walter, *The Good Fight* (New York: Scribners, 2010), 33-34.

[12] Ibid., 56.

[13] Ron Colliver, "Grads Told Protesters Get Results", *Topeka Daily Capital*, Wednesday, May 29, 1968, 2.

[14] Mrs. Paulette Puliam and Mrs. Robert Fay, letters to the editor, *Topeka Daily Capital*, June 8, 1968.

[15] Terry Van Fleet to Jean Dubofsky, December 1968, Dubofsky personal papers.

[16] Robert Coles and Harry Huge, "Peonage in Florida", *The New Republic*, July 26, 1969, 19.

[17] Ibid., 19.

[18] "Harvest of Shame," a *CBS Reports*, aired November 25, 1960, David Lowe, producer, Edward R. Murrow, correspondent. www.cbs.com/shows/cbs_evening_news/video/1662282819/1960-harvest-of-shame-/.

[19] "Migrant: An NBC White Paper," aired July 16, 1970, Martin Carr, producer, Chet Huntley, correspondent. www.nbcnews.com/video/date-line/38248547.

[20] Coles and Huge, 17-21.

[21] Ibid., 19.

[22] Ibid., 19.

[23] Ibid., 18.

[24] *Puerto Rican Farmer Workers v. Eatmon*, Civil No. 69-1417; 427 F.2d 210 (5th Cir. 1970).

[25] Robert D. Clark and Louise Crago, "Suit Says Workers Enslaved At Camp," *Sun-Sentinel* (Palm Beach County), December 12, 1968, 1.

[26] Associated Press, "Farmer Is Accused of Labor Peonage," *Ocala Star-Banner*, December 18, 1968, 25.

[27] Associated Press, "Plantation Terror Charged," *Detroit Free Press*, December 18, 1968, 5.

[28] Associated Press, "Terror of Migrant Workers Bared: Death Threats and Machete Beatings," *Daytona Beach Morning Journal*, Dec. 18, 1968, 10.

[29] Ibid.

[30] Lawrence J. Fox, "Legal Services and the Organized Bar: A Reminiscence and a Renewed Call for Cooperation," *Yale Law & Policy Review*, Vol. 17, Issue 1, 1998, 305. http://digitalcommons.law.yale.edu/ylpr/vol17/iss1/9.

[31] Frank Moya, "Jean Dubofsky Prepared for High Court's Black Robes," *Denver Post*, June 6, 1979, 27, 29.

[32] Dana Parsons, "Ex-Little Leaguer Recalls Hot Summer of Her Discontent," *Denver Post*, July 1, 1984, 1A.

[33] Pat Oliphant, "I'm From the American Civil Liberties Union, and We've had a Complaint," *Denver Post*, June 21, 1974, 22.

[34] "Ann-Marie Plays Ball; Suit Is Dropped," *Rocky Mountain News*, July 9, 1974, 5.

[35] Sandra Dillard, "Legislature Information Session Turns Into Debate— As Usual," *Denver Post*, March 17, 1975, 45D.

[36] Glennys McPhilimy, "ERA's Effect: More Psychological Than Legal" and "A Public Interest Lawyer," *Sunday Camera*, April 6, 1975, 25.

[37] Jack Cox, "Dubofsky Named Colo. Justice," *Denver Post*, June 17, 1979.

[38] Daniel Taylor, "High Court Commission to be Subpoenaed," *Rocky Mountain News*, August 16, 1979, 4.

[39] Jerry Kopel, "Memorial for State Senator Ralph Cole: An Outstanding and Fair Legislator," September 12, 1996. Retrieved from www.jerrykopel.com/b/ Ralph-Cole.htm.ind.

[40] Daniel Taylor, "Wunnicke Silent on Supreme Court Gossip," *Rocky Mountain News*, September 1, 1979, 4.

[41] *Kuhn v. Tribune-Republican Publishing Company*, 637 P.2d 395 (Colo. 1979), No. 79SC160.

[42] *Ortho Pharmaceutical Corp. v. Heath*, 722 P.2d 410 (Colo. 1986) No. 83SA293.

[43] Howard Pankratz, "Supreme Court Justice's Spouse Accused of Inside Information on Lawsuit," *Denver Post*, August 27, 1986, 1A, 7A.

[44] Associated Press, "Justice's Spouse Accused of Gaining Inside Information," *Daily Camera*, August 28, 1986, 9A.

[45] Associated Press, "Justice Dubofsky Denies She Revealed Evidence," *Daily Camera*, August 29, 1986, 15A.

[46] Ibid.

[47] Ibid.

[48] Agreed Public Statement, Exhibit B to Settlement Agreement, December 11,1986, Dubofsky personal papers.

[49] Howard Pankratz, "Supreme Court Justice's Spouse Accused of Inside Information on Lawsuit," *Denver Post*, August 27, 1986, 1A, 7A. "Colo. Supreme Ct Justice, Husband Accused of Inside Information," remains the headline in the *Denver Post* index and likely reflects the headline in another edition.

[50] "Legal Dispute Ends for Justice, Lawyer-husband," *Denver Post*, December 19, 1986, 3B.

[51] Senate Bill 84, 1987. Proposed revision or addition to Colorado Revised Statute 18-8-401; Transcript of Senator Cole's testimony at public hearing, Dubofsky personal papers.

[52] Jean Dubofsky to Governor Lamm, April 2, 1987, Dubofsky personal papers.

[53] Howard Klemme to Faculty Appointments Committee, December 16, 1987, Dubofsky personal papers.

[54] Ralph Cole to Acting Dean Clifford Calhoun, March 11, 1988, Dubofsky personal papers.

[55] Robert Nagel, "Critics of CU Law School Uninformed," Guest Opinion, *Daily Camera*, March 17, 1986, 12A.

[56] Charlie Brennan, "Dubofsky Says Prof Triggered Opposition," *Rocky Mountain News*, March 21, 1988, 9.

[57] Week In Review, *Sunday Camera*, March 20, 1988.

[58] Frank Ruybalid and John Jones, "Dubofsky: Stories the Media Missed," *Colorado Advocate*, Vol. 4, No. 2, Spring 1988, 1.

[59] Dubofsky personal papers.

[60] "A Quiet Trailblazer," news.kgnu.org/2014/11/a-quiet-trailblazer-jean-dubofsky/.

[61] Ibid.

[62] Anita Bryant video collection. Retrieved from http://www.back2stonewall.com/2014/07/achival-footage-of-anita-bryants-save-our-children-campaign-against-gays-video.html.

[63] Erika Stutzman, "Civil Rights, Marching Forward," *Daily Camera*, November 18, 2012, editorial page.

[64] Revised Municipal Code, City of Denver, Title II, Sec. 28-91, City of Denver, CO.

[65] Judy Harrington cover memo, June 1991, EPOC Denver packet, in author's possession.

[66] Brian Weber, "Equal Justice," *Denver Post*, October 21, 1990, 1C.

[67] Kevin Simpson, "Ordinance Signals Public Arrival of Denver's Gay Political Bloc," *Denver Post*, October 18, 1990, IB.

[68] EPOC Colorado memorandum, post-Amendment 2 campaign assessment, undated, in author's possession.

[69] Patricia Calhoun, "Colorado a Swing State in 2012—and a Hate State in 1992," *Westword*, blog, November 5, 2012. Retrieved from www.westword.com/news/colorado-a-swing-state-in-2012-and-a-hate-state-in-1992-5857496.

[70] Carol Chorey, "Council Joins Challenge to Amendment 2, Lawsuit to be Filed in Denver This Week," *Daily Camera*, 1A.

[71] Michael Booth, "Gay-rights Ban Narrowly Winning," *Denver Post*, November 4, 1992, 13A.

[72] Joanne Ostrow, "Sardella Got to Heart of Amendment 2," *Denver Post*, November 5, 1992, 1E.

[73] Roy Romer video interview, "Voices of the Law,"Duke University Law School. Retrieved from http://web.law.duke.edu/voices/.

[74] Ibid.

[75] Linda Cornett "Passage Draws Threats of Lawsuit," *Daily Camera*, Nov 5, 1992.

[76] The plaintiffs' suit was filed in December 1992 as *Evans v. Romer*, the plaintiffs versus the state of Colorado, with Richard G. Evans the named plaintiff and Roy Romer named as the governor of the state. The state appealed the rulings to the Colorado Supreme Court and the U.S. Supreme Court, and the case became known as *Romer v. Evans* 517 U.S. 620 (1996) No. 94-1039.

[77] Lisa Keen and Suzanne B. Goldberg, *Strangers to the Law* (Ann Arbor: University of Michigan Press, 1998), 17.

[78] Lisa Keen, *Washington Blade*, October 29, 1993, 27.

[79] *Romer v. Evans* trial transcripts, Romer v. Evans Collection, Western History & Genealogy, Denver Public Library, Boxes 1-4. All direct quotes by lawyers, witnesses and Judge Bayless in this chapter are taken directly from official transcripts of court proceedings.

[80] Roy Romer video interview, "Voices of the Law," Duke University Law School. Retrieved from http://web.law.duke.edu/voices/.

[81] *U.S. Department of Agriculture v. Moreno*, 413 U.S. 528 (1983) No. 72-534.

[82] *Romer v. Evans* trial transcripts, *Romer v. Evans* Collection, Western History & Genealogy, Denver Public Library, Boxes 1-4. Judge Bayless' comments and ruling are taken directly from official transcripts of court proceedings.

[83] Dirk Johnson, "Colorado Ban on Gay-Rights Laws Is Put On Hold," *New York Times*, January 16, 1993, 1.

[84] Jeffrey Rosen, "Sodom and Demurrer," *The New Republic*, November 20, 1993, 16.

[85] Howard Pankratz, "Sexual Orientation 'Gene-linked'," *Denver Post*, October 14, 1993, 1B.

[86] Al Knight, "A Judicial Circus Is in Town," *Denver Post*, October 17, 1993, 1D.

[87] Dirk Johnson, "Colorado Ban on Gay Rights Laws Is Ruled Unconstitutional," *New York Times*, December 15, 1993, 11A.

[88] "Amendment 2 Struck Down; Amendment Limiting Gay Rights Tossed Out," *Rocky Mountain News*, December 15, 1993, 16A.

[89] Sally McGrath, " '2' Unconstitutional," *Daily Camera*, December 15, 1993, 1A.

[90] "Amendment 2 Struck Down," *Rocky Mountain News*, December 15, 1993, 1A.

[91] Jeffrey A. Roberts, "Gays Equate Court Battle to Brown v. Board of Ed," *Denver Post*, February 22, 1195, A4.

[92] Sue Lindsay and John Sanko, "Amendment 2 Opponents, Supporters Agree Justices' Decision Will Be Pivotal," *Rocky Mountain News*, February 22, 1995, 8A.

[93] Joan Biskupic, "Legal Elite Vie for Court Time in Pursuit of Supreme Challenge," *Washington Post*, December 2, 1996, A19.

[94] Jean Dubofsky to Rick Hills, March 29, 1995, Dubofsky personal papers.

[95] Joan Biskupic, "Gay Rights Case Watched Closely," *Washington Post*, October 10, 1995 1A, 10A.

[96] Charles Brennan, "Stakes High as Amendment 2 Heads for High Court Showdown," *Rocky Mountain News*, October 1, 1995, 2A, 6A.

[97] Lisa Keen, "High Stakes at the High Court," *Washington Blade*, October 6, 1995, 1, 23.

[98] John Brinkley, "Coloradans, Pro and Con, Attend High Court Hearing," *Rocky Mountain News*, October 11, 1995, 1A.

[99] All quotations attributed to the participants at oral arguments are taken from the official transcript provided by the Supreme Court. Retrieved from https://www.oyez.org/cases/1995/94-1039.

[100] Brady's Corner, cartoon, *Washington Blade*, October 13, 1995, 29.

[101] Howard Pankratz, Michael Booth and Adriel Bettelheim, "Court Picks at Amend 2, 'I've Never Seen a Statute Like This', Supreme Court Justices Sharply Question Amendment 2", *Denver Post*, October 11, 1995, 11A.

[102] John Brinkley, " 'I've Never Seen a Case Like This,' Justice Says", *Rocky Mountain News*, Oct 11, 1995, 1A.

[103] Pankratz, Booth, and Bettelheim, 11A.

[104] Linda Greenhouse, "U.S. Justices Hear, And Also Debate, A Gay Rights Case," *New York Times*, October 11, 1995, 1A.

[105] Brinkley, 3A; Pankratz, Booth and Bettelheim, 1A.

[106] Linda Cornett, "Supreme Court Strikes Down '2' ", *Boulder Camera*, May 21, 1996, 2A.

[107] Lourie Zipf, "Reason to Celebrate," *Boulder Camera*, May 21, 1996, color photo, 1.

[108] Karl Gehring, "About 2,000 opponents of Amendment 2 cheer...", *Denver Post*, May 21, 1996, black and white photo, 4A.

Acknowledgments

Writing this book was at once both a solo and lonely journey and a total team sport. From the briefest words of encouragement and cheering on when cheering on was needed, to the steadfastness of the ongoing support and hard work every step of the way, so many people became essential ingredients to the writing of this book. My thanks to family and friends who valued the work and the worth of telling this story, to all who took the time for interviews to travel back many decades to help me unearth the behind the scene stories that gave life to this untold story, and to the many writers, editors, and advisors who provided counsel along the way. They not only taught me much about the writing and publishing life but gave me the courage to jump off the cliff.

Special thanks to two extraordinary people who read and edited, then read and edited again. And again and again. Adele Phelan and Lucie Lehmann fearlessly prodded and challenged me to search for the most compelling pieces of the story, and helped me to tell those pieces of Jean's story with the simplicity and power they deserved. They were by my side every step of the way and I can never thank them enough.

That my two children, Jennifer and Conor, reacted to their mother's "new adventure" with interest, encouragement, and appreciation for the endeavor, and that my husband, Terry, came to think it normal and make it possible for me to disappear from everyday life and exist in the world of the yesterday meant a great deal to me.

And then there is Jean. That she said "yes" when I asked if would agree to be interviewed and be helpful with the book I wanted to write was the first gift. The greater gift was exploring our country's history

of justice through her eyes and her life and coming to a deeper understanding of our country's journey and my own. Her patience with my
continued probing and her openness throughout this long process was
more than any author could expect. I am filled with gratitude.

About the Author

Susan Casey is a respected authority in the field of American politics and government. She served as a top advisor to presidential candidates Sen. Gary Hart, Sen. Bob Kerrey, Sen. John Kerry and Gov. Martin O'Malley, and was an elected member of the Denver City Council when the *Romer v. Evans* decision was handed down. Casey has a PhD in International Affairs, taught at the University of Colorado Graduate School of Public Affairs and at Metropolitan State University in Denver, and led an innovative new media project at the Institute of Politics at the John F. Kennedy School of Government at Harvard University. Her columns have appeared in the *Huffington Post,* the *Denver Post,* the *Rocky Mountain News,* the *Boston Globe,* and the *Concord (NH) Monitor.* This is her second book. She lives in Denver.

About the Author

INDEX

CPSIA information can be obtained
at www.ICGtesting.com
Printed in the USA
FSOW03n2204250816
24032FS